£25.00

The theatres of
Inigo Jones and John Webb

The theatres of
Inigo Jones and John Webb

JOHN ORRELL

Professor of English, University of Alberta

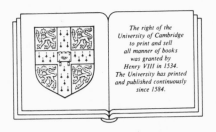

The right of the
University of Cambridge
to print and sell
all manner of books
was granted by
Henry VIII in 1534.
The University has printed
and published continuously
since 1584.

CAMBRIDGE UNIVERSITY PRESS

Cambridge
London   New York   New Rochelle
Melbourne   Sydney

Published by the Press Syndicate of the University of Cambridge
The Pitt Building, Trumpington Street, Cambridge CB2 IRP
32 East 57th Street, New York, NY 10022, USA
296 Beaconsfield Parade, Middle Park, Melbourne 3206, Australia

© Cambridge University Press 1985

First published 1985

Printed in Great Britain at
the University Press, Cambridge

Library of Congress catalogue card number: 84-9623

British Library Cataloguing in Publication Data
Orrell, John
The theatres of Inigo Jones and John Webb.
1. Theatres——England——Construction——
History——17th century
1. Title
725'.822'09032   NA6840.G7
ISBN 0 521 25546 5

WV

For Don Rowan

Contents

Plates

Preface

In 1973 the four hundredth anniversary of Inigo Jones's birth was celebrated by a comprehensive exhibition of his work held within the expressive walls of the Banqueting House in Whitehall. The firm architecture, the energetic craftsmanship, the incisive learning, all the qualities of the man's work were generously displayed. The catalogue of the show, *The King's Arcadia*, remains essential reading for anyone interested in the whole range of Jones's canon, including his work for the theatre and the Court masque.

The quatercentenary also saw the publication of Stephen Orgel and Roy Strong's monumental study of the masque designs, *Inigo Jones: The Theatre of the Stuart Court*. It was a book to catch the imagination, its exhaustive scholarship quickening interest in the study of Jones's scenic art and laying the groundwork for many new discoveries and interpretations, the chief of which have been published in a distinguished series of articles by John Peacock.

Two further volumes placed the architectural and theoretical drawings before the public. John Harris's *Catalogue of the Drawings Collection of the Royal Institute of British Architects: Inigo Jones and John Webb* appeared in 1972 and seven years later was joined by the *Catalogue of Drawings by Inigo Jones, John Webb and Isaac de Caus in the Collection at Worcester College, Oxford*, in which Harris was accompanied as co-editor by A. A. Tait.

Both Jones and his junior associate, John Webb, designed scenery for masques at Court, but their main concern was with architecture. Accordingly they were commissioned from time to time to erect stages and auditoria suitable for the acting of plays, and among their extant drawings are plans, elevations and sections of many theatres, most equipped with scenery, most constructed at Court, and yet nearly all intended for the drama rather than the more specialized requirements of the masque. Some of these drawings were published by Orgel and Strong, others by Harris and Tait; the rest have appeared scattered in books and periodicals over many years. They deserve to be considered as a coherent group, for they are the fruit of Jones's study, of his long experience and deft collaboration with Webb, himself the sole author of several of the schemes. As architecture the drawings belong to a single class, each project representing a new assault on the ancient challenge offered by the theatre's need to bring the performer and the audience profitably together; as theatre history they form by far the richest vein of evidence about English playhouses of the seventeenth century, a period from which only the sparsest graphic documents have survived to illustrate the development of the stage.

I have attempted therefore to assemble all the drawings left by Jones and Webb that show the architecture of the houses they built or fitted out for the drama proper. The masque scenes represent a category of work somewhat removed from the ordinary concerns of the stage and lie beyond the scope of this book. Nevertheless it will often be necessary to refer to them, and I have adopted the convention of using the numbers assigned to them by Orgel and Strong (O & S). The main emphasis lies however on the plans and other architectural drawings by which the theatres are known to us; when the scene designs contribute towards an understanding of the buildings for which they were intended I have of course included them, but they are not the subject of the book. That remains the theatres themselves, their fabric and the traditions of their design.

Parts of chapters 2 and 3 have appeared in somewhat different form in *Shakespeare Survey 30* and *35*, and part of chapter 6 in *The British Library Journal*; I am pleased to have received the permission of their editors to reprint the material here. Much of the research was undertaken with the aid of grants from the Social Sciences and Humanities Research Council of Canada and the University of Alberta Fund for the Advancement of Scholarship. I am grateful to these institutions, but owe an equally important and more personal debt to those whose conversation has made the writing of this book so deep a pleasure: John Harris, Sir Roy Strong, John Newman, Gordon Higgott, Richard Hosley (who rashly volunteered to read the typescript) and – at Cambridge University Press – Sarah Stanton. It was my wife, however, who helped most of all.

A note on terminology

Many of the theatres described in this book derive from the plan and section printed by Sebastiano Serlio in his *Secondo libro di perspettiva* (Paris, 1545). Because the parts of the Renaissance stage and auditorium are not quite the equivalent of modern structures I have adopted a terminology that corresponds to Serlio's. Thus in his plan (plate 3) we find a level *orchestra* labelled E. In Jacobean and Caroline Court theatres a similar area was often used as a *dancing floor*. Between it and the raised stage was a floor-level passage (D), called the *piazza della scena* by Serlio in his later editions and more simply the *piazza* by at least one English designer. I have adopted the shorter form. Beyond the *piazza* is the raised and level *forestage* (C), shown by Serlio with a reticulated surface which distinguishes it from the foreshortened and raked stage proper (B). The latter, being flanked by wings and closed off with a *backscene*, I have called the *scenic stage*. In most designs by Jones and Webb the boundary between the *forestage* and the *scenic stage* is marked by a *frontispiece* or *scenic border*, a feature not found in Serlio. Occasionally an analogous division occurs also in the non-scenic playhouses, as in plate 16, where the stage proper is embraced by the tiring-house front (or *frons scenae*) much as a raked *scenic stage* is enclosed by its scenery. Here the platform is level and continuous with the broad *forestage*, the division between the two being marked only by the return surfaces of the *frons*.

In many of the seventeenth-century scenic theatres the *backscene* was constructed as a pair or pairs of *backshutters* which could be withdrawn to show the *scenes of relieve*, usually a set of profiled flats set up before a *backcloth* (see, for a detailed example, plate 23). Sometimes this back part of the scene was built in two storeys, with an *upper stage* above the *scenes of relieve*; this too was usually fitted at the front with shutters which could be withdrawn to reveal an *upper scene*, often of deities (plate 22). Above the whole was constructed a wooden grid called a *roof*, from which were suspended the *cloud borders* (plate 27).

I Introduction

T HE HALL at Whitehall Palace stood between the river and 'the Street', the highway that ran northwards from Westminster towards the great houses of the Strand. It was built of white ashlar stone, in the late mediaeval style current in the reign of Henry VIII, its lateral walls decoratively battlemented and its roof supported by gilded hammerbeam trusses (plate 1). For generations it served all the expected functions of the public face of the Court, and at festive times was often fitted up as a temporary playhouse where the London acting companies might make their occasional commissioned appearances. In 1665, however, it had been handsomely converted into a substantial Court theatre, and although the plague caused the postponement of most of the first dramatic season planned for the new stage, it reopened in the following year as a permanent scenic house, a notable addition to the small theatre world of London.

Like its temporary predecessors the Hall Theatre was intended chiefly for performances by the professional players, now from Drury Lane and Lincoln's Inn Fields rather than the Globe or the Red Bull, and the first production to be recorded after the enforced closure was a King's Company comedy, *Wit without Money*, on 11 October. A week later the troupe from Davenant's Duke's Theatre appeared in a fashionable heroic drama, Orrery's *Mustapha*, for which several scene designs survive, neatly drawn in the hand of John Webb. Webb had also designed the theatre itself, and the plan, section and elevation of its stage which he has left us make it possible to visualize something of the occasion.

While the actors and actresses dressed in new tiring rooms specially constructed behind the old Tudor screen, an audience of courtiers and their guests filtered through the narrow entrances to take their places in an auditorium set up in the southern two-thirds of the hall.[1] They filled twelve boxes and a gallery built across the end wall, and took up their positions by matted benches placed on the paved floor in the manner of a theatrical pit. Before them rose the stage, almost as high as the ushers who stood at its foot, and reaching all across the room from one wall to the other. At this moment, before the play had begun and the boys were everywhere about the house lighting candles, the scene was still obscured by a great curtain, probably of a serge-like material called 'say' and capable of being taken up in gatherings by means of ropes and copper rings, the whole framed by an architectural frontispiece which soared to so imposing a height as almost to overwhelm the spectators. At its base the upright surface at the front of the stage was painted to resemble rusticated stonework, four courses high with a dressed coping, so that the

1   Wenceslaus Hollar, detail from the *Long View of London* showing Whitehall and the Masquing House

structure seemed massive and impenetrable. The main part of the frontispiece consisted of a border supported by two flat piers, each painted to resemble a giant Doric column, heavily blocked, attached to a pilaster. To either side, beyond the columns, and projecting a few feet forward from them, were balconies set above blind arches of simulated masonry, each topped by a vivid trophy of arms. At the centre, high above the trophies and the columns, a broken segmental pediment sailed over the whole composition, bearing a cartouche with the inscription 'Hi sunt de pace triumphi. Bella dabunt alios': These are the triumphs of peace. War yields others. And higher yet, borne up by this elevating sentiment, sat the pasteboard figure of Fame, a winged woman blowing a long gilded trumpet. Beyond her the gap between the painted pediment and the real roof was filled with nondescript wooden boarding.

Trumpets of a more worldly kind sounded at a doorway in the western side of the hall and with a flurry the royal party arrived, making its way down a special flight of steps through the standing company in the boxes and benches to the special platform at the centre of the auditorium where the state stood beneath its canopy. There followed the customary music, and at length the curtain rose on the first major play to be performed in the new Hall Theatre.

What the audience saw on that night brought them few surprises. John Webb had designed the conversion, and they had known his work before, at the Cockpit in Drury Lane and at the Duke's Theatre, Lincoln's Inn Fields. The stage was gently raked and closed in at either side by four pairs of movable flat wings. At the rear the backshutters carried a painted scene of architecture designed to close the vista framed by the wings. Above, suspended from an unseen wooden grid, a series of cloud borders were disposed between the wing tops, and a second set of backshutters, painted as clouds, stood immediately above the first at the rear of the stage. They could part if necessary, to reveal a skyborne deity perhaps, but on this occasion they were merely louvred as a screen behind which the musicians were installed. As the play progressed, and the scene shifted from 'Solymans *Camp and his Pavillion*' to the Queen of Hungary's chamber, the side wings of the main stage could all be covered simultaneously by a new set slid in front of them along grooves fixed both above and below; at the same time a new set of backshutters could close over the previous one so that the whole scene was transformed at once. Sometimes also the backshutters would part, slid open by the stagehands, to reveal a further scene beyond, like that of Solyman's tent, in which Mustapha's dead body was displayed. Such inner scenes were composed of three or four separate elements cut out in profile and ranged one behind another in front of a backcloth, a layered picture which the designers called a 'relieve', and which gave a delicate sense of depth to the whole work, finely counterbalancing the towering verticality of the architectural frontispiece.[2]

I have said that Restoration audiences would have found little that was new in Webb's Hall Theatre, though certainly they would have been struck, as Webb intended them to be, by its generally fine appearance. For years before the Commonwealth Inigo Jones had been developing the kind of stage which Webb was to exploit during and after it, and to Jones the credit is due for the introduction to England of all the scenic elements I have mentioned, the sliding wings, the movable backshutters, the opening clouds and the deep scenes of relieve. Before him the English stage was quite different, and just how different we may judge from a Works account entry for the preparation of the same hall at Whitehall for the performance of a play in the winter of 1601–2:

. . . making ready the haule with degrees [,] the boordes vpon them [,] footpace vnder the state [,] framing and setting vp a broade stage in the midle of the haule [,] makeing a standing for the Lorde Chamberlaine [,] makeing and setting vp viij particions in the haule and entries [,] framing and setting vp a flower [floor] in it [*sic*] the grownd wyndowe in the haulle for the musitions . . .[3]

Almost the only similarity to Webb's theatre of six decades later is the royal state on its footpace or platform; for the rest the layout is entirely different. The stage is set in the middle of the hall, not at one end, and it is presumably surrounded by the audience. The location of the eight partitions is obscure, but the musicians are removed from the dramatic action on the central stage, being placed on a special floor or gallery constructed in the bay window (the 'grownd wyndowe') near the southeast corner of the room. The Lord Chamberlain has a special standing, perhaps a box, in the auditorium, but the rest of the audience accommodation, apart from the state, is in degrees with boarded seats, presumably arranged along the walls of the hall. Within these walls, where Webb was later to construct his long, uni-directional visual theatre, the Works prepared a theatre-in-the-round, where the player was thrust out into the midst of his audience and no wing, shutter or scene of relieve could ever give him support.

Not all Elizabethan preparations of the hall for plays were as distinctive as this – the habit of placing the stage in the middle of the room apparently having been confined to a few years at the close of the reign – but in the period between the accession of James I and the performance of *Mustapha* at the Hall Theatre the staging of drama underwent changes more radical than any that were to follow before the twentieth century. In part the development may be understood as a seismic shift whose causes lie deep within the religious and political movements of Stuart times; in part also it was the result of the narrower control of the theatre after the Restoration, which confined its pleasures to a small and well-heeled constituency. The courtiers of Charles II, their appetites accustomed to the fare of Paris, and even of Italy, demanded the sort of theatre at home that they had enjoyed in exile. The favourite, Betterton, was commissioned by the king to report on the workings of the French stage from personal observation,[4] and meanwhile a well-known French provincial company, les Comédiens de Mademoiselle d'Orléans, performed spectacular works by Chapoton and Gabriel Gilbert at the Cockpit in Drury Lane.[5]

The new taste for scenes and machines might sometimes be represented as simply a slavish aping of foreign fashions, but in truth it was largely developed out of habits which had long been nurtured at home. The same Cockpit stage that was set for Chapoton's *La Descente d'Orphée* in 1661 had witnessed Davenant's 'operas' two or three years before, dramatic works well equipped with scenes. John Webb's extant designs for one of them, *The Siege of Rhodes*, show how fully their author worked in the tradition established by Inigo Jones, famously in his designs for the Court masque but perhaps more specifically in his scenes created for the Court drama.

That both Jones and Webb designed for the drama as well as for the masque is well known, but the particular quality of their dramatic work has never been adequately distinguished, perhaps because its immediate influence on the commercial playhouses of the London companies was too slight to justify the effort. Certainly students of the seventeenth-century English theatre are right to be sceptical about the extent to which scenery was used in the public and so-called 'private' theatres during Jones's lifetime; what signs there are of its penetration of such stages as the Blackfriars or Salisbury Court are scant and unreliable, and in any case could refer only to a tiny minority of productions.[6] But at Whitehall and Somerset House the situation was different: there from the time of James's Queen Anne a scenic theatre arose and thrived alongside the traditions of the rhetorical drama. Special stages and auditoria were constructed for pastorals and tragedies, akin to those employed for the masques, perhaps, but not identical with them. The intellectual sources which fed the imagination of Jones the masque designer also supplied the raw material of his theatre schemes, though in general the latter drew on the Renaissance classicism of Serlio rather than the flightier mannerism of Vredeman de Vries or the Parigi. In later years, when Webb worked with Davenant on *The Siege of Rhodes* and *Mustapha*, this very deliberate English tradition of Renaissance theatre design was still alive, or at least capable of being revived; so that although during Jones's lifetime it generally ran separate from the mainstream of London playhouse production, after his death it remained available to make a specific contribution to the development of the Restoration stage.

Not only were the Court theatres influential in the shaping of the London stage, but they also had the good fortune to go relatively well recorded. They were designed by men who were conscious of their innovatory role and determined to set it down on paper, in great collections of drawings and even in the margins of their books. By contrast the public theatres of London before 1660 have not been well served by Mnemosyne. Not one of them, from the Theater in Shoreditch to the Red Bull in Clerkenwell, survives in a contemporary plan or elevation, and the historian is hard put to do more than speculate about the details of their structure. Yet many of the theatres constructed at Court – sometimes for the very players whose daily lives were spent at the Globe or the Fortune – are known to us in detailed architectural drawings which convey much information not only about such technical matters as the seating, the stage and the scene, but even about the intellectual provenance of the scheme as a whole. One may dream about discovering Peter Street's plan of the Globe or a detailed survey of the Curtain, but in the technical works of Jones and Webb we already possess ample information about a colourful and important strand in the history of the English theatre. In one set of drawings, indeed, we may have something more valuable still: a full and detailed account of the Cockpit in Drury Lane, one of the most influential 'private' commercial playhouses in seventeenth-century London. No positive documentary confirmation of this identification has yet been discovered, but in chapter 3 I shall present the wealth of circumstantial evidence which supports it, some of it in my view decisive. As for the series of fully documented Court theatres which are illustrated in the ensuing chapters, they constitute a substantial body of work in their own right; not even the masques, copiously documented though they are in scenery and costume, survive in such methodical plans and sections as these designs for the dramatic stage, and I make no apology for singling them out for study in this book.

Nevertheless it was the masques, the costliest and most magnificent theatrical events at Court, that dominated Jones's life as a stage designer. Their performance was as much a matter of political mystique as of mere amusement; through such works as *Tethys' Festival* or *Prince Henry's Barriers* the Court mirrored itself and enacted its sometimes dangerously ideal view of British polity. At Shrovetide and Epiphany, at Candlemas and – after 1605 – on Gunpowder Day Whitehall celebrated the courtly festivals with a purposive cyclical rhythm akin to that of the Church calendar, demonstrating in canvas, paint and rope that infusion of divine order in an otherwise chaotic world which seems so to have enchanted the Jacobean and early Caroline courtier. Repeatedly the personated forces of discord, represented by the passions or caricatures of the baser affections, were first routed and then transformed with a harmony that emanated from recognizably British deities revealed among the pasteboard clouds. Symbols of political order charmed the senses in music and the dance, and the force of the whole was redoubled by the element of surprise, especially in the scenic transformations, whose end was to strike the audience with that wonder which Aquinas called the beginning of knowledge. The object of the Jacobean masque was both to encourage faith in the monarchy and to confirm it. For most of the period it fell to Jones to design these often elaborate productions and, over more than three decades, from *The Masque of Blackness* in 1605 to *Salmacida Spolia* in 1640, he developed a smooth expertise not only in matters of technical administration – the supply and deployment of materials, the supervision of craftsmen, the invention of scenic techniques – but also in matters of the imagination. He soon established dominance over what the published texts sometimes called the 'act' of the masques – their concrete realization on the stage – and although until the 1630s he often shared their 'invention' with the playwright Ben Jonson he was broadly responsible for their visual content, for which he drew on a wide acquaintance with continental *intermezzi* and festival designs as well as those strands of Renaissance and especially mannerist art and architecture that he found most amenable to his purposes. The full story of the masques has been told, with generous scholarship, by Stephen Orgel and Sir Roy Strong,[7] and it reveals how acutely Jones responded to the rich artistic influences of continental Europe, and yet how firmly he remained in independent command of the material he used.

He began as what we should now call a freelance, brought into the circle of Queen Anne of Denmark probably through his association with the Earl of Rutland, in whose household accounts for June 1603 we find mention of a payment to 'Henygo Jones, a picture maker'.[8] On the accession of James I and his queen, the earl made an embassy to Copenhagen to present the Order of the Garter to Christian IV, Anne's brother. Jones was in his train, his presence fortunately noticed by a contemporary diarist.[9] It is fitting that these first records of his courtly activity should date from the very opening of the Stuart era, which he was to do so much to memorialize, but it is certain that before the opening of the new reign he had already laid the foundations of his aesthetic education. According to John Webb he had spent 'many years' in Italy,[10] and although no contemporary documents survive to confirm the nature and extent of his journey he was by 1605 already known as 'a great traveller', one whose exposure to foreign influences suggested that he might provide 'rare devices' when called upon to design the scenes and machines for a season of academic plays at Oxford. In fact 'rare devices' is a fair description of what he did provide when, in the years after 1604, he was invited to provide settings for Court plays and masques: at Oxford he used the *periaktoi* of ancient authority and more recent continental practice;[11] he experimented at Whitehall with the *scena ductilis* (various forms of movable shutters) and the *scena versatilis* (revolves of all sorts); he tried scenic mansions like the pavilions of wood and canvas favoured by the Tudor office of the Revels, and even – in *Prince Henry's Barriers* (1610) – combined them with wing settings derived from Sebastiano Serlio. In style he ranged from the classical setting for a throne of *c.* 1606–9, based on Serlio's description of Bramante's exedra in the Belvedere in Rome,[12] to the pretty gothic revival of *Oberon* (1611), where sophisticated borrowings from du Cerceau enlivened an already elegant design.[13]

During the earlier part of his career at Court Jones's tastes were at their most eclectic, and this was also the time when he was able to continue his travels. His journeys abroad were not frequent, but they were enough to keep alive and significantly to broaden a sensibility already awakened by the sojourns in Italy and Denmark. The sketchbooks and notes he made on his travels, the signs in his subsequent work of a mind opened and disciplined by new experience, the explicit testimony of his associates – all witness the deliberation with which he set out to learn arts that had never been fully understood in England. A year or so after the Oxford plays a friend, Edmond Bolton, presented him with a book inscribed to one 'through whom there is hope that sculpture, modelling, architecture, painting, acting and all that is praiseworthy in the elegant arts of the ancients, may one day find their way across the Alps into our England'.[14] In 1609 he was in France, ostensibly as a messenger,[15] but doubtless seizing the opportunity to renew his acquaintance with foreign architecture: it was after this journey that his masque designs first showed the influence of du Cerceau's *Plus Excellents Bastiments de France* (1607). The journey may even have extended as far as Provence, where Jones 'observed' the Pont du Gard and the ancient theatre at Orange, the former influencing his designs for *Prince Henry's Barriers*, produced in January 1610 soon after his return home.[16]

In 1613–14 came the most fruitful journey of all. It began with an embassy towards Heidelberg, to bring on their way the Princess Elizabeth and her new husband the Elector Palatine after their wedding in London, for which Jones had designed *The Lords' Masque* and *The Middle Temple and Lincoln's Inn Masque*, both at Whitehall. Now renowned, in George Chapman's words, as 'our Kingdome's most Artfull and Ingenious *Architect*',[17] Jones entered the train of the young Earl of Arundel, then at the beginning of his career as one of England's most enlightened art collectors and patrons. Once their part in the embassy was accomplished the earl and his friends set off for Italy, there to spend over a year in the sort of active sightseeing that today would be called research. Jones's learning was by now of such repute that his mere presence with the earl was sufficient to prompt Dudley Carleton to write from Venice (on 9 July 1613) that he did not believe a story which had been put about by some members of Elizabeth's train that Arundel intended to return home from Strasbourg only through France:

I rather believe they were so told to be rid of their companies, and the more because I hear my lord had taken Inigo Jones into his train, who will be of best use to him (by reason of his language and experience) in these parts.[18]

But Jones was no mere cicerone. Through Strasbourg and Basle they came to Milan, and thereafter the exact route of the whole party is difficult to reconstruct. It is probable that Jones sometimes left it to travel by himself: he was in Venice, Parma and Vicenza in the autumn and later Arundel was in Bologna, Florence and Siena, but whether Jones was then with him or not cannot be ascertained. Both dedicated themselves to enquiry and learning. Jones kept a sketchbook which records his interest in Italian painting, and he annotated a copy of Palladio with liberal notes on the buildings he saw and the architectural problems he considered.[19] In September he visited the Teatro Olimpico at Vicenza, carefully describing its stage on the flyleaf of the book. The winter was spent in Rome, where Arundel obtained permission to excavate an ancient site, sending the marbles he discovered back to London.[20] In the new year the little group visited Naples, Venice, Vicenza again, then Genoa and Turin before returning home via Paris. In Venice Jones met Scamozzi, and at some time in the journey – probably before September 1613[21] – he acquired apparently for his own use a great quantity of Palladio's architectural designs. There is reason to believe that he also acquired for Arundel a collection of Scamozzi's drawings, but these were later to be lost.[22]

During this second Italian journey Jones bought books as well as drawings, and we can trace some of his route through his habit of inscribing them with the place and date of purchase. These and other volumes now in the collection at Worcester College, Oxford, show how carefully he read, and how deliberately he noted what he read in marginal comments. The books are as much a witness of his curiosity and readiness to question and learn as the travels are: Serlio, Palladio, Vitruvius and Lomazzo all bear the purposive marks of his pen, and all are incorporated into his growing aesthetic discipline.

It is not my purpose now to trace the adoption and transformation of such sources in Jones's architectural and masque designs, a task already undertaken to good effect by John Harris, Stephen Orgel and Roy Strong.[23] Later chapters will show how deeply some of them shaped his thinking about the theatre, notably the books of Vitruvius and Serlio along with the concrete example of Palladio's Teatro Olimpico. A further influence, less easily documented, was that of the professional theatre world of London, with its business-like commitment to the routines of public performance. The connection which Jones had made with the Court stage in *The Masque of Blackness* and at Oxford strengthened with such rapidity that even before the departure for Italy he had established a dominant position as a designer at Whitehall. He constructed settings for such works as *Hymenaei* (1606), *The Lord Hay's Masque* (1607), *The Masque of Queens* (1609), *Prince Henry's Barriers* (1610), *Tethys' Festival* (1610), *Oberon* (1611), *Love Freed from Ignorance and Folly* (1611), *The Lord's Masque* (1613) and *The Masque of the Middle Temple and Lincoln's Inn* (1613). There were besides many smaller entertainments, each with its own demands for the provision of costumes and settings. Often the masques contained elements of antimasque, chaotic or comical figures played by professional actors, such as the humours and affections in *Hymenaei*. As Jones assumed more and more of the responsibility for staging the whole performance he was brought increasingly into contact with these players, for whom he designed both scenes and costumes. It is likely also that his writ extended to rehearsing and directing their part in the show, in order to harmonize it with the visual transformations, the music and the dance by which the primary purposes of the work were achieved. *Prince Henry's Barriers* opened and closed with long speeches delivered by professionals, who were paid £15[24] and must have worked closely with the designer of the tomb, the cave and the sky from which they emerged on stage. By the following year, when *Oberon* was performed, Jones had been appointed Surveyor to the prince, and warrants dated in the weeks leading up to the production[25] imply that he was largely responsible for its integration of elements, among them the professional players who took the parts of satyrs and fays. Ben Jonson, who as author of the piece bore an equal responsibility for the details of its enactment, was Jones's most obvious link with the world of the London theatre; it was a relationship that grew in something like mutual respect and intimacy for a number of years only to fall into decline and finally to break up rancorously after the poor reception of *Chloridia* in 1631.[26] But for twenty-six years the two men worked together, Jones surviving the setback of the prince's death in 1612 to be granted the reversion of the King's Surveyorship in the following year; in 1615, after the return from Italy, he succeeded to the coveted post itself. As Surveyor, Jones's principal tasks were the administration of the Works, the maintenance of the royal palaces and the design of such alterations and occasional new building as were undertaken by the office. His concern for the masques was a subordinate but recurrent part of his duties, quite possibly the part that called forth the best of his affection. Yet even the succession of great shows, from *The Vision of Delight* early in 1617 to *Salmacida Spolia* in 1640, with all their problems of imaginative creativity as well as of logistics, does not sum up the total of the Surveyor's work for the drama in the period. Every year the professional companies, whether the King's Men, the Prince's or Queen Anne's, performed their plays at Court in auditoria sometimes prepared by the Works, and although the arrangements made for their accommodation in the halls of the various palaces were so routine that they have left little mark on the records the need to provide for them kept Jones in contact with the London stage. Even in the weeks when *The Masque of Blackness* was being prepared by the newly arrived 'great traveller' the rooms of Whitehall were often alive with the King's Men's entertainments: *Othello* in the old Elizabethan Banqueting House was followed by *The Merry Wives of Windsor*, probably in the hall or great chamber. At Christmas they presented *Measure for Measure* and *The Comedy of Errors*. A week before the Sunday staging of *Blackness* the king saw a play 'By the Queens Majesties plaiers', and on the night following the masque the King's Men acted *Henry V*. The next night they appeared in Jonson's *Every Man out of his Humour*, followed soon after, at

Candlemas, by the companion piece, *Every Man in* . . . . Twice at Shrovetide they performed *The Merchant of Venice*, the second time by special request of the king. There were several other performances, including at least eight by the Prince's Men.[27] Similar seasons of plays were mounted at Whitehall almost every year until 1640.

Usually the visits to Court by the public players left nothing in the records beyond a mere entry in the warrant books authorizing the necessary payment, providing us with no information about the stage accommodations the public companies required. They were doubtless fairly simple, capable of being covered by the type of Works account entry that we find enrolled for 1621–2 at Whitehall: 'fittinge the hall and greate Chamber for plays'.[28] Yet it would be unwise to assume too readily that scant records in the rolls always meant scant provisions in the halls. The Chamber accounts for October–December 1621[29] record that the great chamber on the queen's side and the hall were made ready for plays on six occasions, while still others were performed in the new Banqueting House, for which the Works accounts record in greater detail than was customary the construction of ranges of seating in the auditorium:

Ralphe Bryce Carpenter for frameinge and setting vpp xj[en] baies of degrees on both sides of the banquettinge house every bay conteyninge xvj[en] foote longe, beinge twoe panes in every of them; the degrees belowe beinge seven rowes in heighte; and twoe boordes nayled vpon every brackett the degrees in the midle gallery beinge fower rowes in heigthe, and twoe boordes nailed vpon brackettes also with a raile belowe and another raile in the midle gallery being crosse laticed vnder the same; working frameinge & setteinge vpp of vpright postes wroughte with eighte cantes to beare the same woorke . . .[30]

The bays are 16ft between centres, so that the seating will have been ranged continuously along the two side walls for 5½ bays, or 88ft.[31] Between the lower range of seven degrees and the cantilevered balcony which is a structural part of the building a 'middle gallery' of four degrees was erected on canted posts. These degrees, which could be dismantled for storage and re-use on future occasions, were probably prepared for the opening of the new house with *The Masque of Augurs* on Twelfth Night, but it seems likely that they would have been retained for the plays that were performed there in the ensuing weeks. The Works accounts make no mention of a stage, whether for the masque or the plays, though Jones's design for the former (O & S 115) shows an elaborate one with three entrances below and complex flights of steps leading down to the dancing floor. What stage provisions might have been made for the professional players we may only surmise. The same roll of accounts for 1621–2 records preparations for them at St James's in the usual minimal fashion: '. . . makinge ready the Councell chamber with degrees and boordinge them for plays . . .' It is a type of entry that could be repeated from almost any year in the reigns of James I and Charles I and it is unfortunately not of a kind to bring much enlightenment.

Whether Jones had anything directly to do with the majority of these performances by the visiting players from the London theatres is not known, but they must surely have kept him abreast of developments in the professional stage and, perhaps more important, they encouraged his personal contact with particular men of the theatre. Among his friends and acquaintances he numbered not only Burbage, Henslowe and Ben Jonson, but also Edward Alleyn the veteran actor, with whom he was probably associated as early as 1608,[32] and certainly thereafter as a trustee of Dulwich College.[33] His duties were always taking him into playhouses and their tiring rooms, and led occasionally to specific theatrical commissions, as when he was called upon to design a scene at Somerset House for 'her highnes servauntes' in 1616,[34] or, in the same year, turned his attention to the nearby site in Drury Lane where Christopher Beeston proposed to develop a cockpit originally built by Prince Henry's cockmaster into a theatre for these same Queen Anne's Men. The design which Jones then produced (see chapter 3 and plates 6 and 7) owed something to Serlio, perhaps something also to lost drawings by Scamozzi, and even a little to Palladio; but it owed much more to John Best's cockpit building and most of all to the physical requirements of the public players who sought to move their repertory from the open-roofed Red Bull theatre to one of the same type as the enclosed Blackfriars where the King's Men had performed so successfully.

The Drury Lane Cockpit drawings are more complete than any other set dating from the seventeenth century, and give notable insights into the theatrical requirements of one of the leading professional acting companies. Thirteen years later Jones returned to the theme once more, with a second, quite different, commission to convert the more elaborate royal cockpit at Whitehall Palace into a permanent theatre capable of housing the major public companies when they appeared at Court. It was the King's Men who, on Gunpowder Day 1630, opened the so-called Cockpit-in-Court with the first of a season of plays that included work by Fletcher, Beaumont and especially Ben Jonson.[35] Several of the latter's comedies were performed there while he was engaged in his last collaboration with Jones, on *Chloridia*, staged nearby in the Banqueting House. Jones's design for the conversion of the royal cockpit into a small private theatre is known to us in a sheet of drawings by John Webb dating probably from 1660 (plates 16 and 17), which show it to have been a far more resolutely Palladian scheme than that for the other, commercial, Cockpit in Drury Lane. The technical needs of the public players were catered for, but only in a house whose very shape and proportion differed radically from the professional theatres, both public and private. The need to accommodate a royal box to which no member of the audience should turn his back caused part of the difference, but the rest was Jones's own determination to construct a neo-Roman auditorium with a fixed sculptural *frons scenae*, based firmly on Palladio's Teatro Olimpico in Vicenza. The balance between the sources contributing to the design, whether architectural, literary or theatrical, had shifted away from the claims of the actors and towards those of architecture: with the Cockpit-in-Court Jones was already asserting that independent confidence in the designer's art that was shortly to lead to his final rift with Ben Jonson. The building had no successor among English stages, and although it remained useful until after the Restoration it was eventually replaced by the scenic theatre designed by John Webb for the great hall of the palace.

The Cockpit-in-Court is rare among Jones's theatre projects in being known to us both through good drawings and from adequate craftsmen's accounts. In general the documents relating to the theatres fall into two main classes. The more consistent set are the written records found especially in the rolls of the declared accounts of the Office of Works, held in the Public Record Office, and supplemented by a host of warrants, accounts of the Chamber and the Revels, and miscellaneous accounts having to do with the administration of the building projects.[36] The second class, much richer/in detail though less exhaustively representative, consists of the extant architectural drawings of the theatres, chiefly those gathered by John Webb. Plans and sometimes sections or elevations survive for most of the major theatre schemes undertaken by the Works, though many occasions of what one might call the second rank have either slipped from the visual records altogether or are represented only by scene designs. The usual non-scenic stage arrangements at all the palaces were set in train by verbal means alone in warrants and memoranda, and generally were noticed only briefly in the accounts. Occasionally, however, some aspect of them is touched on more fully in the great rolls of the Works accounts. There, for a period of three years from 1629 to 1632, a large number of entries describes the conversion of the Whitehall cockpit into Jones's Palladian theatre. The tasks performed in those years by carpenters, carvers, painters, property-makers and other craftsmen are confirmed by Webb's later set of drawings, and convey a remarkably clear idea of the building's architectural detail, much of which would otherwise be unknown. The Works accounts, but not the Webb drawings, show that in Jones's time the Cockpit-in-Court was sufficiently mechanized, with a single descent machine, to meet the needs of the public players from the Globe or the Fortune without – as the drawings make abundantly clear – raising ranks of pasteboard clouds above their heads, nor wood and canvas houses to compete with their poetic imagery.

The London players for whom Jones designed the two Cockpit conversions performed also on occasion in his most substantial building in Whitehall, the Banqueting House. Constructed after its predecessor had burned down in 1619, this great Palladian hall was never fully fitted out as a playhouse. It was rather a multi-purpose room of state, even more perhaps than those that had stood on the site before it, and both its design and its functions have been well described by the late Per Palme:

It was built for the sumptuous entertainment of foreign princes and ambassadors, for the ratification of diplomatic treaties and agreements, for the gracious reception of the Houses of Parliament, for public audiences, for ceremonies connected with the creation of new peerages, for the pomp of St George's Feast, and for the solemn rite of touching for the 'King's Evil'. In short, it was built as a stage for the display of royal might and glory.[37]

For some years it was used also for the most important masques, but while many of Jones's drawings for the masque scenes survive there are no plans of the arrangements made in it for the accommodation of an audience, nor any records more substantial than those I have already quoted of its fitting out as a temporary playhouse for the non-scenic drama. The building, though extant and well documented, lies beyond the scope of this book.

The two Cockpits and occasionally the Banqueting House were prepared for use by the professional actors, but Jones was often called upon to provide scenic stages for the amateurs at Court. The scene in the hall at Somerset House in 1616 may well have been prepared for the Queen Anne's Men, but others in the same palace were intended for occasions when the courtiers themselves performed. At Shrovetide 1626 Queen Henrietta Maria and her ladies acted Racan's pastoral *Artenice*, Jones providing a standing pastoral scene (plate 12). A Tragic Scene design (plate 14) was probably intended for the same room in 1630, though whether for the enhancement of an amateur courtly production is not known; on 8 December 1629 a warrant was issued to Jones 'for a Stage and Scene to bee made at Somerset House'[38] and the fine Tragic Scene drawing may only tentatively be connected with the occasion, which otherwise went unrecorded. The lack of contemporary comment suggests that it was not a performance by palace amateurs (always a notable event) but one of the usual Court appearances of the professionals. Three years later the queen again appeared with her ladies in Walter Montagu's *The Shepherd's Paradise* for which Jones built a special theatre in the Paved Court at Somerset House; in 1635 he was called on to construct a complete playhouse in the hall at Whitehall for a performance of a pastoral, *Florimène*, by the Queen's French ladies, perhaps with the addition of some English professionals in a concluding antimasque. Both of these occasions called for substantial contributions from the Works, where the Surveyor now had the assistance of John Webb, whose hand appears in the plans prepared for them. The documentation is so full that we shall be able to devote a chapter to each of these important houses (see chapters 6 and 7 below), but it should not be forgotten that many other plays were acted on stages designed by Jones and Webb: at Somerset House, for example, in the summer of 1638 both parts of Carlell's *Passionate Lovers* were performed in the hall by the King's Men, with scenes by Jones, and in 1640 Habington's *Cleodora, or the Queen of Aragon* was staged in the hall at Whitehall by amateur actors drawn from the household servants of the Earl of Pembroke, the Lord Chamberlain, with scenes evidently by Webb as well as by Jones.[39]

These plays were all courtly entertainments, but they were not all performed by courtiers. As we have seen, the professional players from the London public theatres were often involved in the productions, whether in a subordinate role (as in *Florimène*) or as the sole actors (as in *The Passionate Lovers*). Thus while it is true that the scenic plays at Court, to which Jones lent his eclectic talents, were undertaken in a spirit and with resources remote from those customary in the public theatres, the divide between the two worlds was far from absolute. If we exclude the masque designs, Jones and Webb between them probably constructed as many stages for the professional actors as they did for the amateurs at Court, thus forging and keeping in good order a link with the London stage which was a powerful if not always sufficiently decisive influence on their work for the masque as well as the drama.

Professional or amateur, it is the scenic theatres of the Court that survive in the fullest documents. Scenes generally required to be viewed from something more carefully arranged than the sets of degrees put up in the hall or great chamber for an ordinary night's playing at Court, and so the scenic houses appear often to have been more thoroughly designed and more attentively constructed than their non-scenic equivalents. And the more elaborate the Works preparations the more likely they were to be itemized in the accounts. Sometimes, however, even specially built theatres went almost unrecorded, such as the one constructed in the Paved Court at Somerset House for a Court wedding in 1614, when Daniel's *Hymen's Triumph* was played as part of the festivities. No drawing of it survives, nor do the Works accounts offer much more than its cost.[40] But an Italian diplomat reported the event in just enough detail to let us know that *intermedii* were included in the perform-ance, in all probability with scenes, and that the theatre itself was conceived grandly enough to suit the occasion:

After supper their Majesties passed into a little courtyard which the queen had had wonderfully transformed with wooden boards and covered with cloth, with many lights and degrees where all the lords and ladies took their seats. The king sat under a great baldachino; on his right hand sat the queen and on the left the prince . . . . In this same room was performed a pastoral which, for its gestures and its rich costumes, struck me as most beautiful. It had intermedii of two most graceful masques performed by young men in very good order.[41]

The theatre thus described could not have been the work of Inigo Jones, who was away in Italy at the time, but it is a fair example of what the Works officers could do on their own account, or possibly with the aid of the Italian visitor, Constantino de' Servi.[42] Eight years earlier they had constructed a complete Serlian auditorium in the hall at Christ Church, Oxford, for the visit of James I. Here the scenes alone were designed by Jones – it is our first encounter with him as a designer for the drama rather than the masque – and the polygonal *cavea* of benches, deriving from the plan and section of a theatre in Serlio's Second Book, were provided 'with the advice of' the Comptroller of the Works, Simon Basil, and two of his senior carpenters. No Works documents survive for this project, described by observers as 'costly' and 'glorious', but I have identified a useful plan of it among the Additional MSS at the British Library (plate 2). It shows that the Serlian example of a neo-Roman theatre ingeniously compressed into the scope of a palace courtyard or *salon* was not lost on the artisans who were faced with the long, narrow proportions of the Tudor college hall and the injunction to turn it into a theatre fit not only for a king but for scenic plays cast in the three classical kinds. No contemporary evidence credits Jones with anything more of this theatre than the scenes, but it is unlikely that he had no influence over the choice of Serlio as the model for the auditorium, for it was Serlio himself who had most conspicuously publicized the Comic, Tragic and Satyric settings whose characteristics had been described by

Vitruvius in antiquity and by Alberti in the Renaissance, and whose categories formed the basis of the Oxford programme of Latin plays.

Between the Oxford celebrations of 1605 and the entry of John Webb into his office in 1628, Jones must have designed a good many temporary stages and even theatres for the scenic drama at Court, but no plans for them have survived. Perhaps he kept none in the files; if so, Webb very soon changed the habits of the office, retaining and even classifying many sketches and detailed plans related to the drama. Webb had been educated at Merchant Taylors' School, and later claimed that he was then 'brought up by his Unckle Mr. Inigo Jones upon his late Maiestyes command on the study of Architecture, as well that which relates to building as for masques, Tryumphs and the like'.[43] Many of the papers through which we know his work for the drama attest to the care he devoted to its study. He married into Jones's family, and there is about the relationship between the two men something more deliberate and devoted than is usual between a master and his apprentice. The pupil was set to his books and allowed to work freely with the great collection of Palladio and perhaps Scamozzi drawings that Jones had brought back from Italy in 1614. Webb quickly developed a considerable facility as an architectural draftsman. He assisted Jones in the Works office, though he was seldom regularly employed in an official capacity; even in 1643, when he was left alone at Whitehall to deputize for the Surveyor, the delegation was a personal one from Jones.[44]

Most of the theatre plans and sections by which Jones's projects are known date from after 1628 – after, that is, Webb took up his duties in the office[45] – and all of these are actually in Webb's hand. How far Webb may have been responsible for their design, or 'invention', it is difficult to determine, for it was the practice of the office to have clean working drawings prepared by a draftsman from the sketches of the Surveyor. An undated but carefully phrased note by Webb describes the practice as it related to repair works at St Paul's in 1633:

Mr Webbe copied all ye designes from ye Surveyors Invention, made all ye traceryes in great for ye worke, & all ye mouldings by ye Surveyors direction so yt what the Surveyor invented & Mr Webbe made, ye substitute [Edward Carter] saw putt in worke & nothing else.[46]

The Works accounts sometimes include payments for similar tasks, as when Toby Samways was paid 20s for 'drawing the plott for the banquethouse' at Whitehall in 1605–6;[47] Webb's sole appearance in the accounts shows him in an analogous if not identical role:

John Webb Clerke for engrosseinge and makeinge two Copies of a greate Booke of Survey of his Majesties Stables Barnes and Coach howses . . . .[48]

Such documents may scarcely encourage the belief that Webb contributed very much to Jones's theatre designs of the 1630s, but the record of his personal achievement both before and after Jones's death stands to confirm the fact that he was no mere subordinate draftsman. As early as 1638 he appears to have worked on independent commissions for provincial patrons,[49] and under the Surveyor's tutelage he was to develop for a time into the country's foremost architect, though hardly its most justly recognized one. Even in the memorandum quoted above he is careful to assert his superiority over Carter, the superiority of the artist over the craftsman. The surviving architectural drawings of the theatres may sometimes be mere copies by Webb of sketches by Jones; others may represent schemes developed by him independently, or with some degree of direction. Except for those made for projects after Jones's death in 1652 there is little external evidence to make attributions certain, and it is usually necessary to attempt the difficult task of apportioning responsibility for them with only the internal evidence to go on. In the case of *The Shepherd's Paradise* a single meticulous plan survives (plate 18), untitled but evidently in Webb's hand and quite possibly his own invention. All the scene designs for the theatre are by Jones, a fact which may indicate a division of labour by which the Surveyor did the imaginative work while his assistant undertook the more mechanical design of the auditorium. A similar separation of responsibilities is implied by the documents from the production of *Florimène* in 1635: the scenes are nearly all in Jones's hand, while the plan and section of the theatre structure are by Webb, and supplemented by a group of studies – again by Webb – whose purpose is to analyse the structural and geometric details of the perspective stage (plates 20–4).

It appears that the Court pastorals tapped the resources of Jones's imagination more deeply than his contemporary work for the masques at Whitehall. By 1632 he had largely solved the technical problems of scenic representation, whether for masques or plays, and although he never reduced the elaborate business of masque production to a mere routine he did come to rely on a few favoured sources for his imagery: the great Florentine festive occasions designed and published by Giulio and Alfonso Parigi, and especially the former's *Il Giudizio di Paride*, sometimes dominated his work with a force that threatened to displace his own inventive talent. It has been argued, with justice, that Jones never merely succumbed to the authority of the Medician artists, but confidently made it his own, rearranging their scenes and reinterpreting their style to suit the purposes of the Caroline Court.[50] The vigour of his drawing remains unweakened throughout the period, but the frequency with which he returned to the same few pictorial sources in the 1630s does argue a reduction in the range of his imagination, limited perhaps by habit and the pressure of work. The Florentine agent in London, Amerigo Salvetti, was pressed to provide copies of more recent prints, and certainly he believed that they were to be used quite directly as stores of source material. He wrote to Florence:

With your last [dispatch] you told me that you had sent the prints and narrative of the Festival held [in Florence] for the wedding of His Highness. I await them so that I may show them to the Royal Surveyor, who wants to see them.

And later:

If the scene designs for the play arrive, I shall give them with compliments to the Surveyor of His Majesty's Works, who wants them to help him in the opportunities he has to show his art every year in the masques and other entertainments he creates for their Majesties.[51]

The scenes provided for the plays at Court were less spectacular than those that Jones derived from Parigi for the masques, and called for fewer special effects; but they were more various and thoughtful in their inspiration. Their chief source was Serlio's *Architettura*, but on every occasion the Italian models were recast with confident freedom, extensively mingled with an eclectic array of forms derived from artists ranging from Tempesta to Vredeman de Vries. Where the masque designs stayed close to their Italian models the scenes which Jones created for the drama during the 1630s followed a more independent line, chiefly pastoral in nature but inventive and personal in content. Such plays as *The Shepherd's Paradise*, *Florimène* and *The Passionate Lovers* were given wings and shutters owing little to the Parigi, and seem rather to have evoked some of Jones's most lyrical and elegant work, such as the unidentified relieve scene of trees and cottages, O & S 465.

After the staging of *Salmacida Spolia* in 1640 Charles's masquing days were over, and Jones was never again to act the tyrant over his gangs of craftsmen and labourers among the paint and woodshavings at Whitehall. The times turned against him, as they turned against his king, and soon he was summoned before the House of Lords charged with irregularities in his treatment of the parishioners of St Gregory's, a church whose fabric had stood in the way of the restoration works at St Paul's. He was not impeached, but the work at St Paul's had stopped. In 1642 he was with the king in Yorkshire, doubtless advising on fortifications, lending money to the royal cause like so many of his kind, and finally – in 1645 – captured by Cromwell at Basing House, Hampshire. To the Parliamentary press he was known as the 'famous Surveyor and great Enemy of St. Grigory', and the 'contriver of scenes for the Queen's Dancing Barn'.[52] In fact he had been thrust out of the Surveyorship in 1643, his place taken by the same Edward Carter of whom Webb had been so suspicious; now he was brought in custody to London and fined. According to Vertue[53] he had removed his money and plate to Lambeth Marsh and buried them there, so that when his estate was sequestered later on the visitors found less than they had hoped, although they did a good deal of damage in their search.[54] On 22 July 1650 Jones made his will, and almost two years later he died, leaving among many bequests £100 for a white marble monument to be erected where he was buried, close to his parents at St Benet's, Paul's Wharf, between the cathedral and the river. There was a pedestal with a carved bust and reliefs of St Paul's and the Banqueting House. It was destroyed in the Great Fire.[55]

There is no mention in the will of the collection of drawings which Jones had acquired in Italy and elsewhere, and to which he added his own profuse output of more than forty years. In a detailed statement of his possessions drawn up in 1646 as part of his negotiations with the Commons he listed 'Goods and Instruments mathematicall and other things of that Nature belonginge to my profession', valued on this occasion at £500, and 'certain Modelles and other like commodityes which I only used and keepe for my pleasure, but of noe profitt, yet cost mee 200 li and upwards'.[56] Perhaps, for such purposes of fiscal declaration, the drawings were included in these items; they will hardly have been omitted as belonging to the

Works. Whatever the clauses of his will, after Jones's death the drawings passed along with most of his books as a single undivided collection into the possession of John Webb, who added to them many more of his own. His wife Anne, Jones's 'kinswoman', was the major beneficiary of the will, and Webb honoured the memory of his mentor – whose genius he was always quick to defend – by bequesting them in turn to his son William with the injunction that they should not be dispersed. The caveat was ignored by William's widow, but the crucial first generation had successfully been survived. By the time the drawings were put on the market there were interested buyers willing not only to pay for them but to look after what they had bought, and it seems likely that few have been lost.

The greatest collections are at Chatsworth and Worcester College, Oxford, but one group of special interest to the theatre historian is among the Lansdowne MSS at the British Library.[57] The volume consists entirely of drawings in the hand of John Webb, and it seems that he was responsible for assembling it in the first place, for it contains nothing but theatre plans and sections, all of them reproduced in the present book. His handwriting appears on many of them, sometimes with a mere dimension or label, sometimes in a pedagogic vein with extensive marginal notations of an explanatory sort. The collection is further distinguished by the fact that, although it emanates from an office whose foremost theatrical activity was the designing of masques, it contains drawings relating to only one such work – *Salmacida Spolia* – bound up with others made for plays: the Paved Court Theatre at Somerset House as arranged for *The Shepherd's Paradise* (1633), the hall at Whitehall set up for *Florimène* (1635) and the stage of the Cockpit in Drury Lane prepared for *The Siege of Rhodes* in 1658–9. Thus of the four stages represented, three were constructed for the drama and only one for a masque.

At some time after Jones's death Webb appears to have set about preparing various sets of drawings probably for publication: at Worcester College, for example, there are carefully drafted illustrations of the orders, of a quite pedagogical sort. One of his groups may indicate that he planned to present a full-scale study of theatrical scenography. Among the many scene designs which he possessed, and which are now in the Devonshire collection at Chatsworth, is a small but apparently significant number which he endorsed in black chalk with titles and other identifying notes, as if in anticipation of gathering them all together in a single, coherent arrangement. The characteristic annotations are found on twenty-seven drawings altogether, two-thirds of them for plays. They include the following, listed by their numbers in Orgel and Strong:

Unknown tragedy, 1629–30:
141   The Tragick/a standing\seene y^e first sceane
146   5 sceane
The Shepherd's Paradise, 1633:
245   The standing sceane
246   first sceane a pallas in trees painted a shutter
247   The Queenes Throne Act ye 2: sceane ye 4th then changed into ye sheapheards Paradise
249   The 8th sceane a Temple of Releiue

251   The seuenth sceane a Prospect of Trees & howses a shutter
254   Wood of a new forme being a shutter ['Wood of Releiue 6 sceane' deleted]
Florimène, 1635:
327   The shutter [o]f ye Isle of [D]elos being for [y]e standing sceane
328   The first Releiue
329   2 Releiue
331   4 Releiue
332   5 Releiue
333   6ᵗʰ sceane the 2ᵈ Temple [o]f Diana a shutter
The Passionate Lovers, 1638:
397   The wood 6 sceane ['The first sceane' deleted] the wood a shutter in ye 2ᵈ part of Mr
      Lodowicks play
Cleodora, 1640:
444   Cleodora ['first sceane a shutter' in ink] of a fortified Towne & a Campe a farr off.
445   Cleodora
Unidentified play (?):
454   ye 4ᵗʰ sceane a Chamber – a shutter sett back so yt one might passe by

Closely similar chalk annotations are found on a smaller number of masque designs:

Triumph of Peace, 1634:
270   fforum of peace 1 sceane
Coelum Britannicum, 1634:
282   The Cloud which opening Eternity was scene
Britannia Triumphans, 1638:
334   1 sceane with London farr off.
337   3 sceane a forest & Gyants Castell
Luminalia, 1638:
383   The first sceane of night
Salmacida Spolia, 1640:
402   The [?] sceane
403   behind ye 4/side\shutter thrust forth in a groove
409   [contains numerous chalk annotations in the right margin]

In addition O & S 180, one of a set of preliminary costume designs for *Chloridia*, has a more casual note in Webb's hand: 'there is fayre drawings of all these'. This short list includes the first scene of each of *The Triumph of Peace*, *Britannia Triumphans* and *Luminalia* together with two major scenes from *Salmacida Spolia*. There are details from *Coelum Britannicum* and *Salmacida Spolia* and a '3: sceane' from *Britannia Triumphans*, but otherwise Webb seems to have noted only the most complete scenic designs from each of the later Caroline masques, leaving unendorsed many more subordinate drawings. By contrast his inclusion of so many connected with the stage plays designed by Jones in the 1630s suggests that his intention was to assemble a body of documents related chiefly to the scenic drama and perhaps only incidentally illustrated by a few of the choicer drawings from the Caroline masque. Almost all the play-scenes which Jones designed from 1629 to 1640 are touched by Webb's categorizing hand, while only a tiny proportion of the many masque designs are included.[58]

This bias resembles that of Lansdowne MS 1171, but without some further documentary evidence we can hardly know precisely what Webb's purpose was in assembling so exhaustive a collection of work for the Court drama. By far the greater part of the stage drawings in Jones's office, or later in Webb's own possession, recorded the ceaseless commitment of the Works to the production of the Caroline masques; scenic drama constituted only a small and technically uninteresting part of the whole. Possibly Webb annotated the drawings having to do with plays, and collected his theatre plans, at a later time in his career, when his work on the reconversion of the Whitehall great hall into a permanent Court theatre for Charles II rendered this aspect of Jones's canon especially interesting to him, and caused him also to re-examine the principles which had governed his own early theatre designs. Whatever his motives, and whatever the date of his annotations, the grouping of the drawings is itself of some significance, for it argues that Webb found their subject to be worth special study. The scenic drama of the Court was not merely an unmusical extension of the masque, but a distinct category of theatre work. The annotations, in bringing together this coherent group of drawings, constitute in their way the earliest essay in the history of English stage design.

It fell to Webb's lot to become not only the executor of Jones's will but the literary and artistic custodian of his intellectual estate, and there is always a danger that in approaching Jones along avenues signposted by Webb we may see only what he saw. Nor, on the whole, was Webb sufficiently egotistical to assert his own independent claims to recognition, in striking contrast to other Court designers of Jones's time, such as Constantino de' Servi or Balthazar Gerbier. The tight-lipped 'closeness' of the one[59] and the boasting of the other exactly defined the limits of their work in relation to Jones's, for both saw themselves as his competitors. But Webb was an assistant and an interpreter, and it is often difficult to see where his work begins and Jones's leaves off. Perhaps the most obvious example is the book published by Webb in 1655 on the subject of Stonehenge.[60] The text is full of theorizing, of learned exposition and somewhat pedantic classicism. It offers the curious theory that Stonehenge was a Roman Tuscan temple dedicated to Coelus, made round in recognition of the god and proportioned along the lines of an ancient theatre as described by Vitruvius. Webb might have been capable of such a work on his own account, for it shows a good deal of the almost encyclopaedic if not always well-digested learning which he brought to another book in 1669, *An Historical Essay Endeavouring a Probability that the Language of the Empire of China is the Primitive Language*. But he cast the Stonehenge book in the voice of Jones, published it under Jones's name and even included some of the biographical details – offered as autobiography – which still form the basis of our knowledge of Jones's early life and travels. It would be a hard task, perhaps an impossible one, to distinguish the limits of Jones's true contribution to the book, described even by Webb as 'some few indigested Notes', with the result that we can know this not inconsiderable part of Jones's genius only through the eyes of Webb. Similarly the great series of designs for rebuilding Whitehall Palace have come down to us, through Webb's agency, in so convoluted a tangle that at one time it was thought that all were by Jones, then all by Webb, and only now, thanks to the exacting work of Margaret Whinney, by both in four quite independent groups.[61]

At the Restoration it seemed at last that Webb might succeed to the Surveyorship for which he was so thoroughly prepared. His lobbying was vigorous, but not enough to prevent the post going to John Denham; later, in 1669, he was again passed over in favour of Christopher Wren, in part perhaps because he was by now too closely identified with Jones and seen as never quite his own man. After his death his work was cavalierly published by the Palladians of the eighteenth century under Jones's name. In volumes by Kent, Ware and Vardy[62] the authors made no distinction between the two architects, perhaps believing that the 'amanuensis' could hardly be given credit for work that he had simply copied down. But already Kent and Vardy were unconsciously printing what Webb had chosen, preserved and interpreted.

Among the theatre drawings are several where the problem of distinguishing between Jones's original and Webb's copy is of crucial importance. As we have seen, the Cockpit-in-Court is known through a large number of entries in the Works accounts for 1629–32 and in a set of studies by Webb which appears to have been made in connection with a refitting thirty years later. Webb's sheet, among the drawings at Worcester College, omits a section of the theatre as a whole, giving only plans and an elevation limited to the *frons scenae*. The omission focuses attention on the stage and *frons*, leaving the auditorium clear in plan but obscure in elevation, and therefore less immediately present to the modern eye. Yet it appears to have been Jones's intention to design a 'Palladian' theatre along the lines of the Teatro Olimpico in which the auditorium and stage came together in a single entity. The integration is obscured in Webb's drawings, not because he failed to appreciate it, but because in 1660 he was able to take it for granted. Now it must be recovered by a deliberate act of enquiry.

The earliest plan in Lansdowne MS 1171 is that of the Paved Court Theatre, constructed in 1632–3 at Somerset House; the latest is for the stage erected at the Cockpit in Drury Lane and set with scenes when Davenant's *Siege of Rhodes* was performed there. The drawings thus preserved therefore concern theatres designed after Webb entered Jones's office and include one from the period after Jones's death in 1652. Jones had of course been responsible for many court theatres before that built in the Paved Court, but the only playhouse for which we have good drawings probably dating from before Webb's first employment is the Cockpit in Drury Lane, for Jones an atypical commission and one perhaps entailing the sort of royal patronage for which preservable presentation drawings might have been prepared. It is notable that although the masque theatres were constructed routinely throughout the earlier part of the seventeenth century we have no precise architectural record of any of them except Webb's copies in Lansdowne MS 1171 of the plan and section of the stage for *Salmacida Spolia*. A hasty note on the verso of a scene design of 1621 shows the plan of a scenic stage, the only one to survive from Jones's hand. Yet it is hardly conceivable that detailed working drawings were not prepared for all the masques, with their sometimes elaborate machines and always changeable scenery. Possibly they were prepared by draftsmen such as Toby Samways and destroyed as soon as their immediate usefulness was past, Jones's own designs being retained for their artistic merit. With Webb's arrival in 1628 the retention rate improved, but the tally is still highly selective.

The chance survival of particular classes of document brings with it a risk of bias for which the historian must nearly always make allowances. Yet in this case it appears that the bias originated with Webb as a deliberate act of discrimination: for him the material worth preserving was primarily that which related to stage plays, and in particular those plays for which he had himself shared some of the responsibility. The core of his collection is the gathering of architectural drawings in Lansdowne MS 1171, but it is fleshed out by the unusually complete series of scene designs retained among Jones's extant canon, including several for which no plans survive, such as those for *Artenice* (1626) or *The Passionate Lovers*. The whole collection of drama scenes, viewed overall, offers a preponderance of pastoral settings, natural enough in a Court devoted to the headier flights of neo-Platonism. The woodland wings for *Florimène* are interspersed with rustic cottages reminiscent of Serlio's Satyric Scene, a source to which the 'pastoral scene' for *Artenice* was also partly indebted. Other rural scenes are more personal in inspiration, but even those for *The Shepherd's Paradise* and *The Passionate Lovers* seem to have been conceived within the intellectual frame offered by Serlio's adoption, from Vitruvius, of the triad of Comic, Tragic and Satyric kinds. In Serlio the setting proper to the satyr play of antiquity had been appropriated for the pastoral, and Jones in his pastoral settings adopted the identification without demur, though permitting much variety to be introduced, particularly at the changeable backshutters and relieves of his customary scenic system. Examples of the Tragic Scene are fewer, but the beautiful design prepared presumably for Somerset House in 1629–30 again shows how completely Jones accepted the Renaissance classification of the ancient dramatic genres, a habit of mind more customary, perhaps, for an architect than a practising dramatist of the early seventeenth century. Yet if the Satyric and Tragic Scenes are present in the canon in distinguished versions, Serlio's Comic Scene is almost entirely absent, appearing only as a subordinate source in *Artenice* and in some of the masque designs. The omission is perhaps surprising, for we know that many comedies were performed at Court and in general the period was one that saw the strong development of the city comedy and the comedy of manners in the work of Brome and Shirley. Yet with few if any exceptions these plays were staged without scenery even at Court; some of the pastorals were played by distinguished amateurs and all were supported by generous budgets, while the professional actors were expected to perform their work at Court in the non-scenic auditoria customarily fitted up by the Chamber and Revels offices. Yet when Webb constructed the Hall Theatre at Whitehall a few years after the Restoration he prepared for it not merely the pictorial shutter scenes for *Mustapha* whose designs survive, but also – as we shall see in chapter 10 – a complete set of Comic, Tragic and Satyric Scenes to suit an all-purpose stage still cast even at this late date in the mould of Renaissance architectural theory.

Webb's long possession of Jones's drawings, together with his evident desire to classify and present them to the world, may well have allowed him to colour our view of their achievement. His selective labelling favours those that fit the classical 'Satyric' and 'Tragic' mould, but among the miscellaneous designs we find pieces conceived in a spirit far removed from that of Serlio's Second Book, such as the 'Army' and 'Prison' scenes probably made for the Cockpit-in-Court (see p. 111 below), or the various 'Chamber' designs most probably intended for plays rather than masques, but regrettably unidentified. Webb himself, in *The Siege of Rhodes* backshutters and relieves, adopted many of these forms, and it appears that his generic Hall Theatre scenes represent the more serious and theoretical side of his talent. The vigour of the commercial theatre, like Davenant's enterprise at the Drury Lane Cockpit, required a more flexible approach than was taught in the pages of Serlio, and neither Webb nor Jones himself was reluctant to meet its demands. Nevertheless the main corpus of their drama designs, defined as it may have been by Webb's custodianship and selective annotation, may be classified in one or other of the generic 'kinds' of antiquity, and lends to the scenic theatre of the Court, at least in retrospect, a more or less classical canonical authority.

Yet if a kind of high seriousness coloured so much of the theatrical scenery of the seventeenth century it often coexisted with a less solemn playfulness. The masques generally kept the two moods apart, giving all the fun to the burratines and pantaloons of the antimasque and reserving the seriousness for the wonder of the visual transformations, the music and the dances that followed. Plays were more likely to offer a mixed form, and for *The Descent of Orpheus* at the Cockpit in 1661 the French performers provided a spectacular mechanical serpent which slithered across the stage to strike at Euridice. We shall see that even Jones, whose dramatic stages are often chastely ceremonious, let himself go when he offered his first and perhaps his most inventive interpretation of the Tragic, Comic and Satyric scenes to an English audience at Christ Church early in the reign of King James. The present study will close with the version of the same antique triad which Webb prepared for the Hall Theatre after the Restoration. The tenacity of the theme is a sign of the organic continuity of our subject, but in their relative tameness Webb's designs show that the power of the Serlian example was exhausted by 1665. Yet its influence had been long and fruitful. Sixty years earlier the unified perspective scene was a great novelty in England, the Serlian auditorium was a lavish wonder in itself, and Jones, preparing to address his audience of courtiers and academics at Oxford, was at the start of what may properly be called his brilliant career.

2   The theatre at Christ Church, Oxford

INIGO JONES'S first recorded work for the theatre was not for a play but a masque, *The Masque of Blackness*, performed at Whitehall on Twelfth Night, 1605. Its 'bodily part' included a unified perspective seascape, proportioned to the king's station-point in the Banqueting House, and deliberately constructed to strike its audience with wonder, as Ben Jonson claimed in his text:

. . . the *Scene* behind, seemed a vast sea (and vnited with this that flowed forth [a mobile sea of waves and billows]) from the termination, or *horizon* of which (being the leuell of the *State*, which was placed in the vpper end of the hall) was drawne, by the lines of *Prospectiue*, the whole worke shooting downewards, from the eye; which *decorum* made it more conspicuous, and caught the eye a farre off with a wandring beauty. To which was added an obscure and cloudy night-piece, that made the whole set of.[1]

Not everyone was suitably moved by this innovation, Dudley Carleton dismissing it as a 'Pagent',[2] but nothing quite like it had appeared in England before. Within the year, moreover, Jones introduced a series of analogous innovations to the dramatic stage, bringing to it more completely than ever before in England the pleasures of Renaissance learning which had for so long informed the courtly theatres of Italy. The occasion for this assertive display was the week of ceremonies at Oxford called the Act, an annual celebration when public debates were held by day in St Mary's, the University Church, and in the evenings the colleges fell to feasting and sometimes by custom to dramatic entertainments. In August 1605 the Act was favoured with the presence of James I and his Court, and became, under the pressure of Whitehall, as much a courtly as an academic recreation. During the daytime James attended the rhetorical exercises in an auditorium set up in St Mary's; in the evenings he repaired with his courtiers to Christ Church to see the plays. According to an anonymous Cambridge man who wrote a full and critical account of the proceedings for the benefit of his own university,[3] both the Christ Church theatre and the auditorium in St Mary's Church were constructed not by the Oxford academics but by the carpenters of the King's Works from Whitehall, with the advice of their Comptroller, Simon Basil. The plays themselves were of course the university's responsibility, but even here the Court was influential, for the colleges were assisted – at the handsome fee of £50 – by one 'Mr Jones a great travellor', evidently Inigo, whose reputation rode high after the innovations of *Blackness*, but who in our Cambridge narrator's acid opinion on this occasion 'performed very litle to what which was expected'.[4]

This judgment may have been a little coloured by the author's Cantabrigian

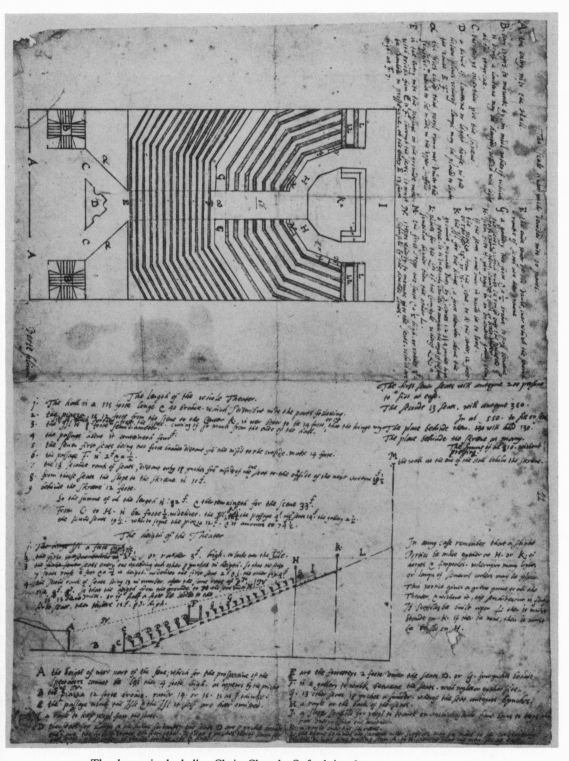

2   The theatre in the hall at Christ Church, Oxford, in 1605

loyalty, for others were more favourably impressed by Jones's work as well as by Simon Basil's. In 1605 Jones still had no official standing with the royal Works, while Basil, already the Comptroller, was shortly to succeed the Scot Sir David Cuningham as Surveyor.[5] None of Jones's designs for the plays have survived, but the original scheme for the auditorium is fully recorded in a drawing at the British Library (plate 2).[6] It shows in some detail what might be expected of a scenic Court theatre at the beginning of the seventeenth century in England, and for that reason must at least be recorded here.

The drawing is on a single sheeet 295 mm by 385 mm, and presents both a plan and a section of the auditorium. The scheme has previously been catalogued as presenting 'some theatre, probably in Germany', but there is in fact nothing German about it. Though the design is unsigned and untitled, it is covered in English-language comments in a neat italic hand of the early seventeenth century which give directions to the workmen for its realization. Occasionally the author changes his mind about a dimension as he works on his drawing, and amends his prescriptions accordingly; evidently the sheet offers a working drawing, not a fair copy. The indication that it shows the hall at Christ Church lies in one of the written comments: 'The hall is a 115 foote longe & 40 broade . . .' No hall in England other than Christ Church possessed such dimensions, which are uncommonly long in relation to the width; but the interior of the hall at Christ Church – and clearly the drawing shows the interior of a room – is commonly stated to be 115 ft by 40 ft (it is in fact 114 ft 6 ins by 39 ft 9 ins).[7] The design also shows places for a king, his lords of the council and his servants. Twice in the earlier seventeenth century a king and his courtiers attended scenic plays in the hall at Christ Church: once in 1636, when Charles I sat opposite a deep scenic stage which according to an eyewitness, the antiquarian Brian Twyne, extended almost to the hearth at the centre of the room;[8] and once in 1605, when James attended the Act.

The British Library drawing is scaled at ten feet to the inch, and shows an auditorium built within a double square, 40 ft by 80 ft. No stage is marked on the plan, but one of the written comments records that 'the summe of al the length is . 82^f· & ther remaineth for the scene 33^f·' Thus the full length of the hall is accounted for (82 ft + 33 ft = 115 ft), though the plan has given the auditorium two feet shorter than it should be. But a stage 33 ft deep is certainly not deep enough to reach to the central hearth, and it appears that the scheme recorded here must relate to the royal visit of 1605 rather than that of thirty years later.

In certain respects the scheme drawn up by the Comptroller did not win the approval of some of the more influential and conservative statesmen of James's Court, and although at first the theatre was erected according to Basil's design, they caused it to be altered before the plays were actually performed. Nevertheless the scheme in its unaltered state, as shown in the drawing, is of considerable interest as showing the tendency of thought among the Works artificers at the beginning of James's reign. It is evidently Serlian in inspiration, though where Serlio's auditorium is segmental in plan within its rectangular boundaries (plate 3) Basil's is

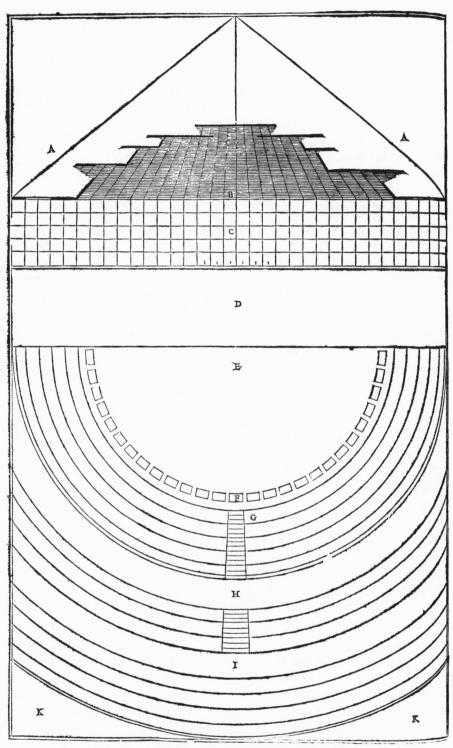

3   Sebastiano Serlio, theatre plan. *Il secondo libro di perspettiva* (Paris, 1545), fol. 66ᵇ

polygonal, arranging straight benches in trapezoidal 'wedges' about a central space whose forepart is occupied by the king's 'Isle' or halpace. In this the English royal theatre differs from its Italian model, where the semi-circular orchestra is left empty but for a peripheral row of noblemen's seats, but the irregular polygons described by the 'Isle', the open space surrounding it and the ranks of degrees behind it are all inscribed, in the drawing, within the arcs of circles scored into the surface of the paper with the sharp point of a pair of compasses whose still foot is placed at what the annotations describe as 'the Center к'. This centre, which appears at the front of the 'Isle', is separated from the stage by what the drawing calls a 'piazza', a term borrowed directly from the later editions of Serlio's *Architettura*, where a similar feature is called the 'piazza della scena' (in the earlier editions, before 1566, it had been called the 'proscenio').[9] As in Serlio also, the seating is arranged according to a social hierarchy: the benches in the front seven rows are for the 'Ladys & the kings servants', and are distinguished by an intermediate gangway from the more narrowly spaced rows behind. At the back, high up, is standing room, presumably for students.

While the plan shows only the auditorium, in accord with the division of responsibility between Basil and Jones, the section does give a hint of a flat forestage with a steeply raked and presumably scenic stage beyond it. Here again the model is evidently Serlian, for this is precisely the pattern of the woodcuts illustrating the *Architettura*, which also present a plan and a longitudinal section. From the written comments we learn that 'the heigth of next [nearest] part of the scene . . . for the prospectiue of the spectators cannot bee less then 4 foote high', and this is the height as drawn in the section, its utility confirmed by a 'prickt line' marking the sightline from the front of the standing places at the rear of the auditorium to the front edge of the forestage.

In all the editions of Serlio before that of 1566 the semi-circular orchestra is drawn as 48 ft wide, the scale being indicated by the reticulation of the forestage into 2 ft squares. The equivalent feature in the Christ Church design, the polygonal area in which the 'Isle' is placed, is just 24 ft across, perhaps indicating that the designer has taken his cue from Serlio's woodcut, following it at a scale of one foot to the square. A similar scale defines the depth of the forestage at Christ Church, which is given as five feet in the section and answers to Serlio's forestage at five squares deep. But the height of the Christ Church stage, at four feet, repeats Serlio directly, for his stage is two squares high at the front; and the 'piazza' at Christ Church, intended by Basil at first to be 12 ft deep, is likewise directly akin to Serlio's, which measures six squares. There is no direct Serlian sanction, however, for two other pieces of proportional decorum in the Christ Church design, where the radius of the incised arc defining the rearmost degrees is 48 ft, or just twice the width of the orchestra; and where the whole plan of the auditorium is drawn within boundaries given by a double square, just 4 in by 8 in on the paper.

Thus far the British Library sheet has offered nothing that could not have been derived from Serlio, modified only slightly to suit English royal conditions – the halpace invading the orchestra, the boxes for the Privy Councillors invading the piazza – and the practical exigencies of carpentry, which doubtless prompted the reduction of Serlio's segmental seating to the straight-sided polygons at Christ Church. For one feature, however, the design (plate 2) looks beyond Serlio to other Italian sources:

In anny case remember that a slight Portico bee made eyther at H. or K. of hoopes & firrpoales. wherupon many lights or lamps of seueral coulers may be placed. This portico giues a great grace to all the Theater, & without it, the Architectur is false.

Such porticos, imitating the grand arcading of the ancient theatre, are found at Vicenza and Sabbioneta, in the work of Palladio and Scamozzi. Basil's construction of hoops and poles sounds more primitive than the exquisite classicism of its models, but one should not be too easily persuaded by the simplicity of the materials. The Italians likewise worked in wood, probably for perfectly good reasons of acoustics, and the Christ Church scheme insists on its own architectural completeness and grace. Basil seems to have intended that a quite regular classical order should round off his composition.

The Christ Church scheme, as it appears in this practical working drawing, gives as clear an indication as one could wish of the international sophistication of the Works early in the seventeenth century. It is perhaps not surprising to discover that Serlio was so assiduoulsy followed, for his great collection of woodcuts was often drawn on by the designers of the grander Elizabethan and Jacobean houses. Many other English drawings of this period, including several associated with Basil by Mark Girouard,[10] show the impact of Serlio's designs, so many that Sir John Summerson has concluded that at the time Serlio 'influenced English architecture more than any other single man'.[11] But in providing a portico at the back of his auditorium, and moreover by arguing that its inclusion was a necessary part of the integrity of its design, Basil shows that he was alive to other treatments of the classical theme than those included in the *Architettura*, where no such feature is to be found.

Indeed it would appear that Basil was ahead of his time in his understanding of the Italian neo-classic auditorium, for when our Cambridge spy looked in on the preparations at Christ Church he found the Earls of Worcester, Suffolk and Northampton with Lord Carey in something of a quandary over what seemed to them the unusual disposition of the house:

They (but especiallie *Suff*:) vtterlie disliked the stage att Christchurch, and above all, the place appointed for the chayre of estate because yt was no higher and the kinge soe placed that the Auditory could see but his cheeke onlie. this dislike of the Earle of *Suff*: much troubled the *Vicechancelor*, and all the workmen, yet they stood in defence of the thinge done, and maynteyned that by the art perspective the kinge should behould all better then if he sat higher. (fol. 30)

Because the stage was a scenic one it made new and special demands on the designer of the theatre. The university was on this occasion at one with the Works (i.e. the vice-chancellor and all the workmen) in defending Basil's Serlian solution against the claims of a more usual courtly decorum most forcefully advanced by the Lord Chamberlain himself, the Earl of Suffolk. The battle was joined by the Chancellor, the Earl of Dorset, who in his younger days as Thomas Sackville had been a noted playwright and now took Basil's part. The matter was important enough to go before Council, who debated it and came to a compromise solution:

> . . . in the end the place was removed, and sett in the midst of the hall, but too farr from the stage (vizt) xxviij. feete, soe that there were manye longe speeches delivered, which neyther the kinge nor anye neere him could well heere or vnderstand.   (Ibid.)

Such a move meant the destruction of the front rank of degrees so that the royal 'Isle' and its flanking boxes for the Lords of the Privy Council could be brought back to a point 28 ft from the forestage. The ladies and king's servants thus displaced were then reseated in the resultant much enlarged 'piazza'. In this revised state the auditorium was described by the former Christ Church man Isaac Wake, now a fellow of Merton, whose elaborate Latin account of the royal visit, *Rex Platonicus*, was printed in 1607 and may be translated thus:

> From the floorboards of the hall right up to the lofty trusses of the roof, wedges (of degrees) were fixed to the walls in a great arc. In the middle of the 'cavea' the royal throne was set up for the princes, surrounded by a balustrade; flanking it to either side lay boxes for the nobles; the remaining space between the throne and the stage was set a little lower, for young women and ladies.   (pp. 46–7)

Here the main elements of Basil's auditorium are all accounted for: the great arc of the degrees is divided, by its polygonal shape, into 'cunei' or wedges of seats ranging high up towards the beams of the hall; in the new position the king's 'Isle', or 'thronus Augustalis cancellis cintus' was indeed in the midst of the 'cavea', and was flanked to either side by the lords' boxes ('que*m* vtrinq*ue* optimatum stationes communiunt'). Between these slightly elevated features and the forestage sat the ladies, doubtless now with a view of more than the king's cheek, for they will have been set sideways, flanking the walls of the hall, and not with their backs to the monarch.

While Basil's Serlian auditorium is fully recorded, in drawings as well as verbal accounts, Jones's work on the stage remains a good deal more shadowy, for no visual records of it remain, and even the verbal descriptions lack focus. Nevertheless it is clear that the plays themselves were deliberately academic in flavour. Of the four, two were certainly in Latin, one probably in Latin and one – the last, not acted before the king – in English.[12] Between them the three major productions covered the three 'kinds' of classical drama as recognized by Vitruvius (Book V, Chapter vi). *Alba*, on the first night, 27 August, was a satyr play, with pans and shepherdesses; *Ajax Flagellifer*, performed the following evening, was a tragedy on a well-known theme; and *Vertumnus* on the third night was a comedy with philosophical overtones. On the last day Daniel's *Arcadia Reformed* was played in English as a treat for the queen and Prince Henry, and although it stood apart from the main programme it was by far the best liked.[13] But Oxford's heart was surely set on the other three. These were the academic plays, illustrating the breadth of classical drama and the vitality of the university's rhetorical culture. To Jones they represented both an opportunity and a challenge. He had already shown his flair for ingenious stagecraft at Whitehall: could he now rise to the learning of the academy with a suitable classicism of his own?

When the anonymous Cambridge reporter comes to render his account of Jones's scenic style his language becomes imprecise, as if he were reaching for words to describe something he has never seen before and does not greatly admire:

The stage was built close to the vpper end of the Hall, as it seemed at the first sight, but indeed it was but a false wall fayre painted and adorned with statelie pillers, which pillers would turne about, by reason whereof with the helpe of other painted clothes, their stage did varrie three tymes in the Actinge of one Tragedye. Behind the foresaid false wall there was reserved 5. or 6. paces of the vpper end of the Hall which served them to good uses for their howses, and receipt of their Actors and souldiors etc. (fol. 30ᵃ⁻ᵇ)

The five or six paces, if we assume them to be Roman paces of 5 ft, amount to 25 or 30 ft, figures consistent with the stage shown in Basil's section and described in his notes. There the forestage is drawn as 5 ft deep and the total space devoted to the stage is 33 ft, leaving 28 ft between what the Cambridge account calls the 'false wall' of the turning pillars and the real wall of the Tudor hall backstage. The stately pillars that turned were clearly some sort of *scena versatilis*, but the details are obscure. Fortunately another, and fuller, account of the stage is given in Isaac Wake's more enthusiastic record, whose language is as fulsome as the other's is dry. After commenting on the beauty of the hall itself, with its eighteen windows and its gilt hammerbeam roof, Wake turns to the stage:

The scene occupied the upper part of the hall; its stage (*Proscenium*) running down to a level part in a gentle incline, which lent great dignity to the entrances of the players, as if descending a hill. (p. 46)

Here is the first record of a raked stage in England, and one moreover that was practicable, for the actors made their entries down it. Wake says that the incline of the stage ended 'in planitiem', as is shown in Basil's section of the theatre, where the flat forestage, borrowed from Serlio, provided room underneath for winches to move the machinery mentioned by the Cambridge reporter and also by Wake in his next sentence:

The cloths and houses of the scene were skilfully changed by means of a machine time and again according to all the necessary places and occasions, so that the whole form of the fabric of the stage suddenly appeared new, to everyone's amazement, not only from day to day for each production, but even in the course of a single performance. (Ibid.)

Here again is the observation that the whole scene changed, together with the point that the changes were made not only from play to play, but also within a single play. Between them, the two commentators show that the same stage was used for all the productions, that it was varied between productions to suit each, and that in the case of the tragedy there were three different scenes.

4 Sebastiano Serlio, Comic Scene. *Il secondo libro di perspettiva*, unfoliated leaf

Wake further complements the Cambridge account by mentioning the moving clouds above, worked by machines and so convincing that one would have thought that they were real. Serlio's perspective theatre, with its capacity for elaborate sky effects,[14] is the closest single analogue to the Christ Church stage, and were it not for his impressive turning pillars one might conclude that Jones's answer to the academic challenge of the occasion was simply to quote the Italian's theatre scheme. But the turning machines, capable of changing the scene before the eyes of the audience, were very different from the fixed angled wings and backcloth illustrated in the *Architettura*. They derived not from Serlio, but from Vitruvius. Unfortunately the combined evidence of the Cambridge report and Wake is insufficient to show precisely how they were arranged, but the fact observed by the latter that the *Ajax* had three scenes probably indicates that they were triangular *periaktoi* capable of presenting one of their three surfaces to the audience at a time. This kind of *scena versatilis* had often enough been used on the Continent, and it had even been seen in a 'Motion' – probably a puppet show – at Blackfriars in the

1580s,[15] but this was the first time it had been employed on a major English stage. Its provenance was antique, and mainly Vitruvian. In the fifth of the *Decem Libri* Vitruvius describes the placing of the doors in the 'scena' of the Roman theatre, and continues:

Beyond [the doors] are spaces provided for decoration – places that the Greeks called περίακτοι, because in these places are triangular pieces of machinery (△.△) which revolve, each having three decorated faces. When the play is to be changed, or when gods enter to the accompaniment of sudden claps of thunder, these may be revolved and present a face differently decorated.[16]

Jones possessed Vitruvius in the fine edition by Daniele Barbaro, published in Venice in 1567, which contained an illustration by Palladio of the plan of a theatre showing the *periaktoi* as very small elements in the large structure of the fixed scene. In one respect Barbaro's commentary anticipated the Oxford programme, for it described the function of the *periaktoi* as reflecting the genre of the play to be staged:

. . . on one surface was the perspective of the Comic scene, on another the Tragic, and on a third the Satyric, and the faces turned to suit the occasion.[17]

The contrast between the diminutive *periaktoi* of Palladio's illustration and Barbaro's claim that they could carry a full perspective scene must have struck Jones, as it had others, as strange. In the margin of his copy of Barbaro he wrote, against this passage:

I thinke that the seane chainged according to the occasiones giuen in the accts by taking of the cloathes painted from the triangles machins as I have often yoused in masques and comedies.[18]

Taken in conjunction with Jones's known habit of creating unified perspective scenes, this passage indicates that he thought of *periaktoi* as something more impressive than those of Palladio's plan. The Cambridge report and Wake agree that at Oxford the whole scene changed in the course of the tragedy. Five years later, when Jones used *periaktoi* again in his staging of Daniel's *Tethys' Festival*, the same effect was noted: it was 'the whole face' of the scene that changed. Although Vitruvius was the ancient authority on whom the modern designer relied to impress his academic audience, antiquity was not slavishly to be followed.

Yet the basis of Jones's thinking is surely to be found in Vitruvius and his Renaissance commentator. Vitruvius himself gave sanction to the change of scenes within a play 'when the gods enter to the accompaniment of sudden claps of thunder', and Barbaro's commentary was helpfully specific:

From the top of these machines (*periaktoi*) spoke the gods; one heard the thunder at their coming, as they made their appearance on the scene. According to Sophocles it was thus in *Ajax Flagellifer*. Pallas spoke to Ulysses, but was not seen by him. He said that the voice of the invisible goddess was like the sound of a trumpet of war, which moves men when it is heard calling to arms. These machines were turned according to need, and became entrance loges, representing streets.

(p. 256)

There is no evidence that Jones used the *periaktoi* for any such purposes at Oxford, but the connection with *Ajax Flagellifer* can hardly be mere coincidence. Faced with the university's programme, he designed a stage with an impeccable ancient rationale, precisely suited to the *Ajax* theme and linked to it by the best recent scholarship.

While the *Ajax* connection increases the probability that the turning machines at Oxford were triangular *periaktoi*, it does little to show how Jones married these ancient devices to the unified perspective scene of Serlio. Yet the indications that he did so are plain: his stage was raked, it had revolving scenery and moving clouds, and the whole presented a vista for which, as in *The Masque of Blackness*, there was an optimum point of view in the auditorium from which 'by the art perspective the kinge should behould all better then if he sat higher'. There exist, in the seventeenth-century handbooks of Sabbatini and Furtenbach, designs for elaborate machinery by which Jones might have achieved these ends, but the handbooks are late, and although in their conservatism they may well reflect conditions he might have seen in his Italian journey of *c.* 1600–1, there is no need to range so far for a probable explanation of his work at Oxford. In 1610, after experimenting with various forms of curtain and the *scena ductilis*, he turned again to the *periaktoi* when he staged *Tethys' Festival* at Whitehall. Here the scene changed, in the course of the masque, from 'a port or haven' to a splendidly ornamented throne scene, and finally to a grove of trees. The textual descriptions of the first and last scenes are perfunctory, but that of Tethys' throne room is minutely particularized and happily includes details which give a good idea of its layout. 'This scene was comparted into five niches . . .', and the plan of the *frons scenae* 'came into the form of a half round . . .' At the centre of the arc was the great throne itself, arranged against a segmental backing. It was conceived as an aedicule or architectural unit, with pillars at either side and an architrave above. Flanking it, and extending forwards toward the audience, were two pairs of great niches, in each of which three ladies sat. These niches were also architectural units, equal in height to the wider central unit. Each was capable of disappearing in a trice, to be replaced by the trees of 'a most pleasant and artificial grove'.[19]

The description of the throne scene shows that the whole consisted of five units, each of which represented a single face of a *periaktos*. That in the centre was probably wider than the four which flanked it, but they were all of similar height. They were disposed about the stage in such a way that their concave segmental faces together formed a semi-circle. This method is far removed from anything in Sabbatini and Furtenbach, but it is very close to a device proposed in E. Danti's commentary on Vignola's *Le due regole della prospettiva pratica*, published in Rome in 1583. Danti had seen *periaktoi* used for scene changes at Florence in 1567, and again later on; they had also been employed by Bastiano da Sangallo at Castro in 1543. The plan Danti illustrates (plate 5)[20] shows the five elements Jones was later to use in *Tethys' Festival*, and may have used at Oxford in 1605. His discussion of the system comes in the midst of his treatment of the practical art of painting perspectives, and it is clear that he thinks of the *periaktoi* scene as an example of what he is talking about. Like Serlio's angled wings, the faces of the prisms are

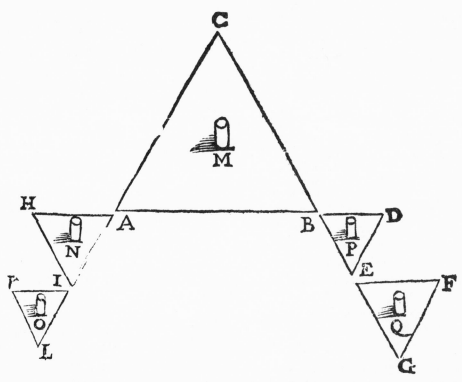

5 A system of *periaktoi*. From E. Danti's commentary on G. B. Vignola's *Le due regole della prospettiva pratica* (Rome, 1583), p. 91

aligned on the orthogonals of the perspective, whose vanishing point therefore coincides with the hidden angle of the centre unit. When all the prisms are turned at once the whole scene changes, just as it did at Oxford. The system used by Bastiano da Sangallo and Baldassare Lanci had the special virtue of combining the ancient motif of the prisms with the modern aim of presenting a unified perspective scene, and it exactly met Jones's needs as he prepared to meet his academic hosts.

The details remain obscure. It is impossible to tell how Jones managed to rotate the prisms above the raked floor of the stage without running foul of it, nor is it clear how he incorporated the cloud borders, if such things are implied by Wake's description. If he followed Danti's system he must have masked the sides of the stage with something like a proscenium border to prevent the 'dead' faces of the prisms from being seen, but neither of the accounts mentions how it was done.

The texts of the two extant plays offer some further information, as do the few facts known about the others. At least two of the plays were costumed in ancient style, suitable to the classical theme of the programme. Lists of the costumes hired by the university from the children of the Queen's Revels for *Alba* are extant, and show that many of them were 'of Antique fashions'.[21] The Cambridge visitor reported that the actors in the *Ajax* 'had all goodlie anticke apparrell' (fol. 37[r]). These touches of antiquity suggest that Jones designed his stage according to the ancient distinction of the Tragic, Comic and Satyric kinds, but enough evidence exists to show that he did so without evoking the example of Vitruvius's best-known Renaissance interpreter in matters of scenography. Wake describes the three scenes of the *Ajax*, and none of them resembles Serlio's Tragic Scene (plate 15):

It is not easy to tell how wondrously all this nourished by turn our ears and eyes. The whole fabric of the scene and its artificial apparatus of hangings was renewed time and again, to everyone's amazement. By which means you saw the living image of Troy, and the Sigean shore; then the woods and deserts and horrid caves, the lair of the Furies; these suddenly vanishing you gazed surprised on the lovely form of the tents and the ships.   (p. 79)

Nothing of what is known about *Alba* or *Arcadia Reformed* gives any specific idea of the designs Jones provided for them. Anthony Nixon, in his account of the royal visit, *Oxfords Triumph*, reported that the latter was 'richlie set forth and performed' (sig. E3ʳ), a judgment which however he applied very freely to the plays.

Alba, written in part by Robert Burton, told the Ovidian story of Pomona and the various disguises under which her lover Vertumnus comes to her. The point of the story, as Ovid tells it, is contained in an allegory of the elm tree and the vine, whose interdependence is an emblem of love. It is possible that Jones provided the tree itself, for a tree seems also to have figured in the setting of *Arcadia Reformed*. In Daniel's play, which was located 'on this Greene' (l. 74), 'in this Grove' (l. 75), Silvia tells Chloris how her lover Palaemon once threatened suicide from the top of 'Yonder craggy rocke' (l. 440) and how she ran to him and led him down

> . . . into this plane,
> And yonder loe, under that fatall tree, –
> Looke *Chloris* there, even in that very place, –
> We sate us down . . .   (ll. 468–71)

Such allusions in the dialogue of a play acted in the public theatres might show nothing about its staging; in a play given a perspective setting by Inigo Jones they are more reliably informative. Indeed there is a glimpse of that stage itself in the shepherds' description of their vale as

> . . . this poore corner of *Arcadia* here,
> This little angle of the world you see,
> Which hath shut out of doore, all t'earth besides,
> And is bard up with mountains, and with trees . . .   (ll. 1023–6)

Just such a 'corner' or 'little angle' was formed by the arrangement of *periaktoi* described by Danti.

The setting for *Vertumnus: sive Annus Recurrens* was very different from the rural scenes of the satyr play and the pastoral. The play is a moral comedy, and its stage as described in a preliminary direction was an elaborate concoction, matching the themes of the text with visual equivalents. The four seasons were present as characters who remained on stage throughout: against their names in the *dramatis personae* is the note '4 tempestae in scena repositáe' (sig. C2ʳ). In the midst was a tree with twelve branches, and above it a cloud-piece painted like a zodiac, through which the sun was made to move, taking in three signs for each act of the play after the first, which was introductory. At the beginning of Act II it left Aries, to pass through Cancer in Act III and Libra in Act IV. Finally, in Act V, it arrived in Pisces, having gone full circle. The four seasons, the four winds, the four humours and the four ages of man: every kind of fourfold division was brought to bear on the central theme of man's development. The compartments of the setting were therefore consistent with the scheme illustrated by Danti and used again by Jones in *Tethys' Festival*, in which four smaller units flanked a large central one. At the centre ('in medio') stood the great tree, its twelve branches lit by twelve lights, thematically if not visually parallel to the twelve signs of the zodiac above. Ranged about the stage were the four houses of the seasons ('Aptum Proscenium ad Tempestates quatuor') with their occupants who remained on stage throughout. Evidently the *periaktoi* were not required to turn during the course of the performance, although the scene, which Nixon reported was 'richlie set foorth and beautified, with . . . curious and quaint conceipts and deuises' (sig. E I^v), was erected in the same theatre that some twenty hours before had witnessed the last transformation in the *Ajax*. Wake states that the same machinery was used to change the scenes between the plays as was used to change it within the *Ajax*, and in any case it is improbable that the system of *periaktoi* would be erected and struck for one production out of the four. *Vertumnus* ended at one a.m. according to the Cambridge report, yet that same morning the stage was cleared of its emblematic tree and houses and a new pastoral setting was introduced. Doubtless the *periaktoi* were simply turned once more, to reveal the 'other painted clothes' which we know were a part of the scheme. Altogether there were six scenes: one for *Alba*, three for *Ajax Flagellifer* and one each for *Vertumnus* and *Arcadia Reformed*. The three used for the *Ajax* needed no special attention during the performance, since all could be made ready beforehand, but the total of six made it necessary that some of the scenes were attached to the prisms rather than painted directly onto their surfaces.

Despite his use of them in subsequent masques, Jones cannot have been happy with the *periaktoi*. Disposed according to Danti's scheme they presented an uninteresting face to the audience, what Daniel rightly characterized as a 'little angle'. The essence of the mannerist stage design which Jones was shortly to master was the sense of recession given by flat side wings standing one behind another and leading the eye on to the exciting veil of the shutters, which would draw back to reveal yet another series of receding surfaces in the relieves set against the infinity of the backcloth. Compared with these delights the *periaktoi* were cumbersome and mawkish. It is little wonder that the productions themselves were enlivened with extrinsic business of a kind calculated to divert the audience's attention from the scene. In *Alba*, for instance, a flock of doves was released from a net and flew out into the hall. One made straight for the queen where she sat in her throne, and there was speculation whether a bird had been specially trained or the trick had been turned by some stage designer's artifice. In the *Ajax* the wonder of the changing scenes was complemented by the noisy madness of the protagonist:

The defeated warrior fills the whole theatre round with his howls; calls on the Furies; execrates gods and men alike; spits out nothing but threats and vengeance.   (Wake, p. 78)

Even the sheep which Ajax mistook for men came and bleated before the king.

Yet, whatever its shortcomings, the Christ Church theatre was a remarkable one for its time. Both Jones and Basil were in fine, aggressive form when they designed it, reaching out well beyond their convenient Serlian source, itself so competently realized and adapted in their work, to riskier but appropriately academic models in the Vitruvian *periaktoi* and the Palladian, neo-Roman 'Portico'. Not for sixty years would England see again so devoted an attempt to bring the ancient theatre alive in modern terms, and that was also to be an Oxford academic building, Christopher Wren's Sheldonian.

3   The Cockpit in Drury Lane

ATE IN 1616 Inigo Jones was starting work on his designs for the king's customary Christmas masque, *The Vision of Delight*. After *Blackness* he had designed most of the major entertainments at Court, but more recently the Italian sojourn had intervened, and this was his first commission of the kind for three years. He turned for inspiration to the book that had shaped the Christ Church theatre eleven years earlier and had been much in his thoughts ever since, Serlio's *Architettura*. Once before, in *Prince Henry's Barriers* (1610), he had plundered its woodcuts for his images of the fallen house of chivalry (O & S 36), a scene which included several monuments culled from its Third Book: a large pyramid, a triumphal arch, a temple and a Roman amphitheatre. In Jones's drawings all are arranged in a scenographic form definitively influenced by the presentation of the Comic and Tragic Scenes in Serlio's Second Book, with their curiously high horizon and steep foreshortening. The same formal qualities distinguish the opening street design of *The Vision of Delight* (O & S 89), but here in addition several of the buildings are borrowed directly from Serlio's two scenes.

The masques of the previous two years were staged without the help of the Surveyor. During his absence in Italy his place was taken by the Florentine visitor, Constantino de' Servi, whose work on Campion's *Somerset Masque* turned into something of a fiasco;[1] and he cannot have been involved in the Christmas masque early in 1615, *Mercury Vindicated*, which was staged before his return. Nor is there any record of his having contributed to Jonson's *Golden Age Restored*, performed at Twelfth Night 1616.[2] Later in that year, however, he was engaged – or so there is good reason to believe – in a theatre project which was to endure far longer than any of these fleeting spectacles. In the closing months of the year, among the muddy building sites of the newly developing area around Drury Lane, close to Queen Street, a brick-built cockpit which had been established seven years before underwent a transformation into a permanent indoor playhouse. It was to prove the most influential house of its type; constructed as it was in the Jacobean heyday, it was home to a variety of professional companies until well after the Restoration, when it stood as a working example to the builders of the Duke's Theatre and the Theatre Royal. No other playhouse so successfully conveyed the dramatic tradition from Shakespeare's age to that of Davenant and Dryden. Not even the Blackfriars, which certainly outshone the Cockpit in Jacobean times, survived so tenaciously all the rigours of the interregnum to live on as a busy and practical place of

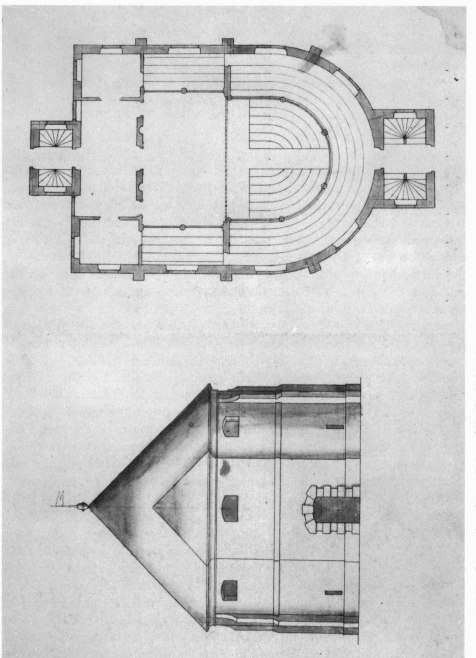

6   Inigo Jones, elevation and plan of the Cockpit in Drury Lane

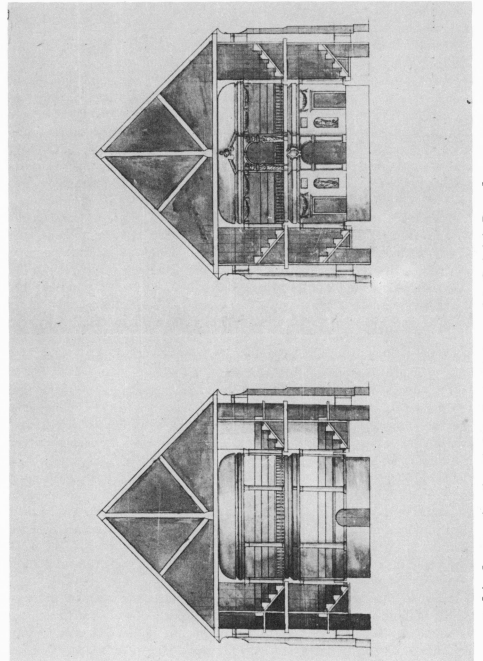

7 Inigo Jones, sections through the auditorium and stage of the Cockpit in Drury Lane

entertainment long after the rhetorical drama had undergone its metamorphosis into the scenic stage.

So crucial is the place of the Cockpit in the development of the English theatre that the lack of any clear idea of its physical form was until recently one of the most serious gaps in our stage history. But a set of drawings by Jones, unpublished until 1969,[3] was first identified in print some four years later by Iain Macintosh as showing the Cockpit itself;[4] others had by then arrived independently at the same conclusion, and now the view is widely shared that in the two handsome sheets among the Jones/Webb collection at Worcester College, Oxford (plates 6 and 7), we possess remarkably detailed designs of this most influential of English playhouses.

The drawings are certainly in Jones's hand, and would merit their place in this book whatever their designation, but their connection with Christopher Beeston's conversion of the Cockpit to theatrical use is so far-reaching in its effect on our understanding of the seventeenth-century theatre that it must be stressed at the outset that the association is still a matter of circumstantial evidence only; no specific, incontrovertible link has yet been found between the drawings and the Cockpit playhouse. In the next few pages I present some reasons for believing that the drawings do show the Cockpit (or Phoenix, as it was sometimes called). More are given in the later discussion of the theatre's conversion to scenic uses in the 1650s; taken all together they seem persuasive enough, and although they do not constitute absolute proof it would be unduly limiting to deny their validity, and with it the important place of Jones's drawings in our theatre history.

If the design does show the Cockpit it must have been made for the owner, Christopher Beeston, an enterprising speculative builder as well as a leading actor and man of the theatre. Jones did sometimes undertake work for private clients, even after he became the King's Surveyor in 1615, but no other example exists of his working for so commercial an entrepreneur as Beeston. Yet, as we saw in chapter 1, by the second decade of the century he was a most practised man of the theatre himself, having designed numerous court masques, with their antimasques performed by the professional players, with whom he had of necessity established close working contacts. At Oxford in 1605 he had used costumes hired from the Blackfriars; at Whitehall he had on occasion arranged for the hall, the great chamber or the cockpit to be made ready for the public companies and must have discussed their requirements with them.[5]

Of course, Jones was not fully a man of the professional theatre, for all his close contact with men like Edward Alleyn[6] and Ben Jonson. Yet at some time in his career he did design the small enclosed playhouse of the Worcester College drawings. It is of the type represented by the Blackfriars or the Salisbury Court, a 'private' house with a U-shaped galleried auditorium surrounding a railed stage with three entrance doors and a balcony above. It possesses most of the character-istics we should expect of a Jacobean private theatre, harmoniously assembled in the idiom of Jones's classicism. In 1973 the drawings were dated on internal evidence by John Harris as 'between c. 1616 and c. 1618'.[7] They are on paper whose watermark indicates a date up to and including 1616, but not later,[8] and though of course the drawings might have been made on the paper at any subsequent date there are general similarities of style between them and other designs made in the years which Harris indicated, such as the scheme supposed to be for Fulke Greville's house (c. 1619) or that for an entrance bay dated 1616 by Jones himself.[9] Their controlled yet painterly handling differs from the freer manner of the drawings for the Whitehall Banqueting House (c. 1619).

The practical theatre projects undertaken in London between Harris's dates 'c. 1616 and c. 1618' were two. One was the abortive project at Puddle Wharf, first broached in 1613, and persisted with until finally suppressed in January 1616–17.[10] Since Jones was out of the country in 1613–14 he is unlikely to have been concerned with this theatre. The other was the Cockpit in Drury Lane. If Jones's designs were ever realized, the circumstantial evidence of the date assigned to them by John Harris points unambiguously to the Cockpit as their object, and indeed Harris, in his official catalogue of the Jones/Webb drawings at Worcester College, now accepts the identification.[11] Nevertheless stronger arguments are needed to justify so important a conclusion, and it will be wise to consider what is known about the Cockpit beyond what is shown in the drawings. The design is a distinctive one quite unlike anything else in Jones's canon, and if the Cockpit in Drury Lane can be proved on other grounds to have been constructed to a similarly distinctive plan the case for the identification will be strengthened.

First, then, to what we can discover about the new playhouse in Drury Lane. The Cockpit was not, as we have seen, built *ab ovo* in 1616. In that year Christopher Beeston leased the site from John Best, who had built a regular cockpit on it in or shortly after 1609.[12] Some accounts of Beeston's theatre say that it was newly erected in 1616, while others speak of his 'converting' the original cockpit to dramatic use. Thus Camden said that it was 'nuper erectum' and Edward Sherburne called it 'a newe playhouse', while to the tatler John Chamberlain it was 'a new play house (sometime a cockpit)'.[13] The major reconstruction work was undertaken even before the beginning of Beeston's lease at Michaelmas 1616 and well before the winter put a stop to the building season, for as early as the middle of October the Benchers of Lincoln's Inn were complaining of 'the convertinge of the Cocke Pytte in the Feildes into a playe house'.[14] Taken together these allusions suggest a conversion so far-reaching as to provide a substantially new building. We know that the resulting theatre was made of brick with a tile roof, in conformity with the Jacobean Proclamations on building.

It is among the Proclamations and the measures taken for their enforcement that we find the next clue to the plan of the Drury Lane playhouse. James I issued a series of Proclamations beginning in 1603 aimed at controlling, indeed almost at preventing, further development in and around London. The policy and its effects are handsomely described in Norman Brett-James's *Growth of Stuart London*.[15] The main object seems to have been to prevent overcrowding, while a good deal of attention was also given to the prevention of fire. The chief means to the latter end was to insist on building in brick or stone, and the former was to be achieved by limiting all new building to old foundations, so that little expansion was legally possible. Of course the Proclamations were especially aimed at residential development, but in practice they were held to cover buildings of all sorts, including theatres.

Not infrequently offending houses were pulled down. One such belonged to Christopher Beeston, the principal in our story about the Cockpit. On 18 September 1616 the Privy Council sent the High Sheriff of Middlesex a list of houses it wanted demolished, including a tenement in Clerkenwell which Beeston had erected separate from his house there, in spite of an undertaking not to. The Sheriff started his work, but his term of office soon expired. When his successor made his report he found that many of the buildings complained of did not exist, others had been pulled down and, 'For Christopher Bastones house, it is for the most parte puld downe, not to be inhabited.'[16] In the following year, however, the Council complained that the house was 'buylt up agayne, and his Majesty of late passing that way hath taken speciall notice thereof, being highly offended with the presumption'.[17] Beeston's tenement was evidently too 'neere unto his Majesties passage' to escape scrutiny, and the Sheriff was ordered to pull the house down to the ground and utterly demolish it.

This little tale of Beeston's Clerkenwell tenement has two points of special relevance to our enquiry. It shows that the king took a personal interest in the execution of his Proclamations on building; and it proves that Christopher Beeston had no special influence with the Privy Council, at any rate at the time when he was building the Cockpit.

Among the developments particularly at risk from the Proclamations were those that the king actually saw on his journeys in and about London. It happened that close to the Cockpit site in Drury Lane there was a private royal road leading out of Westminster towards the hunting country of Theobalds, Royston and Newmarket. East of Drury Lane it became known as Queen Street, after Anne of Denmark, and ran where Great Queen Street runs now.[18] It is not entirely clear whether this section of the route was still private in 1616, but the part north of Holborn certainly was, and James was travelling the whole route frequently during the construction of the Cockpit. From it he could see new buildings springing up around Drury Lane, and he took exception to them. Doubtless he could see the Cockpit too, but there is nothing to suggest that he was the source of complaint against it. Nevertheless the Middlesex Justices could hardly ignore so flagrant a contravention of the king's Proclamations when it was so obviously visible little more than a hundred yards from the king's 'ordinary way'.

That the Justices did move against Beeston in the matter of the Cockpit is plain from the entries in their registers. At the Middlesex Sessions of 5 and 6 September 1616 the following order was made:

Whereas this Courte is informed that there is a new buildinge in hand to be sett up and erected in Drury Lane nere Lincolnes Inne Feildes att and adjoyninge to the Cocke-pitt, contrary to the

Lawe and His Majesties Proclamacione; It is therefore ordered that the said new building shall presently be staid and the workemen committed to prison, that shall hereafter presume to goe forward in the said New Buildinge and also such as shall sett them on worke, havinge had warninge alreadye to forebeare, And further it is ordered that all other new buildinges whatsoeuer be likewise stayed.[19]

In the language of the Proclamations a new building is one that is set on new foundations. Evidently the Justices believed that the development 'att and adjoyninge to' the Cockpit involved the use of new foundations, and indeed an earlier record of the same Sessions appears to confirm the matter (I quote from the calendared version):

John Shepperd of 'Lillypot Lane', London, bricklayer, committed for working upon a new foundation in Drury Lane, and handed in bail to Richard Smith of Holborn upon condition that he shall appear before the Lords of the Council at their first sitting at Whitehall, and in the meantime not to go on in the building and withall to do his best endeavour to bring forth Mr. Beeston to-morrow in court, then his appearance to be spared and Beeston to be bound. On 10 September, A.D. 1616, discharged by order of the Justices.[20]

Since there is no record of any building in Drury Lane by Beeston other than his work at the Cockpit, it is likely that the theatre is referred to here, and that Shepperd was the builder at least of its foundations.

Despite the actions of the Justices the building went ahead, for all we know undisturbed. It duly opened before Shrove Tuesday 1617,[21] by which time it had already worried the Benchers at Lincoln's Inn. Yet the Court's determination to stop the building cannot be doubted. What prevented it from succeeding? Five days after making its order it discharged Shepperd and, we must conclude, closed the case, yet there is no record that Beeston ever appeared before it to state his position.

Who called off the Middlesex dogs? Beeston had no special pull with the Council, as the affair of his Clerkenwell tenement proves. Of course had he the wit to involve His Majesty's Surveyor in his theatre project he might confidently expect some special leniency, even during this singularly inauspicious time when the Puddle Wharf proposal was being so energetically suppressed. But such a notion is merely speculative. A much more telling fact is that Beeston's new building was set largely on old foundations, the foundations, that is, of the Cockpit which had stood on the site since 1609. It was, we recall, as much a conversion as a new establishment. One of the provisions of the Proclamation of 12 October 1607 allowed for the extension of buildings set on old foundations up to a third larger than their original size. If the Cockpit were to be adapted to theatrical use under the regulations of the time, good sense required the incorporation of its original plan, together with an extension built outwards on new foundations continuous with the old, so limited that the new part could be plausibly represented as no more than a third the size of the old. The magistrates stayed the work 'att and adjoyninge to' the Cockpit, using a phrase which precisely indicates that just such a scheme was afoot. Any excuse that it did in fact meet the requirements of the Proclamations (and the original cockhouses and sheds on the property would presumably have entered into the calculations of area) would have been lent colour had it been made by Jones, who as Surveyor was among those charged with seeing that the building policy was carried out.

Plainly we need to know more about John Best's cockpit of 1609. Unhappily the design of cockpits in the seventeenth century has gone almost unrecorded. Much information about cockfighting in general lies scattered in documents and pamphlets, but all too little of it relates to the size and structure of the buildings in which the matches were held. We know most about the elaborate pit put up by Henry VIII in Whitehall, to which I shall turn in chapter 5, but it was an unrepresentative building, quite unlike the more modest ones established elsewhere. A great many are recorded in England before 1700, but apart from Whitehall only five are illustrated in prints. These are at Derby and Leicester (both shown in Speed maps of 1610), Oxford (built in 1672), Dartmouth Street, Westminster (the 'Cockpit Royal', built in 1671) and Gray's Inn Gardens, Holborn (built by 1700).[22] The prints show that each of these was an enclosed, centrally planned building of no great size. Two – those depicted by Speed – were polygonal in plan, while the two close to London were round. To judge from the print, the Oxford pit might have been either. Leicester was domed, and the rest had conical roofs. Both the Holborn and the Westminster pits are also marked on various London maps, usually with a circle, but little credence can be given to what may well be no more than a partly conventional sign.

No seventeenth-century view of the interior of a regular cockpit is extant, though the Dartmouth Street pit – usually known as the Cockpit Royal – appears in an early guise in the frontispiece of R[obert] H[owlett]'s *The Royal Pastime of Cock-fighting* (London, 1709). The round pit is ringed by four tiers of benches, rising to a balustrade behind which runs a level promenade. A similar layout appears in Rowlandson's famous print of the same building as it was *c*. 1808. Hogarth's engraving of a cockpit, usually said to represent this Dartmouth Street building, in fact shows something quite different, a straight-walled, apparently windowless room in which the circular pit and concentric degrees have been arranged on the Westminster pattern. The presence of jockeys shows Hogarth's cockpit to be the one at Newmarket.[23]

Fortunately we have a description of one of the London pits, possibly that at Shoe Lane, made by Thomas Platter in 1599, a mere decade before the Drury Lane pit was built.

. . . I saw the place which is built like a theatre (*theatrum*). In the centre of the floor stands a circular table covered with straw and with ledges round it, where the cocks are teased and incited to fly at one another, while those with wagers as to which cock will win, sit closest around the circular disk, but the spectators who are merely present on their entrance penny sit around higher up . . .[24]

The Holborn pit was described in similar terms in the eighteenth century by another European traveller, Zacharias von Uffenbach:

A special building has been made for [cockfighting] near 'Gras Inn' . . . The building is round like a tower, and inside it resembles a 'theatrum anatomicum', for all round it there are benches in tiers, on which the spectators sit. In the middle is a round table, which is covered with mats, on which the cocks have to fight.[25]

That these descriptions made more than a century apart agree so well with one another and with Rowlandson's nineteenth-century print suggests that the main features of the cockpit were early standardized in much the same way as those of a tennis court or a cricket pitch. Specific regulations governing the size of the pit came too late to be relevant here, but the need for them must have been recognized from the beginning.

Although no direct description of the Drury Lane pit survives, it is safe to assume that it was a round or polygonal building with a conical or domed roof, and that inside there was a circular pit with degrees ranged about it rising up to an ambulatory by the wall. It was probably not very big. At the centre stood the table, which was unlikely to have been more than 12 ft across.[26] Even at the large Whitehall cockpit it was only 'iij yardes everie way' if the dimensions of the mat made to fit it in 1581–2 do indeed give its size; a similar entry in the Works accounts for 1602–3 alludes to 'one thicke bulrushe matt for the rounde table in the cockpitt beinge xj^{en} foote over'.[27] The Royal Cockpit print shows that there were four degrees of seating between the table and the ambulatory, while in Rowlandson's version there are only three, the same as Hogarth found at Newmarket. Allowing a maximum of 12ft for the diameter of the table, the usual sort of cockpit building was probably no more than 40 ft across in all. In one case – that of Royston – no such guesswork is necessary because a precise survey is extant. The cockpit at Royston formed part of James I's 'court house', and was built as part of the general development there in 1609–10. The declared accounts of the Office of Works give details under the heading of Royston:

. . . makeinge and settinge upp a newe Cockpitt there . . . William Pettitt Bricklayer . . . [paid for] digginge the foundacion of the Cockpitt and bringinge upp the same with twoe brickes di*midium* thicke to the water table and twoe brickes thicke the whole heighte conteyninge viij square roddes, xvj foote di*midium* square to the rodde, at xl^s the rodde he finding pencellinge and workmanshipp onely – xvj^l
. . . for new lathinge and tyleinge of the Cockpitt conteyninge xxij squares di*midium* at ij^s x^d the square – lxiij^s ix^d.[28]

Such was the mode of construction of a cockpit exactly contemporary with John Best's building in Drury Lane. It was surveyed by the Parliamentary Commissioners in 1649:

All that Round bricke buildinge called the Cockpitt conteyninge 30.^{ty} foote of Assize in widenes, and 17.^{tn} foote of Assize in heighte, with a substantiall Tymber roofe couered with Tyles . . .[29]

The public pits of London were doubtless somewhat larger than this, for they depended on a paying audience and needed to attract enough of a crowd to cover their costs. Nevertheless the diameter of 30 ft was not greatly exceeded by any commercial cockpit of later times whose dimensions are known: that built in 1785 at Lowther Street, Carlisle, for example, was an octagon 40 ft across.[30] None was large enough to be converted into a regular professional theatre without extensive structural alterations. There is no reason to suppose that the Drury Lane pit differed from the rest in this respect.

The Drury Lane pit was built at much the same time as the one at Royston by John Best, a member of the Grocers' Company whose name often appears in the county records of Middlesex, where he emerges as a small businessman. His interest in cockfighting was not, however, merely speculative. In the Diet Book of Prince Henry's household, 1610, there is a list of miscellaneous tradesmen qualifying for wages. Among them is 'John Beast, cockemaster'.[31] He must have known the Royston pit, and he must have known much else of relevance to this study, for the name at the head of the short list in which his own appears is 'Mr. Inico Joanes, Suruayer of the Workes'.

It is perhaps surprising that Christopher Beeston, involved as he was in speculative building in 1616, could find the capital to finance the thoroughgoing reconstruction of the Cockpit. Yet that he did in fact undertake extensive building work at the site is a matter of record; and we know that the building was so completely converted from its original purpose as to be capable, when the time came, of accommodating the scenic drama of the Restoration, some of it notably elaborate. The question therefore is not whether Beeston could have found the necessary capital, but where he found it. Although the playhouse appears to have remained in Beeston's personal control until his death in 1639 when it passed to his son William, he built it as a regular house for the Queen Anne's Men, who opened in it some time before the Shrove Tuesday riots of 1617, when they were attacked in their new theatre by the apprentices of the city. The Drury Lane site was not far from Queen's Court, Anne's London establishment in Somerset House, located almost at the foot of the Lane by the river. In October 1616 the Benchers of Lincoln's Inn took their complaint about Beeston and his conversion of the Cockpit not to the Middlesex magistrates, nor even directly to the Privy Council in Westminster, but to the Queen's Court at Somerset House. Three years earlier, feeling their amenity threatened because 'some doe goe about to erect new buildinges, contrary to His *Majes*ties Proclamacion', they had complained to the Privy Council, who responded with a prompt memorandum to the Middlesex Justices, a move which the Benchers themselves followed up a few weeks later.[32] When, therefore, they complained to Queen's Council about the Cockpit they must have had a special reason for so unusual an approach, and it may be that they saw the Cockpit as part of the artistic community which Anne was establishing around her at her London residence, where she actively patronized French musicians, Italian designers and English playwrights as well as a large group of sculptors, painters and dancers. Ranked high among these artists by 1616 was Inigo Jones, and in that year, quite apart from his continuing architectural work for the queen, which included extensive projects at Oatlands and Greenwich, he was paid for designing the scene of a masque performed by 'her highnes servauntes' at Somerset House.[33] These performers may have been her French musicians, or even a visiting troupe of French actors led by Anthony Cossart, but the phrase 'her highnes servauntes' most readily suggests the Queen Anne's Men under the direction of Christopher Beeston, for the phrase is of the type that usually denotes players in the records. The entry – among the declared accounts of the King's Works – is unfortunately not clear enough to make the matter certain, and the main financial documents of the Queen's Council, which dealt with her large landholdings and must have been extensive, no longer survive to indicate whether she made payments to her actors for such a performance. But the notion that Jones was engaged in theatre work for the queen, and possibly for a performance by the Queen Anne's Men, at the very time when the Cockpit was being prepared for them up the hill in Drury Lane brings the Surveyor tantalizingly close once more to the mud, bricks and tile of that influential building site. The missing financial records might also have indicated whether the queen paid subsidies to Beeston for the construction of the playhouse: until some further evidence is found the question of his financial sources cannot be answered, though direct patronage from Queen's Court seems not unlikely.

But even leaving the question of costs aside, what sort of a playhouse could possibly be made out of a round, centrally planned cockpit? There can be no doubt that Beeston had to expand John Best's building, which was too small for theatrical purposes. The Proclamations required that he should retain as much as possible of the foundations of the original structure, but had they not done so he would still have been forced either to demolish and begin anew or to adopt a U-shaped plan like that of the Jones drawings. There is no other way of expanding a centrally planned building. Simply to erect a similar but larger building on the same site would require the destruction of the first and the provision of a complete set of new foundations, a possibility excluded as much by common sense as by the Proclamations. It may be, then, that in Jones's drawings the round of the auditorium coincides with half the plan of the original cockpit, retaining its diameter of 40 ft. In this interpretation the stage end is an addition built on the new foundations 'att and adjoyninge to' the Cockpit which so worried the Middlesex Justices, and which may ultimately have been allowed under colour of the provision for expansions up to one-third the size of the previous building. To conclude: what we know independently about the plan of the new playhouse in Drury Lane precisely supports the claim that it is the U-planned building shown in Jones's drawings.

Moreover the Cockpit design, as I shall now provisionally call the drawings, harbours signs within it suggesting that it was made for a conversion rather than an altogether original building. The exterior is exceptional among the architect's canon for its workaday plainness. Here are none of the classical orders, pediments or balustrades of his usual style, but only an unadorned brick shell such as might have come from any mason's hand. The segmental-headed windows do recall some that Jones had used at the rear of the Prince's Lodging in Newmarket, but the buttress piers which mark the structural bays of the outer wall and support the main roof trusses belong in another idiom altogether. These, and almost certainly the whole management of the exterior, continue the style set by John Best in the original cockpit of 1609. But it was surely Jones who added, above the suitably egg-shaped finial, the breezy little pennant which tops the composition, a touch entirely characteristic of his early designs.

The plan of the house is developed according to an equally characteristic modular system. It was Jones's usual practice to assemble his designs using a simple measure from which the proportions of the whole derived. Where orders were employed the module was normally the diameter of a column, though the plan might sometimes be laid out using a larger unit. The Whitehall Banqueting House interior, for example, is 110 ft long and 55 ft wide, and its plan is developed from a 5 ft unit, which represents the width of the windows between their reveals. A similar unit is used for the outer wall of the Cockpit, but it applies to the exterior dimensions, which are all multiples of 5 ft. The radius of the 'round' is 20 ft (69.5 mm on the drawing), the rectangle forming the rest of the U is 40 ft by 35 ft (139 mm by 122 mm) and the overall length excluding the attached stair turrets is 55 ft (191.5 mm). The details of the elevation do not fit the five-foot module. True, the string-course is 15 ft (52 mm) above the ground, but the main door and upper windows are 4 ft 6 in wide (15.5 mm) and the narrow lower windows are 3 ft tall (10.5 mm). Evidently these parts of the design derive from a 1 ft 6 in module, which is incompatible with that of the U plan.

These inconsistencies are not at all surprising. It is only when we turn to look at the internal layout that they assume any significance. Much of the interior is assembled from the smaller module, which I shall call u. The pit door is 2u wide (10.5 mm), the centrepiece of the *frons scenae* is 4u across (21 mm), the benches are 1u apart (5 mm). One measure, however, fits both modules because it is a multiple of both. This is 10u (i.e. 15 ft, or 52 mm on the plan), and it is precisely the depth of the stage. Moreover, the outer stage doors are separated by 10u, so that a square 10u across placed centrally at the front of the stage defines both the depth of the stage and the placing of the entrance doors. The stage front bisects the overall length of the playhouse (again, excluding the stairs), so that it is just 5u (i.e. 7 ft 6 in or 26 mm) distant from the centre of the 'round'. The centre of the gallery rail which defines the round itself has a diameter of some 21 ft 2 in (73.5 mm on the sheet), a dimension which at first sight appears to have nothing to do with either module. It is, however, 15 ft × √2, or the diameter of a circle described around a square 10u across. A 10u square, constructed on the auditorium side of the stage front, thus defines the width of the pit and the relation of the pit to the stage (plate 8).

The plan of the outer wall, then, is designed in multiples of 5 ft; but details of the elevation and of the interior use a 1 ft 6 in module. The modular armature of the interior, a pair of 10u squares either side of the centre line, fits both systems. Jones might of course have used the 1 ft 6 in unit for the exterior also, and so have achieved a fully consistent plan, had he not been constrained to use the foundations and perhaps much of the wall structure of Best's original cockpit, itself presumably 40 ft across.

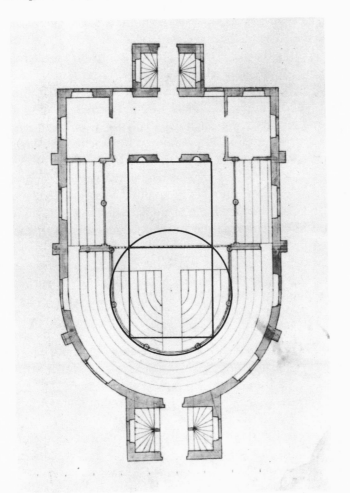

8 *Ad quadratum* relation of stage to auditorium at the Cockpit, Drury Lane

If the quirks introduced into the modular system suggest that Jones's design is a practical one in which the accidents of particular reality are accommodated, the disposition of the stage and auditorium shows evidence of much practical thinking. The section of the stage end of the house does not show the stage itself in place – evidently it was thought of as a removable structure independent of the frame of the building – but the sills of the doors of entrance required it to be elevated to a height of 4 ft. The plan shows that it was equipped with a rail, which slotted neatly into the transverse wall which separated the stage end of the house from the round of the auditorium. Of the three stage entrances the two smaller, flanking, ones were only 5 ft 6 in high clear space, and though doubtless fully practicable could hardly have been used for impressive entries. The taller, arched central entry was made wide enough to be used as a discovery space, and above it the central part of the balcony was cleared of degrees and framed architecturally with terms and a broken pediment to provide a music room. The rest of the balcony was set with degrees which doubtless extended into the corners of the house to meet those in the upper galleries over the sides of the stage, so that at this upper level the audience sat entirely surrounding the players below, the continuity of the degrees being broken only by the music room above the stage. Access to most of this upper part of the house was by a passage running behind the degrees, lit by a series of small segmentally headed windows. Although the light from these was visible from many parts of the auditorium, it was high up, well away from the stage and would not have caused a distracting glare. The windows also functioned as vents to remove the smoke of candles and the spent air of the assembled company.

At the lower gallery level the encirclement of the stage by the audience was only slightly less complete. The round of the auditorium connected directly with boxes flanking the stage to either side, but of course there was no room for the audience upstage at this level. Although the four rows of degrees were reached, like those above, from an open passage or gangway at their rear, this was not lit by windows, whose glare in the daylight hours would have annoyed those sitting opposite; the artificial lighting of the auditorium may have sufficed for the purpose, or there may have been additional sconces attached to the wall. At both levels the stage boxes were separated from the main auditorium by being stepped back by the width of one degree, and in the plan a partition wall is shown marking the boundary between them. It may be that this wall was intended to be built only at the lowest level, beneath the lower gallery, as shown in the two sections; if so it will almost certainly have supported a partition rising through both storeys of the house to the coved plaster ceiling above, so making possible a satisfactory junction between the boxes and the galleries. I shall return to this curious partition later on.

At the lowest level stood the pit, in this case we may suppose quite literally the original cockpit of John Best's time, where the birds had been incited to do battle on their matted table. In the section Jones omits the degrees with which it was fitted, though he shows them in the plan. Perhaps they were removable like the stage, which is also omitted in the section. The degrees consisted of six risers, but the total height available for them before the foot of the lower gallery rail was only 3 ft, so that each riser was no more than 6 in high and the rake of the degrees much shallower than in the galleries, where it was uniformly 40°. In plan they repeated the D-shape of the galleries, with the curious effect that the spectators placed at the front faced one another rather than the stage, just as they did in the Court theatres. Access to these pit degrees was through a vomitory at ground level whose upper part was high enough, even at 6 ft, to have to cut through the front of the lower gallery.

The Cockpit, if that is indeed the theatre shown in these drawings, was essentially a free-standing brick shell elaborately fitted out inside with woodwork and plaster. The inner faces of the house – the parts immediately surrounding the stage and pit – were constructed in a classic decorative mode, with turned posts at the lower level given Doric capitals to make them into an order. Above them the upper gallery had posts with taller capitals, proportioned as Corinthian, though in the drawing they are without the acanthus carving. For some reason both orders were given Tuscan bases, consisting of a single torus and a plinth. At the upper level a handsome balustered rail encircled the room, distinguishing the higher part from the lower, where the gallery was fronted by a blank parapet that did little to interrupt the continuity of the degrees as they ranged outwards from the pit. Standing at the centre of the house a spectator might have looked around him to see a series of half a dozen shallow degrees rising gradually to the blank rail of the lower gallery, then stepping up more sharply for four degrees to the passage by the dark rear wall. Where the rhythm of the degrees was broken by the rail, functional posts rose to support the upper gallery, and here the balustered rail made a clear decorative impact. The 'Corinthian' posts of the upper level were perhaps something of a surprise, for they had no structural function to perform, the ceiling above them being attached to roof trusses whose load passed directly to the brick walls of the shell. That Jones should have provided these upper posts, so carefully distinguished in mode from those below, may suggest that he had in mind the encircling galleries of the Jacobean public theatres, but there is also, in the distinction between the lower degrees reaching forward into the pit and those above contained by their balusters, a suggestion of the *cavea* and *porticus* of the antique Roman theatre.

The drawings give no explicit programme for the interior finishing of the house, but one may at least hazard a few informed guesses about it. Jones was the designer, and as Surveyor of the King's Works he exercised a general control over the Sergeant Painter and the craftsmen responsible for maintaining and decorating the rooms at Court. It is a reasonable assumption that he would have employed a scheme at the Cockpit similar to those he was accustomed to at Whitehall and Somerset House, though he might have been more sparing than usual in his use of such expensive finishes as gilding. We shall have occasion in chapter 5 to notice the records in the accounts of the Office of Works describing the craftsmen's tasks performed at the Cockpit-in-Court in 1629–32, where some of the older painting and gilding was refurbished along with the new work. Using these documents and other Works accounts pertaining to the palaces generally – and especially to the Whitehall Banqueting House of 1606–7 (PRO E351/3242–3) – we may deduce some fairly reliable guides to the colours and finishes used at the Drury Lane Cockpit, though at best, in the absence of any direct evidence, our conclusions can only be statements of probability.

With this caveat, then, let us colour the drawings. We may begin with the general aim of the style of decoration, which is so to treat an interior constructed of wood and plaster that it takes on the appearance of stone. A visit to the Sheldonian in Oxford will show how the trick was turned, for there much of the woodwork is still painted in what the seventeenth-century accounts call 'stone colour', usually the pale yellow of Caen-stone, and much of it is veined artificially to represent marble. If the Cockpit was decorated like most contemporary semi-public rooms at Court its orders – the turned posts with their entablatures, as well as the woodwork of the *frons scenae* – will have been painted stone colour, and the shafts of the columns marbled. The upper gallery balustrade and the stage rail will have been treated in the same way, to give the impression that their turned wooden balusters were carved out of stone. The plaster surface of the walls behind the lower gallery will have been lined with a trowel's edge to resemble courses of masonry, and the vertical surface of the stage front will almost certainly have been painted to the same end, though here the masonry will have appeared to be rusticated in three or four substantial courses, with a coping of dressed stone at the top. The central aedicule of the *frons* may well have been distinguished by being painted 'rance', to give the effect of a blushing red marble veined in blue and white. The statuary on the *frons* will have been made of plaster of Paris, though the bust at the very top may have been a bronze. The friezes in all the entablatures were probably painted with 'rich bice', a pale blue pigment derived from smalt, in oil. If the triglyphs, capitals, bases and other details were enriched at all, it will have been with 'gold colour' (i.e. yellow) pigment in oil, and the same treatment will have been given to the iron-work of the lighting equipment, the 'branches' or candelabra, the candlesticks and sconces. It is possible that some of the most visible work about the stage may have been gilded, including perhaps the swags on the stone-coloured *frons*.

The door leaves in the *frons* and elsewhere will have been painted 'walnut colour' in oil, and grained artificially; their iron furniture was probably painted lead colour in oil, and their cases stone colour like the rest of the woodwork. The lower slit window frames will also have been lead colour, while the upper casement frames will have been white. I have been unable to discover the usual colour for degrees of seating in the halls at Court, but outdoor wooden seating was customarily painted russet, and it may be that this colour was used also for the degrees at the Cockpit. The seat surfaces themselves will have been covered in rush matting. The surface of the stage will more probably have been covered in stretched green baize, a material also used to line the tiring rooms, though there it is likely to have been a neutral grey–brown colour.

Thus far, with its enriched stone-coloured columns containing russet, matted seats, the appearance of the theatre might almost have recalled an outdoor setting. The *alfresco* conceit – it will hardly have been intended as a convincing illusion – was probably continued in the ceiling. Here the flat plastered surface was deeply coved where it met the upper storey entablature, and although it was not compartmented it was divided in two by an architrave or coved lintel above the front of the stage. The part of the ceiling over the pit will have been painted sky blue, while over the stage it will have been decorated with clouds and very probably with allegorical representations of the planets or signs of the zodiac. The walls behind the upper gallery seating may also have been painted blue, like those of the Cockpit in Whitehall, reinforcing the colonnade effect of the stone-painted columns and entablature. In sum, with its russet and green lower surfaces and its stone-coloured structural elements, the interior will have borne more than a passing resemblance to the open-air theatres of antiquity, an allusion continued in the sky-like treatment of the ceiling and upper walls, calculated to throw into relief the arc of the columns as they stood like an ancient *porticus* around the circle of the *cavea*.

To find examples of the rounded auditorium in enclosed theatres at both Christ Church and Drury Lane so early in the seventeenth century is something of a surprise. So far as is known, no Parisian theatre had yet been constructed to this plan, which had been established in Italy and promulgated in the Second Book of Serlio's *Architettura*, first published in Paris in 1545. There, as in all the Italian examples, it is specifically intended to recall the *cavea* of the ancient theatre:

And because halls, no matter how large they are, are not large enough to be theatres I have – in order to come as close as possible to the Ancients – tried to include as many parts of the antique theatre as I could in a great chamber . . . the larger the room, the more the theatre can approach to its complete form.   (fol. 65ᵇ)

Serlio's scheme offers as much of the 'perfetta forma' of the antique theatre as may be accommodated 'in vna gran sala'. At the Teatro Olimpico in Vicenza, which Jones had visited and recorded in his copy of Palladio, the classicism of the auditorium is as explicit as that of the *frons scenae*, for a colonnade closes off the rear, enlivened with statuary in the manner of an ancient *porticus*. There is no evidence that Jones visited that other famous Teatro Olimpico, at Sabbioneta, but he met its designer, Vincenzo Scamozzi, and may well have had access to his designs for this notable scenic house. According to the drawing now at Milan[34] a raked stage some 4 ft high was faced by a rectangular auditorium in which the degrees were arranged in a U shape, their curve returning at the front to give the outline of a bell. Behind them stood, and stands, for the theatre is extant, the loggia, its non-functional decorative columns supporting only an entablature and a dozen small statues. The purpose of these columns was to evoke the ideality both of an ancient *porticus* and of a Roman townscape, and the theme was continued throughout the theatre, in the perspective vistas and triumphal arches of the flanking walls, with their *trompe l'oeil* figures leaning over a painted balustrade at the level of the loggia, and in the permanent standing scene itself, with its evocation of Serlio's Tragic Scene.

It is tempting to look for some direct influence of Scamozzi's theatre on Jones's. We recall that on their Italian journey of 1613–14 Jones and Arundel acquired a great collection of drawings by Palladio, and perhaps some by Scamozzi; possibly the original designs for the theatre at Sabbioneta were among them.[35] They have unfortunately now vanished, along with the rest of Arundel's Scamozzi drawings, but if they were acquired during the Italian tour Jones might have had them before him as he worked on the Cockpit design. The two projects were similar in scale, Scamozzi's being 23¼ braccia wide internally with an auditorium 32⅔ braccia long; modern measured drawings show the building to be 38.30 m long by 12.97 m wide externally (125.65 ft × 42.55 ft).[36] Yet the differences between the two theatres were very marked, Scamozzi's offering a scenic stage and a playfully illusionistic decorative scheme, where Jones's was fitted out to suit the demands of the predominantly oral drama of Jacobean London, with no illusionary trappings at all and the audience almost entirely surrounding the stage. There is one detail in Jones's plan which suggests that from the beginning he may have intended this playhouse to have been capable of conversion into a scenic theatre, but it is far from suggesting the Sabbionetan model. Scamozzi, taking his cue from Serlio, thought of the place represented by his standing scene as visually continuous with the structure of his auditorium and the illusionistic vistas painted on its walls. His audience sat, as it were, in the forum and watched the play being acted out among the neighbouring streets. Save for the necessary elevation of the stage itself, his theatre set no visual boundary between the audience and the scene; there was no scenic frontispiece or border, no hint of a proscenium arch. By 1616 Jones had experimented a good deal with such a feature in his masques – for example in *The Masque of Queens* and *Tethys' Festival* – and may well have come to think of it as having value for the drama too.[37] We have noticed that in the theatre plan he provides for a heavy brick wall between the main part of the auditorium and the stage end of the house. On the audience side the wall extends to meet the posts and rails of the galleries, and in the left-hand section is shown sufficiently wide to do so. On the stage side it stops short at the front of the boxes flanking the stage, as shown in the right-hand section. The presence of this wall is puzzling, for it appears to have no special function. The roof trusses are sufficient to span the full width of the theatre without additional support, and the outer walls are buttressed specifically to take their load. The sections do not show the wall extending upwards above the level of the foot of the lower gallery, yet the plan appears to indicate that it did so. Had Jones intended to render only the ground level at this point in the plan his inclusion of stage and gallery level features immediately next to it would seem perverse, even for a drawing of the seventeenth century, when inconsistencies of level were admittedly common. One would surmise that the wall did in fact support something, and the most likely possibility seems to be a structural frame within which a stage frontispiece or proscenium border might on occasion be erected. Certainly some visual interruption of the ceiling must have occurred at this point, in line with the stage front, for its coving had here to adjust to the different widths of stage and auditorium, a break perhaps best managed with the aid of an architrave supported to either side by the partition walls registered on the plan.

In the latter part of its life the Cockpit was frequently used for the scenic drama, and it is therefore certain that the building was capable of accommodating scenes, some of which we shall notice later in the present chapter. In so far as the heavy partition wall marked in the plan broke across the visual articulation of the playhouse, separating the rectangular stage end from the rounded auditorium, it compromised the building's quality as a theatre in the round, setting the stage side in opposition to the house side. Whether or not the wall supported a partition, the rhythm of the room was broken by the wider separation of the stage boxes in comparison with the galleries, a break which was repeated in the coving of the ceiling and accentuated by the stage front and its rail. This architectural interruption likewise made more difficult the achievement of the sort of scenic integrity attempted by Scamozzi at Sabbioneta. If Jones was indeed influenced by the Italian the debt on this occasion was not profound, and the managment of the theatrical space at Drury Lane owed more to English Court and private theatre traditions than to the illusions of late Renaissance Italy.

The circular basis of the Cockpit's auditorium side was inherited from John Best's original building, but once incorporated into a theatre it came to have some more fanciful, even mystical, associations. It might be treated as an analogue of the heavens, as it was in Ford and Dekker's Cockpit play, *The Sun's Darling* (1623/4), when the Sun speaks:

> We must descend, and leav a while our sphere,
> To greet the world – ha, there does now appear
> A circle in this round, of beams that shine,
> As if their friendly lights would darken mine.   (p. 7, sig. B4^a)

A more abstract application of the idea occurs in Shirley's *The Coronation* (1634/5), when the Female Prologue addresses the gentlewomen in the Cockpit audience:

> You are the bright intelligences move,
> And make a harmony this sphere of Love.   (sig. A2^b)

To Apuleius, speaking to Midas about the audience in Heywood's *Love's Mistress* (1634), the auditorium offers an analogue of the night sky:

Seest thou this sphear spangled with all these stars, all these Loue-arts; nor shall they part from hence with unfeasted eares.   (1636 sig. B2^a)

Of course similar allusions to the theatre's shape can be found in plays written for other houses, notably the Globe and the Salisbury Court; in this the Cockpit is not by any means unusal. The shape of any auditorium based on the figure of a circle might prompt the poets to associative fancies, and not the poets alone, as Henry Wotton showed in his *Elements of Architecture*:

Now the exact *Circle* is in truth a Figure, which for our purpose hath many fit and eminent properties; as fitnesse, for Commodity and Receit, being the most capable; fitnesse for strength and duration, being the most vnited in his parts; Fitnesse for beautie and delight, as imitating the celestiall *Orbes*, and the vniuersall *Forme*. And it seemes, besides, to haue the approbation of *Nature*, when shee worketh by *Instinct*, which is her secret Schoole: For birds doe build their nests *Spherically* . . .[38]

Such thinking, with its architectural antecedents in Vitruvius and Alberti, is commonplace by the seventeenth century; in the particular matter of theatre design we notice that the circularity of the ancient *cavea* was persistently retained in the period even where its practical disadvantages were manifest, as in the scenic theatres of Serlio and his followers, where much of the audience was left seated sideways-on to the visual spectacle. Moreover a certain schematism in some of these theatre plans suggests that their authors were concerned to incorporate the very *idea* of circularity, with all its analogical possibilities, into schemes which were customarily set up in rectangular halls or courtyards. At Christ Church, Simon Basil went to great lengths to establish a radial auditorium centred on the 'Isle' or state, even though the hall was long and comparatively narrow. At Vicenza Palladio pressed his *cavea* into a semi-ellipse where his room was too shallow for the full antique semi-circle. And Serlio adopted a scheme designed to reduce the half-round form of the Roman theatre to a modern and constricted rectangular site.

In their theatre designs after 1630 both Jones and Webb owed particular and detailed debts to the Serlian scheme, as we shall see in later chapters, but at Drury Lane, possibly because he was building within an established private playhouse tradition, Jones felt less need to draw on the authority of the *Architettura* than Basil had done at Christ Church in 1605. Yet even at the Cockpit Serlio's presence could not lightly be put by, and it is felt in several parts of the design. In order to understand these Italian and humanist aspects of the Cockpit drawings it will be necessary to make a brief excursus into the methods used by Serlio to develop his theatre scheme, methods understood by both Jones and Webb and used, with particular literalness by the latter, in most of their theatre designs. The analysis which follows therefore bears more strongly on the later designs, but even the Cockpit's plan cannot adequately be understood without some recognition of its debt to the Italian model.

It was Serlio's expressed aim to reinterpret the Roman theatre for Renaissance courts and audiences. His scheme proceeded by a deliberate method to accommodate the circular and radial inheritance from antiquity to the rectilinear demands of modern theatre conditions. In order to achieve his practical end while retaining a firm sense of mathematical order, Serlio had recourse to the mediaeval system of *ad quadratum* design, used since at least the time of the d'Honnecourt MS in the thirteenth century to lay out large buildings such as churches and cloisters, and also to design their details, in windows and finials.[39] The *ad quadratum* designer proceeds from a square, whose diagonal he uses typically as the measure of the next stage of his scheme. Thus the method described in the d'Honnecourt MS to set out a cloister begins with the square of its outer wall; one half the diagonal of this square then becomes the measure of the sides of the square yard set up within it.[40] Similar methods might be used for proportioning the nave and aisles of a church, or even for setting out the beds of an Elizabethan knot garden. A series of proportions ensues when one takes half the diagonal of each smaller square as the measure of the next step in a continuous sequence, and this method was taught in masons' lodges as a means of establishing the diminishing stages of a tower or finial.[41] Each successive stage is smaller than that preceding it by a factor of $\frac{1}{\sqrt{2}}$ and the sequence may be represented by a series of squares and circles inscribed within each other, the proportion between the stages being precisely that between the diameter of a circle and the sides of a square inscribed within it so that it touches at the corners. Just such a diagram is illustrated, as one of the great commonplaces of geometrical design, on the title pages of the first editions of Serlio's First and Second Books. It is this form of the procedure that most obviously represents the accommodation of rectilinear design to circular, and which therefore appealed to an architect proposing to establish the semi-circular *cavea* of antiquity within a modern rectangular hall or courtyard; in the Second Book, bearing the *ad quadratum* scheme like a banner on its frontispiece, Serlio turns to the design of theatres.

A building proportioned by *ad quadratum* means will normally be characterized by the incommensurability of its parts, for they will be related to each other in the ratio $1:1.414$ $(1:\sqrt{2})$, and if the outer wall of a cloister is 80 ft its yard will measure $\frac{80}{\sqrt{2}}$ ft across, or 56.57 ft. If the one figure can be given as a whole number, the other cannot. There is however one rather special sequence of $\sqrt{2}$ values which, though strictly irrational, are so close to whole numbers as to be practically indistinguishable from them in matters of building design. The sequence is based on 3 and continues [4.24], 6, [8.49], 12, 16.97, 24, 33.94, 48. Here the figures in square brackets are not close enough to whole numbers to be rounded out, but the larger values of 16.97 and 33.94 are so close to 17 and 34 as to be almost indistinguishable from them, so that for practical purposes they may be used to proportion a building as if they were commensurate.

The proportions of Serlio's theatre plan are measured by the square units into which he divides the forestage. At the front centre he marks off six of these units into a scale of twelve parts, which in the text he suggests should be thought of as feet.[42] The six units of the scale are proportioned to the radius of the orchestra, which is twelve units; the twenty-four unit width of the orchestra answers to that of the 'occhio', or opening between the front wings of the scene. And the width of the theatre is proportioned to that of the orchestra in the *ad quadratum* ratio of 34:24 (i.e. $\sqrt{2}:1$), again as measured by the squares of the forestage. The back wall of the theatre, behind the backcloth, is not shown on the plan, but its location is given in the section as 17 units from the centre of the composition at the front of the orchestra. It would be possible therefore to superimpose over this theatre plan an *ad quadratum* diagram of precisely the sort that Serlio includes on his title page, so that the main lines of the plan coincided with the squares and circles of the scheme. But it is to be doubted whether Serlio intended his woodcut to be dealt with quite so painstakingly: the *ad quadratum* proportions can be read from it merely in the counting of the squares of the forestage, so that one need not go to the trouble even of manipulating the dividers over it to find the method of its construction.

In later chapters of the present book we shall find that both Inigo Jones and John Webb understood the method by which Serlio had developed his plan to incorporate both the rotundity of the antique theatre and the rectilinearity of the modern hall or courtyard; their persistence in following it, though by no means absolute, was devoted enough to suggest that they thought of it as something more important than a convenient drafting technique. Possibly they saw in it the mystery of the squaring of the round, familiar from Euclid and from the attempts of geometers of all ages to define the area of a circle; perhaps too they associated it with the Vitruvian *homo ad quadratum*, illustrated by Scamozzi with a human figure standing within a circle inscribed within a square and illustrating the notion, itself derived from antiquity, that in the human body could be found the proportionality of both perfect figures.[43]

There are, in the Cockpit designs, only slight recollections of Serlio's theatre plan, for Jones's purpose was to provide a sound architectural assemblage of the parts of a Jacobean private playhouse, complete with its stage boxes, permanent *frons scenae* and upper level music room, the last to be capable of occasional use as an elevated acting area. Yet in the half round of the auditorium there is surely an echo of Serlio, however fortuitous its origin in the original cockpit. The width of the house being thus defined by the existing round, Jones did not use it as part of his commensurate modular scheme; nor did he attempt to incorporate it into a Serlian *ad quadratum* reconciliation of the round part of the house to the square. Instead he established the gallery fronts, over whose placing he had full control, on a circle described about a 15 ft square, yielding a pit diameter, measured between the gallery rails, of 21 ft 2 in, or 15 ft $\times \sqrt{2}$. Because 15 ft is ten modules of 18 in the width of the pit and galleries is incorporated into the modular plan of the whole; it now appears that this accommodation is made by means of an *ad quadratum* construction adapted from Serlio (see plate 8).

Like Serlio, Jones leaves a 'proscenio' or 'piazza della scena' between the stage and the auditorium, but he departs from his model in filling the remainder of his orchestra or pit with degrees. Whatever the possible humanistic associations of his *ad quadratum* method, Serlio in one respect firmly relates the whole of his design to the proportions of the human body, for he takes the depth of each of the degrees as the measure of the square units into which he divides the forestage; his plan is scaled by the very basic theatrical need to put bottoms onto seats. So also Jones, whose module at the Cockpit is 18 in, chooses a measure which is exactly the depth of a seating degree, a notion to which both he and Webb would return in later designs.

For all the humanistic quality of its method of design, the Cockpit remained essentially a Jacobean playhouse best suited to the poetic, non-scenic drama of the age. As T. J. King has shown, in a definitive study of the dramaturgy of plays acted there before the closing of the theatres,[44] the house must have had a raised stage with three entrances, the largest of which was capable of providing a very small discovery space; the plays required a small upper acting level, but there is no reliable evidence in them of the use of a descent machine or a trap. And indeed Jones's drawings, while clearly showing the three entrances and the balcony, give no hint of a trap or winch for flying effects. They are, that is to say, exactly consistent with the evidence of the plays performed at the Cockpit in the years before the scenic potentiality of the house was at last exploited.

There are a few indications that the Cockpit may have been used for occasional scenic shows even from its earliest years, but none is sufficiently reliable to make the matter certain. In 1639, however, Jones prepared a freely drawn sketch of a full scenic stage set up behind a proscenium arch, with wings, cloud borders in an upper stage, and a 'citti of rileve' before a backcloth. The scene is typical, in its technical proficiency, of his contemporary work for the Whitehall masques, but it is

9   Inigo Jones, scene design for the Cockpit, Drury Lane, 1639

distinguished by the endorsement: 'for y^e cokpitt for my lord Chamberalin 1639' (plate 9). It is not impossible that the phrase 'for y^e cokpitt' is merely an address, for the Lord Chamberlain's lodgings were at the Cockpit in Whitehall, but if so the form of the words would be unusual, and it seems more likely that they refer to the place where the scene was to be erected. Orgel and Strong, in their fine study of Jones's scene designs, assume this to be the Cockpit-in-Court at Whitehall, which had been converted into a regular theatre by Jones in 1629.[45] The Lord Chamberlain did produce a play at Court in 1639/40, but in the hall, not in the Cockpit, and in any case it is hard to see how the tall arch of Jones's design could be accommodated within the much more horizontal scope of the Whitehall building after its conversion.

The sketch is freely, even roughly, drawn, but it shows very clearly the main parts of the scenic structure including a stage rail apparently in the same plane as the proscenium arch. Such rails were common enough in the playhouses, public and private, but were not a feature of the scenic theatres at court where they would have interfered with important sightlines to the wing feet. The rail in the 'cokpitt' design is therefore unusual enough to suggest that Jones prepared the work, not for any of the usual Court theatres, but for a playhouse, presumably one or other of the two Cockpits. The Whitehall Cockpit had a thrust stage whose ends returned to join the permanent *frons scenae*, and after 1660 there was a low rail following its front edge back to either side. It is possible that a rail had been fitted in 1629, but if so it went unrecorded. Were an arch to be erected on this stage in the same plane as a front rail it would stand some five feet forward of the *frons* and any members of the audience sitting to either side of the apron would have to view the scene from behind the arch. If the arch took up the full width of the stage, and so was co-extensive with the rail as shown in the 'cokpitt' sketch, it would be 34 ft wide. The sketch shows the arch just as high as it is wide overall, so that it would have reached some 34 ft high to the top of its central cartouche. This is much higher than the coved ceiling shown in John Webb's careful drawing of the stage at the Cockpit-in-Court (plate 16), and it is clear that the 'cokpitt' scene could not have been mounted there without very considerable alterations to the house, alterations of which the extant and detailed Works accounts of the period give no sign.

It could, on the other hand, readily have been set up on the stage at Drury Lane, as Iain Mackintosh has shown.[46] The railed front of the stage, included only in Jones's plan, is some 21 ft 6 in wide as measured between the centres of the gallery posts closest to it which define its visible width. The height of the ceiling above the floor of the stage is 21 ft 9 in, and an arch made to the pattern of Jones's sketch would neatly fill the opening onto the stage as seen from the auditorium. That such an arch could in fact be inserted into the structure of the Cockpit in Drury Lane we know from the text of Davenant's *Cruelty of the Spaniards in Peru*, an operatic drama staged there in 1658, in which the frontispiece is described as 'An Arch . . . rais'd upon stone of Rustick work; upon the top of which is written, in an Antique Shield, PERU . . .'[47] Beyond the arch was a curtain, drawn up at the beginning of the performance to reveal a scenic stage.

The 'cokpitt' sketch includes clear indications of four pairs of wings beyond the arch, each flat representing a tent; beyond these the backshutters have been opened to reveal a city made of cut-out relieves. At the upper level horizontal lines mark the presence of several cloud borders answering the wings below, and closing towards the backcloth; above the backshutters is a cloudrow evidently included to hide the upper grooves of the shutter assembly. The cloudrow therefore marks the boundary between the upper and the lower parts of the scene, for the cloud backcloth can be seen above it. It is drawn on a level with the capitals of the columns or pilasters which support the arch, its upper edge just over half as high as the whole. This part of the scenic apparatus, essentially similar to that shown by John Webb in his section of the *Florimène* scene (plate 22), therefore occurs at just the level of the gallery rail in the Drury Lane Cockpit; set up in that playhouse, it would be readily supported by the existing structure. The lower edge of the cloudrow, coinciding with the top of the backshutters as visible in the sketch, would have been about 9 ft above the stage, at just the level of the gallery floor in the Cockpit. That such a scene, complete with its changeable shutters and relieves, could be accommodated in a platform only 15 ft deep, as here in the Jones drawings, is proved by Davenant's staging of *The Siege of Rhodes* at Rutland House, where he tells us the scenes were 'confin'd to eleven foot in height, and about fifteen in depth, including the place of passage reserv'd for the musick'.[48]

The difficulty of placing the scene shown in the 'cokpitt' sketch in the Cockpit-in-Court suggests that it was intended for the other Cockpit, in Drury Lane; the ease with which it may be fitted into the building shown in Jones's drawings further suggests that we are right to identify it as Beeston's private playhouse. Yet the sketch was directed to the Lord Chamberlain, within whose care the Whitehall Cockpit certainly lay, while Drury Lane did not. By 1639, however, much had changed at the latter house. Christopher Beeston, who in 1616 had successfully opposed the Middlesex Justices, confident perhaps in the knowledge that he had Queen Anne's support, by now had established a unique and very convenient relationship with the Lord Chamberlain himself. In that officer's warrant book there is an entry dated 21 February 1636/7: 'A Warrant to sweare Mr Christopher Bieston his *Majesties* servant in ye place of Gouuernor of the new Company of the King*es* & Queenes boyes.'[49] This status of governor was, as Bentley remarks, 'unprecedented since the time of the Elizabethan and early Jacobean boy companies'.[50] A short time later, moreover, despite a flagrant violation of the plague prohibition at the Cockpit, Beeston was granted unusual privileges by the Lord Chamberlain in the matter of the possession of disputed playscripts. After Christopher's death in 1639 his son William inherited the special relationship, and by a warrant of 5 April he was sworn 'vnder the Title of Gouuernor & Instructer of the Kings & Queens young Company of Actors'.[51]

In 1639, then, first Christopher and then William Beeston enjoyed a direct contact with the Lord Chamberlain. This is the context in which Jones's drawing 'for ye cokpitt for my lo*rd* Cha*m*beralin' must be placed. The particular play for which the design was made remains unknown, but the difficulty of trying to fit it into the Cockpit-in-Court now disappears. The sketch is the earliest surviving scene design for the professional theatre in England, dashed off by Inigo Jones to fit a theatre which, there is every reason to believe, he had himself prepared almost a quarter of a century before for just such an eventuality.

The best evidence of the scenic use of the Cockpit's stage dates from the last years of the Commonwealth and the first of the Restoration. By this time there was certainly some machinery in the house for spectacular effects, as well as room for the frontispiece used in *The Cruelty of the Spaniards in Peru*. This last was presumably expensive, and was retained for Davenant's *History of Sir Francis Drake*, performed like its predecessor 'daily at the *Cockpit* in *Drury-Lane* at Three Afternoon Punctually'.[52] Both productions were 'Exprest by Instrumentall and Vocall Musick, and by Art of Perspective in Scenes, &c.' In *The Cruelty* the music room appears to have been on or close to the stage, for a Priest waves 'his Verge towards the Room where the Musick are plac'd behind the Curtain'. In the same production some elementary spectacular machinery was used, as when 'a Rope descends out of the Clouds, and is stretcht to a stiffness by an Engine . . .' A pair of apes then danced on it, after which it ascended whence it came.[53]

Far more elaborate machinery was called for by the published scenario of a 'machine play' put on at the Cockpit by a visiting French troupe in 1661. The fashion for richly spectacular shows had been fostered by Denis Buffequin at the Marais in Paris, and inspired by the example of Torelli, whose work was seen at the Petit-Bourbon. A few French provincial companies soon developed the necessary techniques for taking productions of such works as Corneille's *Andromède* or *La Toyson d'Or* on tour, and it was one of these companies that appeared in London for a season at the Cockpit. English synopses of two of their productions survive, but have not been given the attention they deserve by theatre historians. They show that the Cockpit was capable of housing complete systems of scenery and machines, and that the English stage was exposed, at this crucial moment in its history, to the full force of the French enthusiasm for the drama of spectacle. The influence of the troupe's presence on later technical work at the Duke's Theatre and even on the design of the King's must one day be assessed; for the moment we are concerned rather with the fact that it was the Cockpit in Drury Lane which housed the evidently elaborate equipment used for the French productions.

The Description of the Great Machines, of the Descent of Orpheus into Hell. Presented by the French Commedians at the Cock-pit in Drury Lane was published in the year of the performance and calls for such traditional spectacles as a flying dragon breathing fire, a scene of rocks with a great grotto, lightning and winds.[54] But it also includes a heaven which can open to reveal Juno in her chariot 'drawn up and down the Ayre by two Eagles of Gold', and, after a clash between Juno and Envy, 'a great disturbance in the Ayre, or rather an Irregular motion of several wonderfull Machines'. The action that follows involves a succession of wondrous scene changes, probably effected by means of movable flat wings set in grooves. From the rocks and heaven of the opening we move to a magician's palace, built in the Doric

order; in the twinkling of an eye the place changes to a garden, in which a
mechanical serpent 'by an admirable Machine creeps over the Theatre' to bite
Euridice. Now the scene is suddenly rocky again, and Aristeus plunges to his death.
The banks of Acheron appear, depicted apparently on one half of the rocky scene;
in a moment all this vanishes to be replaced by 'a dismal Hell' with the palace of
Pluto; as Orpheus returns with Euridice half of this is changed to Acheron again,
with Charon's ferry. At the end Orpheus is installed at Mount Rodophe, beneath an
arcade of trees and flowers flanked by cypress walks; here he is murdered by the
Bacchanales, who then suffer a miraculous transformation into trees.

So spectacular are many of these effects that one may be led to conclude that they
could not have been attempted at the Cockpit. In fact the drama was a well-
established 'machine play' by Chapoton, in the repertory of the Comédiens de
Mademoiselle d'Orléans, a provincial company which enjoyed close links with the
actors of the Marais in Paris. The Comédiens are traceable in Brussels, Ghent and
Rouen in the months before their arrival in London, and while in Brussels in March
1661 they performed *La Descente d'Orphée aux Enfers* which, according to the
journal *Relations Veritables*, was 'merveilleuse pour ses rares machines et magnifiques changements de téâtre, qui ont ravit et parfaitement satisfait toute la cour et
les autres spectateurs'.[55] It was their custom on their journeys to have theatres set
up for them by local carpenters in public halls of various sorts, but especially in
indoor tennis courts. In March they had rented the Théâtre de la Montagne Sainte-
Elisabeth, but on their return to Brussels after their London season they entered
into an agreement with a carpenter, Estienne Mees, for the construction of a
temporary theatre in le Fossé-aux-Loups. The contract is extant and, like many
similar documents drawn up for the travelling players on the Continent, shows that
an entire stage, with 'deux aultres téâtres dessus' (presumably an upper stage and a
relieve area behind backshutters) was specially constructed for the season, which
included among other works Corneille's 'machine play', *La Toyson d'Or*.[56] The
spectacle of *La Descente d'Orphée*, which so pleased the Brussels audiences in
March 1661, could be equally successful at the Drury Lane Cockpit a few months
later simply because the company had developed the expertise necessary to take the
production on tour. Doubtless their staging of Chapoton's play would not have
matched the quality of its revival at the Marais in the following year, with new
scenes by Buffequin, but nothing we know about the troupe suggests that its works
were at all incompetent or unpleasing.

Nothing, that is, except the *Diary* of Samuel Pepys, who attended the Cockpit on
30 August to see the 'French Comedy, which was so ill done and the Scenes and
company and everything else so nasty and out of order and poor, that I was sick all
the while in my mind to be there'.[57] Yet the Florentine agent in London reported
that the king, the queen and the Duke and Duchess of York all went to see for
themselves and marvelled at the spectacle; later in September they went again and
greatly enjoyed a piece based on 'li amori di Diana e Endimion'. The agent wrote
admiringly of the production, which lived up to the honour of its distinguished

audience 'as much for the variety of the scenes and machines as for the excellence of the voices and music'.[58] This play was evidently Gabriel Gilbert's *Les Amours de Diane et d'Endimion*, for which an undated four-leaf programme survives among the Malone pamphlets at the Bodleian Library, with the title 'The designe or the great peece of MACHINES of the Loves of DIANA and ENDIMION'.[59] The pamphlet names no theatre as the site of the production, but it is generally similar to the *Descent of Orpheus* synopsis in the same collection and evidently belongs to the season at the Cockpit. In stilted English, awkwardly translated from the French, it briefly summarizes the legend of Endymion before passing on to a longer summary of the play, with special emphasis on the scenic effects. At first, for the Prologue, there is a forest 'Composed of trees of different natures' in which 'by the appearance of a Machine well fancied, there is to bee seen a young Lover peircing the Clouds, and descending to the Earth, with so great a swiftness, that the quickest and the nimblest eye cannot but with admiration give a great deal of praise to our most famous Machinest . . .'

The 'Machinest' of the Comédiens de Mademoiselle d'Orléans was Charles Rousselle, described in a Brussels document in February 1662 as their 'décorateur'.[60] His scenes for Gilbert's play at the Cockpit may well have retained the 'trees of different natures' as standing wings, changing only at the backshutters to a view of dark clouds which subsequently withdrew to reveal Mount Latmos in its 'stateliness', probably also a shutter. Much of the play is served by this scene, a fact excused by the synopsis in confident terms:

It is always that Lofty mountain, *Lathmos* that serves as an ornament to this Act; also it would not be just if it withdraw so soon, since it is not to be denied that our Machenist has done what the art of man could to render this mountain as renowned upon our Theater as it is in Caire . (p. 5)

The verb 'withdraw' suggests that sliding flats were employed, an indication repeated at the next change of scene:

. . . this great mountain *Lathmos* withdraws it selfe to give place to a stately garden filled with all the Rarities of Nature and Art.   (p. 6)

Perhaps this last scene was of relieve, but in general the scenery seems to have been a good deal simpler than that required for *La Descente d'Orphée*. Rousselle reserved his most stunning work for the descent machinery used by many of the characters, including Amor, Diana, Night, Aurora, Apollo and Mercury, most of them claimed by the pamphleteer to be of surpassing beauty and ingenuity.

The spectacle was enlivened with lighting effects. In the opening scene of the play proper, amidst a perspective of clouds, two chariots appeared:

. . . the one looking towards the East, the other towards the West, these two Chariots are not of equall beauty, the one being the Chariot of the Moon, the other of the night; one is all of Silver adorned with rich Diamonds, and drawn with four beautifull Grayhounds, and the other drawes its light from her proper obscurity, yet nevertheless doth not cease to glitter by the help of a great number of stars that are round about . . .   (p. 2)

Apollo appeared in a 'flaming Chariot drawn by these four burning horses . . .

laden with all the most rich stones that the East produces . . .' (p. 5). The jewels were probably miniature lights, and all the various cars were adorned with them, including that of Aurora, who appeared

. . . in a Chariot where Rubies and the Opalls are sown in such rare order and in such a quantity that this mixture makes a fire not only to enlighten, but to make her appear more admirable . . .
(p. 4)

The composer of the synopsis bears in mind the danger of an actor placed upstage in the deep scene going unheard. The chariots of the Moon and Night 'do approach neer enough the spectators, that they may understand the fair *Diana* . . .', and when Endimion awakes from a deep sleep 'in the loveliest part of this mountain . . . hee is not so far off, but that it is easy to be understood, that he thinks of the fair *Diana* . . .' (p. 3). The effect of the machines, on the other hand, depends on the invisibility of the means used to move them. The chariots draw near 'by an undiscernedness' (p. 2), and for Mercury's descent in III, ii the synopsist makes his most enthusiastic claims:

In this Scene is to be seen *Mercury* from the very top of Olympus, descending to the earth; it is here where the most wise & the most knowing in the motions of the rare Machines, ought to be at a stand, and to admire the rare inventin [*sic*] that causes the motion of this god of diligence, since that the most clear-sighted, and most refined cannot discover the subtilty, but with labour. . .
(p. 6)

Although the French players left behind them such gratifyingly explicit descriptions of their work we cannot be quite sure how far their ambitions were realized within the narrow scope of the Cockpit's stage. It is in the nature of such synopses to exaggerate, and doubtless the productions did not live up to the effusive claims made for them, but nowhere are the effects described inconsistent with contemporary scenic practice, at least in France. On a bad day, when things went wrong, they might have been 'nasty and out of order and poor'; but when their changeable wings, inventive scenes of relieve and elaborate flying effects all worked harmoniously together they must have made as impressive a sight as any that had ever graced the public stage in London, fit indeed to honour a king. That the players were used to mounting their machine plays on small stages is a matter of record, confirmed time and again by the contracts they entered into in such cities as Brussels and the Hague, and it is likely that the upper and back scenes they then constructed to supplement their main raked stages were sufficient to create decors of considerable sophistication.[61] Nevertheless their London records do lack the particularity of those connected with Davenant's production of *The Siege of Rhodes* at the Cockpit two or three years earlier, in 1658–9, and it is to these that we must turn for an exact understanding of how the scenic drama of the Restoration could be accommodated in Jones's Jacobean playhouse.

Davenant knew the building well because in 1640–1 he had run it as its officially patented governor in succession to William Beeston, though his career there had been cut short by the Parliamentarians.[62] As Leslie Hotson has argued,[63]

Davenant's whole dramatic enterprise in the 1650s was directed at loosening the ties which held the drama down. He began in a small way, with 'entertainments', but aimed at nothing less than the restoration of drama to the London stage. He made his first, tentative, essays at his home in Rutland House, but his intention was to move back into the theatre proper. So much at least is clear from his Preface to the published text of his *First Day's Entertainment* . . .

By 1 April 1656, Davenant had chanced his arm at four London houses: the Apothecaries' Hall, Rutland House itself, Gibbons' Tennis Court (not yet properly fitted up as a theatre, though it would be in a few years' time) and the Cockpit. Of these only the last was a full-fledged theatre, properly and newly equipped. In 1649 it had been broken up by the Parliamentary soldiers, and two years later it had been refitted at a cost of £200 by William Beeston.[64] If Davenant was aiming to establish himself at any one of the four buildings he tried, it must surely have been the Cockpit that he had his eye on. And that indeed is where he did mount his productions of *The Siege of Rhodes* and *The Cruelty of the Spaniards in Peru* in 1658–9.

Thanks to John Webb's thoroughness we possess his measured scene designs for the *The Siege of Rhodes*; we also have, collected in the Lansdowne MS folio of Webb drawings at the British Library, a plan and section – clearly in Webb's hand – of a stage which appears to be related to them (plate 10).[65] A simple frontispiece with a straight border or lintel opens onto a raked stage with three pairs of flat, fixed wings. The scene is changeable only at the backshutters, whose assembly is neatly drawn and shows grooves capable of holding three pairs of shutter leaves. Beyond the shutters is housing for relief scenes. Compared with the French spectacular machinery that was later to be installed at the Cockpit this stage is a simple affair; it lacks changeable side wings, an upper stage and even the customary forestage or indeed any acting area in front of the border. The dimensions marked on the plan and section are generally similar to those of the *Siege of Rhodes* frontispiece design, though not in all respects identical; and between them the drawings contain enough detailed information to relate them not only to each other but to the Cockpit playhouse as it appears in Jones's design.

In his preface to *The Siege of Rhodes*, dated August 1656, Davenant apologizes for the small scale of his scene at Rutland House:

It has been often wisht that our scenes . . . had not been confin'd to eleven foot in height, and about fifteen in depth, including the places of passage reserv'd for the musick.[66]

Eleven feet is apparently just the height of the frontispiece designed by Webb (plate 11), where the scenery is shown mounted on a stage 3 ft high, giving a total elevation of 14 ft. But it must be acknowledged that the scale of the frontispiece drawing is a little ambiguous. Ruled divisions across the border top are marked in one-foot intervals for a total of 22 ft 4 in. Similar divisions mark the blocking of the support columns and appear to indicate the height of 11 ft above the stage, confirming both Davenant's observation about the scene at Rutland House and the scaled height of

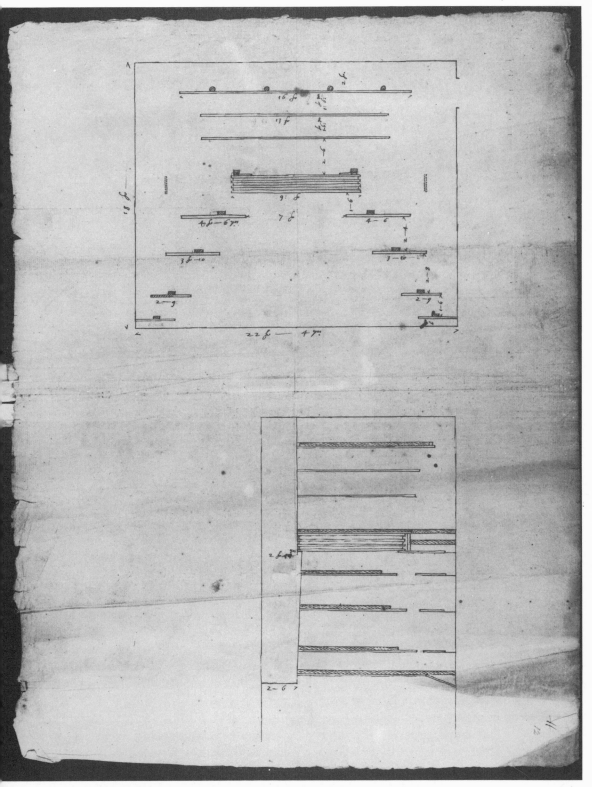

10   John Webb, plan and section of the stage at the Cockpit, Drury Lane

11   John Webb, frontispiece for *The Siege of Rhodes*

the frontispiece as shown in the Lansdowne MS section. In fact, however, Webb altered the scale of the design during the course of its development with the result that it is no longer quite consistent. Judged by the numbering along the top of the border the height of the frontispiece scales at a few inches more than 11 ft, and each of the vertical divisions ruled across the supports exceeds 1 ft by a small amount. A series of intervals marked off in lead along the right side of the foot of the stage gives a scale agreeable with that of the supports rather than the top, but the inked dimensions of the latter confirm it as the one intended to be final. Probably the drawing should be interpreted according to its ruled divisions rather than any precise scale.

The plan and section of a stage in the Lansdowne MS show a frontispiece 11 ft high by 22 ft 4 in wide, measurements which both exactly accord with the divisions ruled on the elevation, and have led to the conclusion, often stated, that all three drawings represent the Rutland House stage. But in fact the plan and section, while largely agreeing with the frontispiece design, differ from it in at least one important respect. In them the raked stage slopes upward from a marked height of 2 ft 6 in at the front to 2 ft 10 in halfway back, where it steps down 4 in to conceal the backshutter grooves. These measures are quite certain, and are confirmed by an accurate scale bar. In the elevation, whatever its slight ambiguity of scale, the stage is given as approximately 3 ft high, six inches higher than that in the section. Moreover the plan and section both show a stage 18 ft from front to back, and fail therefore to agree with what we know of the Rutland House arrangements, where only 15 ft could be spared for the scenes, 'including the places of passage reserv'd for the musick', which themselves are not shown in the drawings.

It is clear, therefore, that historians have been wrong to identify these British Library drawings with the Webb design at Chatsworth. Yet just as clearly they are related, and the simplest way of accounting for the relation is to suppose that they show an identical set of scenery put up in two different places. We know that *The Siege of Rhodes* was acted in both Rutland House and the Cockpit, and we may surmise that when Davenant put it on at the first he already had in mind a transfer to the second. Though small, the scenes were not cheap. They were designed by the nation's foremost expert in that line of work, the direct inheritor of Jones's reputation (and the owner, incidentally, of Jones's drawings of the Cockpit).[67] Not for many years would scenery come to be thought of as a temporary decoration, to be abandoned when the production came to an end. It was used again and again, often in quite various plays. Small wonder, then, that Davenant should take his scenery for *The Siege* with him along Holborn to Drury Lane when he opened the opera at the Cockpit in 1658–9.

The stage shown in the plan at the British Library is 18 ft deep, and makes no allowance for the places of passage for the music. It follows therefore that this is not the Rutland House stage, but that of the other theatre where the Webb scenes were used: the Cockpit.[68] Rutland House, we may fairly conclude, had the 3 ft high stage shown in the elevation, and was only 15 ft deep. The Cockpit stage, which is shown in the Worcester College drawings as 4 ft high and 15 ft deep, had been demolished in 1649 and rebuilt in 1651. Evidently it had been rearranged to be capable of supporting scenic productions. The new 18 ft depth of the stage probably indicates that the old decorated *frons scenae* – an obvious target for the wreckers – had been demolished, leaving part of the room backstage to be devoted to the new backcloth and relieves.

When we transfer the Webb designs at Chatsworth onto the stage shown in his plan and section and place the whole ensemble in the Cockpit playhouse we find that everything fits together very well. The section in Jones's Worcester College drawings does not show the stage itself in place, but defines its width between the foundation walls to either side as just 77.5 mm on the sheet, a measure which scales at 22 ft 4 in. Into this space the stage in Webb's drawing exactly fits, its sides making direct contact with the piers supporting the gallery posts. In Jones's section of the stage end of his theatre the top of the lower storey entablature is about 13 ft 8 in (47.5 mm) above the floor. The *Siege of Rhodes* frontispiece is ruled up 11 ft high; mounted on the 2 ft 6 in stage shown in Webb's section it would rise to 13 ft 6 in, a mere 2 in from a perfect match. Perfection is probably not to be expected in such matters as these; we have noted ambiguities in the scale of the frontispiece design, and in any case Webb may have needed to take into account small deviations from the original drawings in the Cockpit building as constructed. Even so, his decorated border is based on a Doric entablature presented as 2 ft tall, exactly the height of the lower storey entablature in the Jones drawings (7 mm on the sheet), the architectural feature it was designed to meet.

The ruled divisions along the border entablature mark intervals of 1 ft, but the supports are divided by a quite separate series of vertical lines into intervals of 9, 9 and 6 inches, counted inwards from their outer edges. The inmost pair of lines defines the inner edges of the support piers, excluding the profile of their rusticated blocking. The second pair marks the limits of the attached columns, measured at their capitals; but the third pair, 9 in in from either end of the frontispiece, seems to bear no relation to any feature of Webb's design. They do not mark the centres of the columns, for these occur just under 1 ft from the ends. If they mark nothing within the drawing, it is possible that they indicate something outside it, in the building, that is, for which the frontispiece was intended. Both supports are drawn in perspective so that they would represent a continuation of whatever structure they were placed behind, and when we turn to the Cockpit drawings we find that the width of the auditorium as defined by the inward surface of the gallery rails is 20 ft 10 in (72.5 mm on the sheet). The mysterious lines in Webb's drawing occur 9 in from either end of his frontispiece, or likewise 20 ft 10 in apart. The correspondence is exact: the lines precisely mark the width of the galleried pit in Jones's auditorium, just as the frontispiece and stage are precisely as wide as the space available for them.

Once they were installed Webb's frontispiece supports, which his plan shows were mounted 6 in back from the stage front, extended the architectural treatment of the playhouse by continuing its features in a modified form. His columns were stepped down $1\frac{1}{2}$ ft and with their pronounced blocking gave a massive appearance in keeping with the heroic spectacle they were to contain, but they were set so as to give the illusion of continuity with Inigo Jones's building. The shafts themselves (of course they were only flat painted representations) are shown in the drawing to be 1 ft in diameter within their blocks, like the posts at the Cockpit. Above them the Doric entablature exactly repeats that found in Jones's auditorium, with a single triglyph placed above each column. But the most remarkable indication that Webb's Doric order was intended to match the building shown in Jones's drawings lies in the bases of its columns. In the theatre sections the turned posts are given tall 'Corinthian' capitals above and simple Doric ones below, but all have the abbreviated bases proper to the Tuscan or possibly the Doric as interpreted by Vignola, with an astragal and a single torus. Jones was never one to be limited by too strict an adherence to the rules, and it is no surprise to find him working beyond them in this way, avoiding too fussy an articulation in the confined space of the auditorium. But Webb generally speaking was a stickler for correctness in such matters, as may be seen from his studies for door and gate aedicules as well as for the orders themselves. Yet in the *Siege of Rhodes* frontispiece he breaks the rules for once, giving the Doric columns Tuscan bases consisting of a plinth, single torus and astragal, exactly following Jones's pattern at the Cockpit. When he returned to this theme of the blocked Doric column in the frontispiece design for the Hall Theatre at Whitehall (1665: see plate 31) he returned also to correctness, and drew the proper bases. The eccentricity of the *Siege of Rhodes* design was an isolated case, a matter simply of repeating Jones's tune.

The Webb drawings make it possible for us to follow Davenant's production of *The Siege of Rhodes* from Rutland House – now seen as a kind of trial run – to the Cockpit, for whose stage the Rutland House arrangements were in truth a mock-up. As a result of his foresight, Davenant was able to transfer his expensive scenes from the one stage to the other with little alteration. More important, the dimensions of the Webb designs clinch the identification of the Worcester College drawings as showing the Cockpit in Drury Lane. Webb's scenery was certainly used at the Cockpit, and it fits our drawings not in an approximate or imprecise fashion, but exactly, with a perfect identity of measurement in most cases and a direct correspondence to what is idiosyncratic in their style.

There is evidence that Webb may have made one change in the proportions of his frontispiece when he took it to Drury Lane. Such an arrangement as I have outlined would leave the supports shown in the Chatsworth elevation partly obscured by the forward gallery posts at the Cockpit. It would be desirable to step the painted frontispiece columns inwards 9 in to each side, thus narrowing the scenic opening somewhat but bringing the frontispiece supports into clearer view. In the right margin of the frontispiece design a comment is inked in Webb's hand:

Memorandum. because I cast the odd 4:inches to one end ye middle of ye Compartiment falls not vpon one of the square lines though in ye middle of the roome.

Clearly these words refer to the ruling of the top part of the frontispiece into one-foot measures; spaced beneath them, and presumably therefore added later, is a curious column of figures rendered in lead:

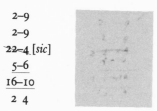

2–9
2–9
22–4 [sic]
5–6
16–10
2 4

This too presumably refers to the width of the frontispiece, for it includes the measure of 22 ft 4 in, but it is not clear what the other figures mean. Turning to the plan of the scene (plate 10) we find that most of the measurements have been noted first in lead and then, with the drawing inverted, rewritten in ink. One dimension – that of the width of the frontispiece supports – appears only in lead, and is given as '2–9'. The scenic opening between the supports is therefore 16 ft 10 in, a figure which, though not marked, may readily be calculated from the overall width, given in ink as '22 fo – 4 yn'. Some such calculation appears to be the aim of the column of figures added in lead to the frontispiece design: between them the two supports, at 2 ft 9 in each, take up 5 ft 6 in of the whole width of 22 ft 4 in, leaving a clear space of

16 ft 10 in. These dimensions differ from those of the frontispiece design, where the supports are 2 ft wide and leave a space between them of 18 ft 4 in.

The precise purpose of the lead figures in the margin of the Chatsworth elevation is certainly not clear, but it does appear to have something to do with a slight modification of the frontispiece *after* the original design had been made and in order to make it fit the requirements of the stage shown in the Lansdowne MS plan. Other measurements in the frontispiece design conform very closely to those of the plan and section: thus the wings converge precisely as shown in the plan, stepping in at 2 ft intervals to leave a 7 ft gap before the backshutter assembly. Only the stage height (about 3 ft in the elevation as against 2 ft 6 in in the section) and the width of the frontispiece supports appear to have been changed, and these changes are exactly consistent with what would be required when the frontispiece was re-erected at the Cockpit. The lower stage brought the border in line with the lower storey entablature of the playhouse, and the increase in the width of the supports, from 2 ft to 2 ft 9 in at either side, achieved by the narrowing of the scenic opening from 18 ft 4 in to 16 ft 10 in, allowed Webb's attached and rusticated columns to be stepped inward so that they could be seen beyond the gallery posts at the Cockpit, while retaining the necessary overall width of 22 ft 4 in.

In Webb's section of the stage some parts of the structure, such as the wings and backcloth, are shown erected as free-standing elements based on the platform alone, but others, including the upper grooves of the backshutter assembly and all the cloud borders, are suspended from a grid or roof of which no details are given. By 1658–9 Webb had used such grids many times, and had left a careful record of one in his drawings of *Salmacida Spolia* (plate 27), where he calls it a 'roofe'. At the Cockpit the bottom of this 'roofe' was evidently set on a level with the top of the frontispiece border, on a level, that is, with the upper gallery floor. Attaching it to the structure of the playhouse would therefore have been a simple matter, but the whole of the upper part of the stage above this level must have been blanked off, or perhaps converted into a music room for the occasion. That this was a temporary and unsatisfactory shift is confirmed by the fact that Davenant replaced the low frontispiece of *The Siege* with an arch for *The Cruelty of the Spaniards in Peru*. The border for *The Siege* was made horizontal to fit beneath an upper music room at Rutland House for the original performances; the arch for *The Cruelty* could be built higher because it had to suit only the Cockpit, and the music could be moved elsewhere.

Both forms of frontispiece were capable of accommodating a rising curtain, though this was used only to open and close each performance and was not lowered between the acts. With the aid of Webb's designs it is possible to reconstruct almost the entire scenic business of *The Siege of Rhodes*. Davenant divided the work into 'entries' rather than acts, borrowing a word made familiar by the masques. He describes Webb's 'Ornament' or frontispiece, adding the information that the drapery incorporated into its border was crimson. After the curtain was drawn up a 'lightsome sky appear'd, discov'ring a maritime coast, full of craggy rocks, and high cliffs . . .'[69] This was the set of flat wings, three to a side, which are shown in the frontispiece drawing as well as the plan and section of the stage.[70] Beyond it was a shutter, the design for which is at Chatsworth, showing Rhodes in its prosperity, with the Turkish fleet visible on the horizon. This scene served for the whole of the first entry, but was changed for the second at the shutter alone. In the stage plan Webb shows grooves capable of taking three pairs of shutters: evidently the forward pair, bearing the view of Rhodes in its prosperity, were drawn aside to reveal a picture of Rhodes besieged, the design for which is also at Chatsworth, labelled by Webb, '2:sceane The Towne beseiged A Shutter'. At the beginning of the third entry this shutter parted to reveal a relieve scene set beyond it, showing Solyman's throne. The design is extant, labelled '3.ᵈ scene Releive'. During the entry the scene changed again at the shutters, where the pair bearing the design of 'The Towne beseiged' were closed together to block off the view of the relieves. While these shutters were in place the relieves were changed behind them, and at the opening of the fourth entry they were revealed, presenting Mount Philermus with Solyman's army drawn up on the plain below. The design is at Chatsworth, labelled by Webb, '4: scene Relev'. During this entry the scene changed back to the shutter of Rhodes besieged (Webb's '2:sceane'), so that once more the relieves were obscured. For the fifth entry a third pair of shutters closed the scene, showing, in Webb's title, 'The Towne generally assaulted especially in the English Bulwarcke a shutter'. Later these shutters opened to reveal the relieves of Mount Philermus once more; at the end the shutters of the besieged Rhodes closed for the final moments of reconciliation.

In his discussion of these scene designs and their place in English theatre history, Richard Southern has convincingly shown[71] that Webb did not seek to provide a naturalistic setting for the action of Davenant's opera, but rather a series of pictorial backgrounds which, while providing an apt if only loosely applicable location, primarily aimed to counterpoint the action with images of threatened 'prosperity', the encirclement of the 'Towne beseiged', the splendour of Solyman's throne and the violence of the general assault. The settings provide pictorial themes rather than logically consistent *loci*. Nevertheless most are coherent landscapes, and Webb appears to have thought of them as fitting some sort of perspective scheme. The three backshutter scenes, of Rhodes in its prosperity, besieged and generally assaulted, all include a foreground of the island with the sea visible beyond, its horizon clearly marked. We shall find in a later chapter that Inigo Jones employed the uncompromising line of a marine horizon to establish the vanishing point for his shutters in *Florimène* in 1635; here more than twenty years later Webb follows his master very closely. The designs are ruled up in squares for the transfer to the shutters themselves, each square representing one foot each way and indicating that the shutters were 7 ft 6 in high by 9 ft wide, as they are in the stage plan and section. In the first scene Webb draws the marine horizon just 5 ft above the foot of the shutter; in the two remaining shutter designs it is about 5 ft 4 in high.

A similarly high horizon is maintained in the one relieve design that shows a landscape, that of Mount Philermus, where the horizon is about 5 ft above the foot. At the bottom of this drawing a strip representing a height of 4 in is hatched to represent the part of the relieves not seen by the audience by reason of the 4 in deep step down of the stage behind the backshutter assembly; Webb has noted the interval, '4 yn.', but then changed his mind and cancelled the note. The other relieve design, not of a landscape but of Solyman's throne surrounded by tents, is more explicitly ruled with a '4-yn' strip at the bottom, seven rows of squares and a further '2: yn' strip at the top for a total of 7 ft 6 in. Both this and the Mount Philermus design are ruled into 9-square widths just like the shutter designs, even though the plan and section call for the relieves to be 13 ft wide and up to 8 ft 6 in tall. No indication is given of what appeared on the necessary lateral extensions, but Webb does seem to have taken care of the greater height, marking no actual limit on the Mount Philermus design and adding a marginal note to Solyman's throne: 'To draw ye vpper part of ye balcone of ye Canopy at [gap] fo: high.' This drawing is, however, made on a sheet of paper different from all the others in size (165 mm by 197 mm as against about 157 mm by 189 mm for the rest) and it differs from them also in establishing a much lower horizon, deducible from the ruled orthogonals at about 3 ft 6 in above the foot of the design.

It is hardly possible, from this evidence, to discover what Webb's intention was in marking the horizon of the throne relieve so much lower than in the other designs. Perhaps he found simply that the lower horizon better suited the larger foreground of the scene, while the landscape backings could be made more explicit with a high horizon. His criterion for choosing the specific height of this horizon is a matter to which we shall return in a later chapter. That there was to be no rigorous perspective continuity between the standing wings and the shutters and relieves beyond them is clear from the frontispiece design at Chatsworth (plate 11). Here the inked drawing is laid over a pencil under-drawing which does not clearly emerge in photographs; and this in turn is established on a basis of lines ruled with the scorer. In a few parts these lead and scored lines offer useful information not conveyed by the ink. Thus the craggy tops of the wings, which look as though they might have been intended for cut-out 'relieves' to be seen against the background of a series of cloud borders, are rendered in lead as straight, and the wings themselves as regular rectangles. It is possible that Webb meant these flat-topped wings simply to join the cloud borders, for he shows them in line with one another in his section of the scene. Scored lines joining the inner top corners of each set of wings show that they were arranged to converge in a straight line, but these lines of diminishment slope downwards shallowly and stop with the furthest wings, so that they do not converge at a vanishing point. A vertical axis is scored down the centre of the drawing, and onto this three separate sets of orthogonals converge. From the top inner corners of the frontispiece scored lines cut through the upper parts of the wings and are continued until they converge on the central axis at a point 43 mm above the stage front, a measure which scales at just 3 ft. Scored horizontal lines apparently mark the top and bottom of the shutter assembly, on which two groups of orthogonals are rendered lightly in lead, one converging on the same vanishing point as the scored lines, the other set a few millimetres higher. Such a vanishing point is consistent neither with the wings (assuming that their bases are aligned on orthogonals) nor with the 5 ft 4 in horizons of the landscape scenes. It comes fairly close to that of the Solyman's throne relieve, but does not match it exactly. Though aiming for the kind of perspective consistency which we have noted, Webb did not require all the elements of his scene to conform to a single unified system.

With Webb's drawings our graphic records of the Cockpit playhouse cease, but the building was much used after the Restoration, along with the two other survivors from earlier days, the Salisbury Court and the Red Bull. George Jolly performed his repertory of old-fashioned plays at the Cockpit in 1661 and again from 1664 until he was arrested for doing so in April 1667. But if Jolly's largely Jacobean repertoire suggests that he had restored the theatre to its Jacobean form, it should not be forgotten that his reputation had been made in the 1650s in Germany as 'Joris Jollifus', who claimed to work in 'a theatre decorated in the Italian manner'.[72] He would have been well placed to exploit a stage equipped to service *The Siege of Rhodes* and *The Descent of Orpheus*, yet it can hardly be doubted that many of his old dramas were acted in the old-fashioned way without scenes. The French actors too were not exclusively devoted to machine plays, for they included among their number the playwright Dorimond, one of whose many modest, unspectacular works may have been the 'French comedy' seen by Evelyn and recorded in his *Diary* for 16 December 1661. In its last years the Cockpit was versatile enough to contain both the scenic and the older rhetorical drama. That indeed was its genius. Jones's drawings show that he considered it to be a fully articulated Jacobean private theatre, its audience disposed so that it entirely surrounded the stage; but even in its original state it stood ready to accept the sort of frontispiece that Jones had already by 1616 introduced to his masque productions. By Davenant's time this potential of the house could at last be realized, at first a little tentatively with *The Siege of Rhodes*, then more ambitiously with *The Cruelty of the Spaniards in Peru* and by the Comédiens de Mademoiselle d'Orléans. Especially through its influence on Davenant and John Webb the Cockpit shaped the expectations of Englishmen as they addressed the theatre of what Webb was to call 'the Scenicall Art, which to others than himselfe was before muche unknowne'.[73] It had been known to Jones, and it was the Surveyor's recognition that the private theatres of his day might serve also the demands of a newer kind of entertainment that ensured that his conversion of the Cockpit should survive for more than half a century, and teach the theatre men of a new age how to build.

4 Perspective scenes at Somerset House

OR MANY YEARS after his conversion of the Cockpit in Drury Lane Jones's theatrical commitments were restricted to the temporary arrangements made for masques and plays at Court. The stages and their auditoria were fleeting things, soon dismantled, and even the scene designs have not copiously survived. Those that have come down to us show that his prime source at this time was the set of woodcuts of the generic scenes published by Serlio, with their single point perspective presented in that curious, even idiosyncratic, up-tilted fashion that gives them their disturbing blatancy. The 'Street in perspective of faire building'[1] which Jones prepared for Jonson's *Vision of Delight* not only took individual buildings from the Comic and Tragic Scenes, but disposed them in the Serlian way, the ground rising abruptly towards a high vanishing point, the wings steeply foreshortened and the backscene filled with the elevation of a triumphal arch. Through this scene, indeed through the arch at its deepest part, advanced a bevy of the social graces, creating a pattern of motion down the stage which Jones had repeated in many of his earlier masques where the performers moved forwards through the perspective structure without apparent regard for the consequent incongruities of scale. Serlio himself does not seem to have encouraged such invasions of the sharply diminished upstage area by actors whose stature, of course, remained constant and therefore out of scale with their surroundings, and he rather grudgingly recommended the use of painted pasteboard figures to represent motionless human beings in the deeper parts of the scene. But as early as *Prince Henry's Barriers* (1610) Jones provided that the knights and their trains should make their entry through St George's Portico (O & S 37), a structure placed behind the backshutters and containing an axial corridor down which the participants passed in a regular progress towards the main stage. Even earlier, in 1605, Wake had noted how the perspective scene at Christ Church, with its raked stage 'running down to a level part in a gentle incline . . . lent great dignity to the players, as if descending a hill'.[2] The main physical action of *Oberon* (1611) consisted of Prince Henry's triumphal progress from the back part of the scene to the front:

There the whole palace open'd, and the nation of Faies were discouer'd, some with instruments, some bearing lights; others singing; and within a farre off in perspectiue, the knights masquers sitting in their seuerall sieges; At the further end of all, OBERON, in a chariot, which to a lowd triumphant musique began to moue forward, drawne by two white beares, and on either side guarded by three Syluanes, with one going in front.[3]

The design for the palace (O & S 62) shows a deep corridor of entrance similar to that framed by St George's Portico. Evidently the risk that such uses of the perspective construction might lead to ridiculous disparities of scale made little impression on Jones, and he emphasized the depth of the scene in his drawing by showing the upstage projection filled with bright artificial light.

Almost all Jones's earlier architectural scenes are conceived as great passages through which the masquers pass in their triumphal entries. A drawing for a barriers of *c.* 1613 (O & S 39) reduces the theme to its simplest expression: an aedicule with an opening 11 ft wide and 11 ft tall to its blind arch fronts an entrance corridor drawn in sharp foreshortening. Through it the knights passed on their way to the barriers, just as in *The Vision of Delight* the milder figures of Delight, Grace, Love and the rest were 'seene to come as afarre off' through the centre of its complex Serlian street scene. In *The Masque of Augurs* (1622), another Serlian scene in structure, Apollo descends from the clouds and calls forth his 'sacred sons' from their tombs, presumably in the Pantheon-like building at the back of the stage. In Jones's sketch (O & S 115) three of them are shown descending its steps, ready to make their downstage progress.

There is evidence that on one occasion at least Jones was disturbed by the clash of scale which inevitably followed his usual practice, and went to some lengths to avoid it. A design for the unknown masque of 6 January 1619 (O & S 100), labelled 'Pallace of Perfection', shows an upper level architectural scene of the Serlian kind, its wings diminishing sharply and forming a vista of rich buildings closed by a palazzo with obelisks. On the main stage below it a cloud has descended, containing a group of masquers. Lacking the text of the masque to aid us in interpreting this vision, we are fortunate to discover a description of its action among the diplomatic dispatches sent home to Turin by the Savoy agent in London, Giovanni Battista Gabaleone:

. . . at the foot of the room opposite his Majesty a curtain which hid all the wall at that end was let drop, revealing a perspective with very lovely ornaments which stood in the air between the ceiling of the room and the solarium. In it were seated all the lords of the masque, in the most beautiful order. By means of a hidden device it descended very, very gently to the ground. Behind this perspective, in proportion as the lords' seat descended, and at their backs, there were seen in another perspective castles, towers, palaces, rooms and pictures in foreshortening. In truth it seemed to me that I had never seen anything that gave more cause for wonder.[4]

The first perspective – the cloud machine on which the lords rode – closed off the audience's view of the second, architectural, one until after the all-important triumphal progress of the masquers had begun to leave it behind. It was doubtless a complicated way of wedding the idea of the progress, now downwards as well as forwards toward the stage, to the foreshortened perspective scene without risk of incongruity, but Gabaleone seems to have been pleased enough with it. Perhaps it was too expensive a stratagem to be often repeated, for in general Jones continued to think of the perspective masquing scene as something to be penetrated, whether it was the simple gateway of the barriers of *c.* 1613 or the more elaborate architectural vista of *The Masque of Augurs*. By 1625, however, he was beginning to develop some of his perspective stages in new ways, more closely akin to those described by Serlio and apparently intended for the drama proper, as distinct from the masque or barriers.

These neo-Serlian scenes are first recorded in designs prepared for plays staged by Queen Henrietta Maria at Somerset House beginning in 1626, but their style may have been set earlier. Jones had provided scenes for performances there as much as a decade before, though no drawings of them survive. Some account must therefore be given, before we turn to the designs of the later 1620s, of the earlier but more sparsely documented stages at Somerset House, a building which had always been a showplace for the courtier arts since it was erected by the Lord Protector in the time of Edward VI. Even from the beginning it became a particular source of French influence, its Strand façade – precociously classical for London – having probably been constructed with the aid of French craftsmen.[5] Many of the details, including the treatment of the windows, were French in origin. Under Elizabeth it languished, but Anne of Denmark made it her own, establishing her household there so that it came to be known, familiarly at first but by 1617 with official sanction, as Denmark House. In several of its larger rooms, but especially in the great hall which flanked the riverside gardens, theatres were routinely prepared for the performance of masques and especially of plays.

A plan of Somerset House made by Robert Smythson[6] indicates that the hall was 30 ft wide internally, a dimension more or less confirmed by a Works account entry of 1611–12 which records the fitting of a new floor 60 ft by 31 ft.[7] The room was made ready 'with the State and hangings there vpon the Stage of the pastorall' performed at a Court wedding early in 1613,[8] and several plays were given there in the summer of the same year. Some hint of what these routine arrangements consisted of is given in a detailed 'particular book' listing the tasks undertaken by the Works in 1614,[9] when King Christian IV of Denmark made a surprise visit to London and was richly entertained by his brother-in-law, James I, with a week or two of hurriedly improvised festivities. They included a 'play and dancing' in the hall at Somerset House. The footpace for the state was 10 ft square in plan, and over it there was a framework of boards supporting the canopy. The usual timber degrees – seven cartloads of them – were brought in from their storage place in Scotland Yard, close to Whitehall. Their frames were altered so that they might stand even, and wooden brackets were attached to them. The boards which made the bench seating were nailed in their turn to the brackets. An elevated place was made from boards mounted on trestles for the lords and ladies to sit in; below, beside the pit or orchestra, there were ordinary forms and benches. More boards were placed on trestles for the music, and posts and rails were provided on each side of the hall door, presumably to contain the movement of the crowds.[10]

Similar arrangements to these were probably made for appearances of the King's and Queen's Men at Somerset House in December 1615,[11] but in the following year Inigo Jones was commissioned to design what appears to be the first scene to be erected in the hall:

. . . for the workes of the Sceane for a maske presented before the late Quenes Majestie at Denmarke House in the Straund by her highnes servauntes in the year 1616. the which Sceane was afterwardes made new with more workes for the presentacion thereof before his Majestie at the said house, the said Inigo Jones fynding all the clothe Colours golde sylver and all the workes of the paynters and guilders, by agreemente betwene the late Quenes Majestie and him . . . the some of xlij^li.[12]

There were frequent masques and plays in the hall after this date, partly perhaps because in the spring of 1617 Anne took up permanent residence at what was now officially renamed Denmark House. A new lantern was installed in the roof, designed by Jones who was currently engaged on several other projects for the queen.[13] Two years later, however, she died, and for a time the hall was quieter than it had been. Nevertheless the accounts of 1619–20 record that somewhere in Somerset House – presumably in the hall – the carpenters were engaged in '. . . makeinge degrees and fitting dealebordes on them for plaies, laying a false floore of tymber and boordes for the Prynce and Noblemen to daunce vppon. . .'[14]

After James's death Henrietta Maria took up residence at Somerset House and made the hall the centre of the scenic drama in England. Her first production, in which she shocked contemporary opinion by taking a part herself, was Racan's *Artenice*, performed on 21 February 1626. It was, as such things went, a fairly lavish occasion, its cost recorded in the annual Works account for Somerset House: '. . . *Clxviij^li xxij^d ob* for the Pastorall Comody in the Hall there. . .' and requiring special payments 'to Raphe Brice Deputy Carpenter for his attendaunce early, and late, and sondry nightes to see the service of the Pastorall performed. . .'[15] In the Houghton Library at Harvard there is a copy of the play marked with annotations of the scene changes made at the performance, which have been transcribed by Orgel and Strong:

Opening:	La Seine (= scene) est vng village
I.i:	La Lune se Leuue dune nue por monstrer quil est nuict
II.i:	La Seine se change en vng bois
II.iv	(*two stage directions*): Icy tonneres et esclairs et La lune sobcursist, *and* Icy La lune deuient Claire
III.i:	La Seine se change et devient en village pastoralle
III.iii:	La Seine se change en La [several letters indecipherable] de Seine
IV.v:	La Seine se change en vng village pastoral
V.i:	Le Seine se change encore vne fois en vng bois
V.v:	La Seine se change en vng village pastoral
end:	Quand La pastorelle est finist La Seine se change en vng mont desus Lequel sont assis les masques qui dessendent pour danser et puis apres se change La seine en la maison de Soumarcet et sy voit Le fleuue de Tamise qui est La fin[16]

The action of the play appears to have taken place in two alternating settings of a village and a wood. At the end two quite different scenes were introduced: a mount was revealed, presumably by the parting of shutters, with masquers sitting on it, ready to descend to the dancing floor in front of the state; afterwards these ideal rural images were replaced by a vision of the real, tangible Somerset House within whose walls the audience were seated. This closing transformation still strikes one

12   Inigo Jones, standing scene for *Artenice*

as a fine conceit, bringing the philosophical pretentions of the pastoral and the sensuousness of the masque to focus on Queen's Court itself, as if the real world might be tuned with the harmony of what went before.

But how was it done? Jones's design for the stage is extant (plate 12), labelled simply 'pastoral sceane Som: House 1625'.[17] It is squared up in lead for enlargement, and measures 31 squares wide by 28 squares high to the top of the border. We know that the floor fitted in the hall in 1611–12 was 31 ft wide, and this was presumably the internal measure of the room. Jones must have intended his stage to reach all across it from wall to wall, for he provided no pilasters at either side to support the entablature. If each square is 1 ft across the design precisely fits the space available for the scene. The stage in the drawing is heavily rusticated, 5 ft high, with steps leading down from it to the orchestra, the route followed by the masquers at the end of the play. The scene opening is 19 squares high, and as wide as the hall, giving it approximately the proportions of a Golden Rectangle.[18] The top border, shaped as a Composite entablature, is presumably supported by brackets at either end where it abuts the walls, but these are obscured by the bunched curtain.

13   Sebastiano Serlio, Satyric Scene. *Il secondo libro di perspettiva*, fol. 70ᵇ

The scene is of the Serlian type, and not only in its imagery. The rustic cottages which crowd in at either side are drawn from the Satyric Scene in the *Architettura* (plate 13), while the building at the left with the open upper storey and large eaves recalls one in a similar position in the Comic Scene (plate 4), the source also of the pattern of the forestage steps. Like Serlio's, the stage was capable of sky effects, the moon disappearing behind clouds and then emerging again after thunder and lightning. The Works accounts, unfortunately very brief on this occasion, record an expenditure of 2s 1d for 10 lb of 'soape for the engines of the Pastorall'.[19] A more modern device, not found in Serlio, is the heavy decorated border, used to support the curtain and the pulleys by which it was raised, but it is remarkable that no pilasters supported it at either side.[20] The wings therefore could not have been sliding flats, capable of rapid change. The structure shown in the drawing could not be moved at all except at the deeper part of the vista, there being no free space available to either side of the stage for withdrawing the wings. They are clearly drawn as angled or 'book' wings, their inner faces aligned on orthogonals which converge towards a vanishing point, as in Serlio. Serlio's scene was not, however, intended to be a changeable one, yet we know from the Harvard annotations to

Artenice that Jones's scene changed many times. It could have done so only at the backshutters:[21] the village buildings shown closing the deepest part of the design could be withdrawn to reveal a second set painted with a woodland. The two pairs of shutters alternated during the action of the play proper, then both were opened at once to reveal the masquers seated on a mount. These courtiers left their station at the deepest part of the scene, moved forward through the cottage wings, and passed to the dancing floor down the rusticated steps at the stage front. After the dancing, the mount was obscured by a third pair of shutters closing in front of it, painted with a view of Somerset House and the Thames.

The Works accounts for the pastoral note that a 'Lardge Theater' was built at the upper end of the hall, the word 'Lardge' doubtless indicating that it was what we should call 'deep'. It was usual for the carpenters or their accountants to reserve the word 'long' for the greatest dimension of a stage, and 'broad' or 'large' for its secondary dimension. The stage at Somerset House was 31 ft wide, and presumably rather less than that deep, yet deep enough to be called large. A fairly deep stage is required to hold the Serlian angle wings, and in the accounts there is some indication of how substantial one of these foreshortened structures might be. An entry concerns a 'Tabernacle' constructed for the scene 'standing vppon viij pilleres with Architrave, ffreeze, and Cornish', a reference to the temple shown in Jones's design:

John Hooke Turnor for turning viij^t pillers for the Tabernackle at iiij^d the peece *ij^s viij^d* [22]

The hexastyle temple in the *Artenice* scene has one of a pair of further columns visible behind the portico, and the fact that John Hooke turned eight columns for it shows that the structure was a solid construction, not simply painted canvas.

Orgel and Strong tentatively assign a second drawing to *Artenice* (O & S 136), on the supposition that it shows the woodland which alternated with the village setting. It is roughly drawn, and includes a temple thrust in among the trees at the right. This temple is, however, tetrastyle and without the pediment shown in the village scene; moreover the tree wings are shaped as flats, not angled wings. The size of the drawing, 119 mm by 169 mm, is such that it precisely fits the scenic opening in a design for the frontispiece of *The Shepherd's Paradise* (plate 19), a play for which a tetrastyle unpedimented temple was designed to be thrust out between the flat tree wings. O & S 136 is therefore a drawing intended for *The Shepherd's Paradise*, and should not be taken as proof that the *Artenice* stage was movable anywhere but at the backshutters.

While the play itself was in progress the scene was closed at the back with shutters; the end was marked, not by the descent of a curtain nor even by an Epilogue, but by the opening of the shutters to reveal the masquers on their mount. What had been an action played across the stage in front of the standing scene now became a deeper vista through which the masquers advanced towards the rustic steps at the front of the stage, and thence to the orchestra.

A masque performed by the queen and her ladies in the following year at

Somerset House, presumably in the hall, has left no record of its scenery, but an entry fortuitously slipped in among some other Works accounts for the period gives a useful note on the way in which the hall floor was prepared for dances such as those that followed *Artenice*:

Item to Raph Grinder for one hundred fower-score and three yards of greene Cotton to Couer a floore at Denmarke house Where the said Masque was performed and for threed and Workmanship in fitting and laying the same, and two thousand black tacks imployed therein xvj^{li}xix^s vij^d[23]

It seems likely that the green cloth was tacked to a wooden dancing floor of the type that had been installed for Prince Charles in 1619–20. Whether or not such particular arrangements were made for the dancing that followed *Artenice*, it is clear that the occasion used Jones's scene in two ways, first as a background for drama and then as an entry for the masquers. For the play the backshutters closed the vista; for the masque the longitudinal axis of the theatre was extended backwards into the relieve of the mount and forwards to include the dancing floor, the whole work stepping downwards to decant the performers at the feet of the king in his state. Finally, when the dances were done, the shutters closed once more to present to the assembled company a reminder both of the physical limitation of the real world and of its beauty. The vision of Somerset House and the Thames seen through the cottages and beyond the Temple of Arcadia was more than a mirror image or solipsism. It was an affirmation of the human order that could be enshrined in good architecture.

Somerset House was extensively developed by Henrietta Maria, and Jones was soon occupied in work on a new cabinet room, new river stairs and a new chapel, most showing the influence of the French courtiers and artists who surrounded the queen.[24] On 8 December 1629, at a time when he was engaged in the conversion of the old cockpit in Whitehall into a small Palladian theatre, Jones received a warrant 'for a Stage & Scene to bee made at Somerset House'.[25] No details of this stage are given in the Works accounts, which do however refer to its cost in the sum of 'all the chardges of the saide woorkes and Reparacions donne and bestowed att Denmarke House . . . with xlv:^{li} v.^{s} for the Seane there'.[26] A notable design by Jones is linked to this occasion by Orgel and Strong (O & S 141; plate 14), and while it cannot be confirmed their attribution is entirely convincing. Neither the warrant nor the Works account specifies the particular chamber in which the scene was erected, but Jones's design shows a stage running all across a room, with no side supports but a heavy decorated border attached to the side walls by means of enriched consoles. The drawing is squared up with a pointer, and the scene is 30 units wide from wall to wall. If, as is likely, each square scales at a foot across, the scene would approximately fit the hall at Somerset House, and that appears to be its intended location. Above a great cartouche at the centre of the border is a crown made to a fleur-de-lis pattern, indicating that the scene was prepared for Henrietta Maria. John Webb later added the chalk inscription, 'The Tragick/a standing\seene y^e first scene', but unfortunately without a localized title.

14   Inigo Jones, Tragic Scene

The general construction of the scene resembles that of the *Artenice* design. The border hides the pulleys and ropes by which a curtain could be raised, and the lack of side supports shows that the wings were constructed Serlian style with two angled faces, the front pair evidently abutting the walls of the hall. The tall front wing at the left appears to have been drawn originally as a single foreshortened face aligned with a ruled orthogonal, but a heavy ink overdrawing corrects its shape at the head and foot by indicating the return face, parallel to the front of the stage. The smaller wing at the right seems to have needed no such correction. At the rear an arcaded building is shown, evidently painted on backshutters whose bottom edge is clearly indicated.

The border is decorated with figures of Hercules and Truth, and on a separate sheet (O & S 144) appear studies for them both. On the verso of the sheet is a list of the shutters by which the standing scene of architecture was varied during the course of the unknown play for which the stage was prepared:

Shuters. the com*m*on sceane [Tra] g [ic?]
[cabinett 1, struck out]   cabinett   1

a wrak & port	I	the dreame	I
prinses/hir\chamber	I	cabinett varied	I
a desartt	I	a cattafalk	
too campes	I		
prinses chamber	I		
the kinges chamber/or prospectt\	I[27]		

The subjects of these designs cannot all have been consistent with the architecture of the standing scene. Some are exterior views ('a wrak & port', 'a desartt'), some interiors ('prinses hir chamber', 'the kinges chamber . . .') and others indeterminate ('the dreame', 'a cattafalk'). None constitutes an obvious point of entry, like the mount with its seated masquers which followed *Artenice*, but there are so many that some at least – possibly the righthand column – must have been scenes of relieve, deepening the vista apparently during the course of the play. If 'the dreame of relievo' which appears on a separate sheet (O & S 146) is identical with 'the dreame' mentioned in the list, as Simpson and Bell first proposed, it shows that the theatre at Somerset House had an upper as well as a lower stage. The scenic opening in the Standing Scene design is proportioned as a double square, 30 ft wide and 15 ft tall, and the provision of a two-storey set of backshutters within such limits of size, though difficult, would not be impossible. Each set could be some 7 ft tall, and indeed 'the dreame of relievo' shows the large seated figure of Pallas in the lower part, with a cloud 'of past bord finto' in the upper. Many figures are represented in the cloud, but they are much smaller than the goddess below and the discrepancy of scale suggests that they were merely painted representations, not human actors. It is important to recognize that when the wings shown in the Tragic Scene were mounted on a stage raked at anything like the ratio shown in most of the extant sections of Jones and Webb theatres, the backshutter assembly and rear wings would all appear much lower relative to the stage front than they do in the drawing, leaving an empty expanse of sky over them. The designer could readily use this space to introduce an upper stage for relieves even within a scenic opening as low as 15 ft.

The Tragic Scene is a more eclectic and sophisticated drawing than the pastoral setting for *Artenice*. Although its angled wings derive from Serlio (plate 15) its architecture is more various, owing debts to theatrical sources such as Bartolomeo Neroni's set for *L'Ortensio* and G. B. Aleotti's Ferrara Tragic Scene.[28] The building on the backshutters is a regularized version of one in Vredeman de Vries's *Perspective* (1605), and the arcading which flanks it stems from Giulio Parigi.[29] As in *Artenice*, however, the perspective of the scene was violated in the production with apparent impunity by the introduction of human actors or masquers among the steeply foreshortened – and therefore miniature – objects at the back of the stage. In *Artenice* the masquers descended from their mount and entered the main scene among the rearmost wings, where they will have seemed taller than the ridges of the cottage roofs. Towards the stage front they will have come into scale, their heads about as high as the house door at the left or the eaves of the very humble little cottage to the right. In the Tragic Scene Pallas, seated beyond the backshutters,

15 Sebastiano Serlio, Tragic Scene. *Il secondo libro di perspettiva*, fol. 69ᵃ

will have loomed vast in comparison with the architecture of the rear wings. Even after moving downstage an actor would still have looked uncomfortably tall in relation to the buildings, especially the smaller one to the right. It is possible that a level forestage was erected in front of the scene, and that most of the action took place on it, as in Serlio's theatre scheme. The scale of the buildings might then have seemed more correct, but there is no specific evidence that such a platform was built.

Somerset House remained the chief London centre for the production of the scenic drama until 1640. A special theatre was constructed in the Paved Court for a production of Montagu's *The Shepherd's Paradise* in 1633, the extensive drawings for which will be examined in a later chapter. On Twelfth Night 1634 Fletcher's *Faithful Shepherdess* was produced in the Presence Chamber[30] and a scene and 'diverse motions' were set up for it.[31] In November there were two performances of Heywood's masque-like play, *Love's Mistress*, with scenes by Jones which included a machine descent, but the designs have not survived and whether the production was in the hall or elsewhere in the palace is unknown.[32] French players performed at Somerset House in the new year, and in August a play was acted by the ladies of

Henrietta Maria's Court.[33] None of these productions left any detailed record; not until Lodowick Carlell's *The Passionate Lovers* was staged in the hall in the summer of 1638[34] is there any further graphic evidence of the theatrical arrangements made there, and this is only a backshutter design of woodland, squared up 11 units wide by 9 high. It has nothing new to offer. Several other plays were performed at Somerset House in that year, and a special Works account for two of them gives some idea of the variety of materials and workmanship required for mounting the type of production reviewed in this chapter:

. . . for fittinge of *Somsett house for twoe Playes* acted there before the kinge and Queene in December 1638 The particulareties whereof hereafter ensewe viz' for Empcions and Provicions viz' of Dealeboordes v^s vj^d slitt deales xxxij^s. Candles xxiij^s Ironwoorke xxiiij^s Baskett*es* xij^d Oyle xx^d Rozen and ffrankincense xviij^d. Birchen Bromes ix^d. Packthreed iiij^s x^d Soape iiij^s ij^d. Nailes xlvij^s Glewe vj^d. Mapp vj^d Baserope iiij^s viij^d. In all the saide Provicions vij^{li}. xij^s j^d. Carryadge by land & water, xvij^s. Wages of Carpenters at ij^s and xviij^d p*er* diem and asmuch p*er* noctem ix^{li}. xij^s. x^d. Laborers at xij^d. p*er* diem and viij^d p*er* noctem xlj^s. Clarke of the workes at xx^d p*er* diem xxvj^s. viij^d. and Purveyors at xx^d p*er* diem xxv^s In all the saide wages xiiij^{li}. v^s. vj^d. *In all* the charges for fittinge the house for twoe Plaies . . . the sume of xxij^{li}, xiiij^s, vij^d.[35]

5   The Cockpit-in-Court

WHEN, in the closing weeks of 1629, Jones designed a scene for Somerset House, probably the Tragic Scene described in the previous chapter, he was also engaged in preparing what a subsequent Works account called 'Designes and Draughtes'[1] to convert the famous Cockpit at Whitehall into a small playhouse. Both theatres seem to have been intended for the professional players: the lack of Court gossip concerning the production at Somerset House suggests that the scene constructed there was not meant for eminent amateurs, and the new Cockpit was planned to accommodate the public companies for those of their Whitehall performances that would not require the larger auditorium available in the hall. It is probable, then, that Jones had similar users in mind as he prepared both schemes, the one for a scenic house derived from Serlio and the other, as we shall see, an exercise in Palladianism. Yet the physical requirements of the actors can hardly have been his prime concern, for the designs ignore the deep thrust stages and encircling audience of the Globe, the Blackfriars and Jones's own earlier Cockpit coversion in Drury Lane. If the two theatres of 1629–30 have anything in common it is an acting area whose size and proportions derive more from Italian example than contemporary usage in the commercial playhouses of London. They are informed, even learned, variations on themes borrowed from Renaissance architecture rather than the daily experience of the players who were to use them.

For years the Cockpit had served, in its flexible way, for stage plays as well as cockfighting, but after Jones's conversion it remained exclusively a theatre until a decade before its demolition in the 1670s. It had originally been erected, *c.* 1530–2, as a regular if rather splendid cockpit, part of the sports complex established by Henry VIII on the west side of Whitehall. Its long life is documented in many entries in the declared accounts of the Office of Works, especially for refittings in the years 1581–2, 1629–30 and 1660. It appears in early drawings and maps, and in its final phase – after it had ceased to be used as a theatre – in a detailed topographical painting by Hendrik Dankerts.[2] Its relation to the other buildings of the palace is given in an engraving dated 1680, but based on a survey made ten years before.[3] By far the best documentary source recording its design is a sheet of drawings (plates 16 and 17)[4] among the collection at Worcester College, in the hand of John Webb and probably arising from the refitting of 1660. Here are registered not only many details of Jones's earlier scheme of 1629, but also the size and proportions of the original building. The Works accounts for 1629–30 are particularly full, and together with Webb's drawings convey a fairly good idea of what was built at that time, though the plans introduce subsequent alterations. Nevertheless it is unfortunate that Webb's sheet includes no section of the theatre as a whole, for the facts recorded about its interior, though plentiful, are ambiguous. An understanding of its layout must find room for them all, even those that appear to be contradictory, and it must be reached – if indeed it may be reached at all – only through an acknowledgment of the building's history as both cockpit and playhouse, for even after the conversion of 1629 most of the original fabric remained intact.

Jones's theatre was largely a matter of surfaces, even though it did reorganize the space within the Tudor structure. No cockpit is altogether adequate, in itself, for the staging of plays, and even the lavish royal pit at Whitehall needed some alteration if it was to become a regular Court theatre, as distinct from a place where plays might occasionally be performed alongside cockfights, as they were in the reign of James I.[5] Exterior views of the building appear in an early drawing of Whitehall by Wyngaerde, in the so-called 'Agas' map of London which shows the area as it was *c.* 1560, and in a drawing by the architect John Thorpe made *c.* 1606.[6] All give bird's-eye surveys but more or less confirm the accuracy of Dankerts' ground-based perspective view, showing the Cockpit to have been a battlemented square-planned structure with an octagonal tower which rose at its centre and supported a pyramidal 'cant' roof topped by a lantern. All except Dankerts agree that the central tower was a full storey higher than the square surrounding it, with large lights (most fully described by Thorpe) in its upper walls. Dankerts' lower angle of view may have prevented him from seeing these windows, which he does not record, but there is also a possibility that the outer square had been built higher by the time he made his painting in 1674. A Works account of 1670–1 records a quantity of new construction at the Cockpit without specifying its exact location;[7] if Dankerts' view is correct in showing the square as higher than in the earlier drawings and maps, some of the new work may have been done at the upper level, which was at this date converted into part of the new lodgings for the Duke of Buckingham.

Webb's plan precisely records the relation of outer square and inner octagon. The square is large – some 57 ft across externally – but the octagon within it is 39 ft overall in diameter, just about the size of a conventional cockpit building. The nature of cockfighting is such that the 'audience' are almost participants; they crowd the table (known from the Works accounts to have been round and 9 ft in diameter in 1581–2[8]), coming close enough to touch it. Later engravings by Hogarth and Rowlandson[9] give a good idea of the nature of the sport, while the frontispiece to R[ichard] H[owlett]'s *Royal Pastime of Cock-fighting* (London, 1709) shows the intimate scale of the Royal Cockpit across the park in St James's.[10] The proceedings required small structures, as we saw in connection with John Best's house in Drury Lane. At Whitehall, if they bore any resemblance to those recorded elsewhere, the cockfight table and chief degrees must all have been contained within the diameter of the central octagon. That degrees did surround the table is suggested by the Works accounts for 1581–2, when the pit was equipped with 'new settell*es*', elsewhere described in the same account as 'seates', which were to be laid 'with verditur'.[11] Eight years later they were repaired in terms that go some way towards describing their structure, for carpenters were paid for 'shoringe up newe joysing and boordinge sondrye decayed seats in the cockpitt'.[12] Such fixed degrees, raised on sloping joists, resemble what Hogarth and Rowlandson show later on, but they were provided also, constructed as 'ryngs', at another of Henry's VIII's cockpits, the one built at Greenwich in 1533:

CARPENTERS . . . making a new cocke place in the tilt yerde with iiij ryngs for men to sytt upon also a cocke cope in the este lane [Eastney Street] for the Kings cockes with vj rooms in the same
PLASTERERS . . . also lathying and seyling with lyme and heyre a place in the galary over the bowling allaye for the Quene to syte in to see the cocks fyghting
CARPYNTERS makyng of a seyt for the Kyng to syte in within the new cocke place[13]

Here are all the main constituents of a cockpit: the rings of seats about the table, a group of cockpens or coops, and, because this is a royal pit, two special seats, one for the king 'within' the main circle and a second elevated in a gallery outside it for the queen. At Whitehall we may suppose that Henry's seat was similarly close to the action, but in 1581–2 we hear of Queen Elizabeth's 'privy gallorie', doubtless removed from the table a decent way, like that which Anne Boleyn was able 'to syte in to see the cocks fyghting'. Any space provided for spectators at the Whitehall pit beyond the rings of seats about the table would need to be raised high enough above them for the fights to be visible, as in the prints mentioned above and in Platter's description of 1599 (see p. 46 above). Beneath the elevated gallery the cockpens were installed, conveniently surrounding the pit.[14]

Such is the configuration of the house as recorded by a Spanish visitor, Don Andres de Laguna, who attended a fight there in 1539:

King Henry the eighth of that name had had a sumptuous amphitheatre of fine workmanship built, designed like a colosseum and intended exclusively for fights and matches between [cocks]. Round about the circumference of the enclosure there were innumerable coops, belonging to many princes and lords of the kingdom. In the centre of this colosseum, if I remember correctly, stood a sort of short, upright, truncated column about a span and a half high from the ground in height and so thick that a man could scarcely get his hands around it . . . the cocks were brought out from the cages already mentioned . . . They were placed two at a time on the column in full view of the great number of spectators. The jewels and valuables which were bet on them were placed in the middle.[15]

In every age, it seems, the intimacy of the cockpit derives not only from the small scale of the combat, but from the need of the spectators to lay their bets and deliver their pledges.

Beyond the main 'colosseum' contained within the central octagon (the 'ryngs' of Greenwich) stood the cockpens, above which ran an elevated gallery somewhat removed from the fray and extending all round the house. An early reference, c. 1532, to gilding the 'Roofe of the galarye aboute the [Cockep] ittehowse'[16] confirms that the structure was not set within the central octagon, which opened upwards towards the lantern, but ran 'aboute' the building in much the same way as Webb shows it to have done in his later drawings. Part of it was designated as a privy gallery for the queen during the reign of Elizabeth, but there is no sign in the records that the rest of it was equipped with seats or degrees until the conversion of 1629. Rather it remained a level ambulatory on the regular cockpit pattern, though further removed from the action than was customary elsewhere.

Webb's drawings record some details of Jones's conversion, together with other work done at the Restoration, but they also happily preserve the ground plan of the whole and show it to have been set out according to the mediaeval *ad quadratum* method. The corners of the lower square structure are closed off to form a large brick octagon. Within this, five foundation walls of the smaller octagon are shown, together with sections of six of the posts which supported the high pyramidal roof. Where Webb records the curve of Jones's *frons scenae* he omits two posts, but indicates by means of a broken line the extent of the inner structure. The octagon thus defined coincides with the inner surfaces of the low walls which front the gallery, and its diameter is close to that of the larger octagon (formed by the closed-off square) divided by $\sqrt{2}$. This method of planning is characteristic of mediaeval practice, as we have seen, and almost certainly originates in the use of surveyors' or masons' lines in setting out the footings of the walls. The proportion is not quite exact in Webb's drawing, as it would have been had he been developing an *ad quadratum* scheme directly on the paper; the inexactness argues that his plan is a survey of what was actually built, with all of its material imprecisions, rather than a copy of a theoretical drawing.

The form of the Cockpit was unusual but not unprecedented. Its closest analogues are to be found in a class of structures associated with monastic or royal kitchens. The Livery Kitchen at Richmond, for example, built early in the sixteenth century by the same Works office that developed Whitehall, was described in a Parliamentary Survey of 1649 as

. . . consisting of one square building called the Livery Kitchen floored with stone . . . this roome is tyled a good parte thereof, and hath in the midle a large spired turret; leaded all over which renders it a speciall ornament unto the rest of the buildings.[17]

The Whitehall Cockpit also had something of a 'spired turret' at its centre. It was made of timber, with decorative battlements of lead and wood like those of the inner court at Nonsuch, Henry's showplace palace in Surrey. At 39 ft its external diameter was large; much larger than the celebrated corner towers of Nonsuch, themselves a high point of the Tudor style, which were only 25 ft across.[18]

The original cockpit was lavishly decorated, containing 'seatts, borders, pendans, chappitrells, armys, baydgs and dyvers other thyngs' and 32 'chaptrellis with their basis sette up within [the saide C]ockepitthowse'.[19] Outside, the cants of the roof were adorned with great posts or columns, surmounted by carved figures of the King's Beasts. Several of these are clearly visible even in Dankerts' view painted in the 1670s, and they appear in greater detail in Thorpe's much earlier drawing.

Such decorations were customary at Whitehall, and often reported by foreign visitors.[20] Above the lantern was a 'type' or domed top, with a carved lion supporting a vane.[21] Much of this work was installed or renewed in 1581–2, when Elizabeth refurbished the cockpit in preparation for Alençon's embassy. Artisans were then paid for

. . . workinge and makinge of Bases of Cann-stone and settinge them in soundrie places vnder the main post*es* their . . .[22]

The 'main post*es*' in question appear to have been the exterior masts on which the beasts were mounted, rising from each of the angles of the larger octagon. Among the taskwork related to this project was an item for painting 'the stooles of xvj carued beast*es* with black and white' – the usual outdoor colour scheme – and a payment of £16 to 'Richard Dickson Caruer for Caruing xj*ten* [*sic*, read xvj*ten*] new beastes and bases at xx*s* the pece . . .' The Caen stone bases housed the footings of the larger posts where they sprang from the roof, and the whole set of sixteen new beasts joined others already in position, as a further item makes clear:

. . . paintinge and mendinge soundrie old beast*es* and vaines and the old and new supportinge poostes of Timber . . .

Like the painted beasts, the leaded roof of the central turret and the flats surrounding it proved troublesome and often needed repair, as in 1581–2:

Rippinge vpp of thold leade vppon the roofes, layinge new leade vppon the same, in soundrie places and also sowdringe diuerse places vppon the said roofes and Batlementes . . .

Evidently the decay had reached the timbers of the building, for the Works accounted for 'settvnge vpp diuerse post*es* with frayminge them for stainge of the house . . .' Other work done on the interior included the provision, which we have already noted, of 'new settell*es*', repairing 'the Tables whear the Cockes feight', 'new mattinge of the gallorie with ordin*a*rie matt*es*', 'Paynting of the hornes Cloas Crownes Cheines and all other places around with fine gold', and 'layinge of the seates with verditur . . .'

When, therefore, Jones came to refit this building as a theatre he found, not some characterless arena or squash court, but one of the most assertive examples of the Tudor festive style. He might perhaps have attempted to clear much of the decorative work away in favour of detailing closer to his own thoughtful classicism, but in fact he did not do so. Instead Mathew Goodricke was paid for painting in stone colour 'divers Cornishes pendaunt*es* and mouldings in the viijt Cant*es*', and 'for Clenzinge and washinge the gold of the pendaunt*es* and Cornishes and mendinge the same in divers places with gold Cullor in oyle and mendinge the blew of the same in sondry places . . .' The upper parts of the walls within the larger octagon were already painted blue, which Goodricke was to make good: 'for new Couleringe over with fayre blewe the viij*t* upper squares on the wall three of them beinge wholy shaddowed and the rest mended . . .'[23] Golden and painted within, enlivened without by rampant beasts guarding its battlements, Henry VIII's cockpit remained one of the marvels of Whitehall long into the seventeenth century.

Jones's conversion of this colourful building contained some elements at least of a Palladian evocation of the antique theatre. His delicate *frons scenae*, with its classical articulation and five doors of entrance, was a sophisticated variation on the theme of the Teatro Olimpico, and one would expect him to provide a neo-Roman *cavea* to correspond with it on the house side, as Palladio had done at Vicenza. Unfortunately Webb's drawings are incomplete, and fail to show how effectively Jones's new work was able to counter the vigorous Tudor style of the old auditorium. Indeed most previous accounts of the Cockpit-in-Court have assumed that the theatre inherited from the original building a two-tier system of galleries, the upper storey superimposed on the lower, so that the playhouse when complete bore a marked resemblance to the galleried theatres to which the professional players were accustomed. According to this argument Webb's plan shows only the lower storey, the upper level being implied by the heavy posts shown at the angles of the lower gallery front. Certainly the cockpit, both before and after its conversion, contained at least one gallery running all around the auditorium, but Jones might readily have incorporated it into a single sweep of seating rising continuously from the pit floor to the rear wall, as had been done at Christ Church in 1605. The resulting *cavea* would have been interrupted by the substantial posts which supported the inner octagonal roof of the building, and to that extent its neo-Roman character would have been compromised; but a second level of galleries strung between the upper reaches of the posts might have negated the Roman allusion altogether.

It would be prudent, then, to settle this matter of the galleries before we proceed to the analysis of Jones's alterations. To what extent was the original cockpit a galleried room? In 1532 we hear of 'the galarye aboute the [Cockep] ittehowse', and the Works account for 1581–2 alludes to 'new mattinge of the gallorie'; but if the turn of these phrases suggests a single level there are several entries made in later years that seem to imply a second constructed over the first. We hear of 'the galleryes over the Cockpitt' and 'the postes both belowe and in the gallery aboue' in 1629–30,[24] and of the 'vpper gallery & boxes lookeing down into ye Cockepit playhowse' in 1670–1.[25] Jones's stage was certainly equipped with an upper level where a music room opened through the *frons* towards the auditorium; here, in what the Works accounts called 'ye Gallery ouer the stage',[26] a tiring room was established in 1660 suitable for both men and women. Dankerts' view shows two storeys of windows in both the northern and the western walls. At first sight, therefore, the evidence for the existence of the upper gallery seems persuasive.

Nevertheless there are reasons for doubt. The use of the plural 'galleryes' cannot by itself be taken to mean two or more storeys, for it was commonly applied to a single level built along more than one wall of a room. Nowhere do we find an explicit description of the Cockpit as housing superimposed levels of galleries, yet when such things were installed in the public halls of the palaces the record in the

Works accounts was generally unambiguous in its phrasing, either describing the structure fully, as at the Banqueting House in 1621–2,[27] or employing a precise formula, as at Westminster for the coronation in 1661, where the galleries, each lined with three degrees, were fitted 'one above thother'.[28] The words used to describe the gallery or galleries at the cockpit refer rather to an upper area beyond the main circle of seats around the cockfight table, or later on beyond the pit of the theatre. From the beginning such a gallery had to be located above the cockpens and high enough to provide sightlines above the seats about the table. If it were a level ambulatory it would have required only some 7 ft headroom below any upper gallery, which would have needed rather more clearance beneath its gilded ceiling. All this might readily have been erected within the building known to us from Dankerts' painting, but in 1629 the 'galleryes over the Cockpitt' were equipped with degrees constructed with the unusually high rise of 'three bourd*es*' apiece.[29] Degrees were often made with level seating surfaces only two boards wide and an equal or lesser rise, and it appears that these at the Cockpit-in-Court stepped upwards more abruptly than was customary, doubtless to give better sightlines to the stage. We do not know how many degrees were provided, but their total ascent must have been considerable, a minimum of 6 ft but probably approaching 9 ft.

The height of the outer parts of the Cockpit – at least before any reconstruction of 1670–1 – may be estimated with the aid of Webb's drawings, where the upper level is pitched 15 ft above the floor. A Works account of 1663 records the construction of 'a paire of staires of 12 stepps goeing vp from the vpper tiering roome into ye leads at the Cockpit playhowse',[30] and because this upper room is identical with the space behind the upper storey of the *frons* it follows that the height of the flat leaded roof around the building was 15 ft plus twelve steps. Part of the *frons* fabric was constructed underneath the beams of the octagon where they supported the joists of the flat roof, so that the roof cannot have been lower than Jones's entablature. Neither, if it were to be reached by twelve steps, could it have been much higher, and it follows that the outer roof was pitched at the same level as the top of the *frons*. The coved ceiling could rise 3 ft higher within the octagon, and the central pediment appears to have been attached directly to one of the great beams of the octagon's frame.

Whatever the configuration of the galleries, they had to be contained within an elevation of 24 ft 6 in above the floor, a height inadequate for two storeys of steep degrees with headroom at the rear, all constructed above the level of the original cockpens. Moreover, Webb's plan shows that the upper tiring room could be reached by doorways leading directly from the passage at the back of the degrees. This level was 9 ft 6 in below the flat roof of the outer part of the house, giving plenty of headroom for members of the audience passing along the rear gangway, but certainly not enough for a second gallery as well, not even one constructed with a slanting floor. Even a sloping gallery would need headroom at the rear, and 9 ft 6 in is simply too small an interval to contain two gangway passages one above the other.

Nor perhaps was it simply a matter of allowing enough room for a live theatre audience to circulate behind the degrees: there may have been presences of another sort to be considered. Among the Sergeant Painter's items of taskwork relating to the Cockpit in 1631–2 is an entry for the repair of an impressive array of paintings:

. . . ffor repayring & mending twoe great peeces of paynted woorke that were done by Palma, thone being the Story of Dauid and Goliah, thother of Saules Conuersion which were much defaced . . . for repayring mending and new varnishing vij:en of the greate Emperoures Heades that were done by Titian being likewise much defaced . . .[31]

In the same year the section of the accounts relating to St James's gives information about the framing of these pictures:

. . . for painting two lardge picture frames for twoe peeces done by Palma being xij:ve foot one way and vij:en fo: the other way . . . And alsoe for Painting xij:ve picture frames being vj:fo one way & iij:er thother way for peeces or pictures of Emeroures heades that were done by Titiano . . .[32]

It appears that the frames were made in St James's while the pictures themselves were repaired at Whitehall. It has been supposed, by Bentley and Wickham, that they hung in the Cockpit-in-Court, possibly 'about the back of the house, as statues were in Jones's model at Vicenza'.[33] There seems to be little reason for certainty in the matter, for although the item relating to their repair appears among the series of Cockpit tasks in the Declared Accounts the conjunction means very little, the works being generally listed merely in the order of their completion.[34] The paintings could well have been repaired elsewhere in Whitehall, and it may be that they were actually displayed in the gallery at St James's, for that is where the two Palmas and seven of the Emperors' heads were located when the palace collection was catalogued c. 1640.[35] Yet the evidence is uncertain and it must be admitted that they might originally have been installed at the Cockpit-in-Court, where they could only have been placed on the peripheral walls of the auditorium, beyond the furthest degrees and well above them if the defacing were not to be continued by knocks and scuffing from the feet of people using the access gangway at the rear. A minimum clearance of 3 ft beneath the frames would surely have been required, and the panels themselves would have taken up at least a further 6 ft,[36] for a total of 9 ft above the highest level of seats. The provision of so much wall space above a second gallery would have required a taller building than the one shown by Dankerts, and even if there were room for them at the back of a lower gallery – as there was not – it is hardly likely that a dozen Titians would have been packed away in the darkest corners of the house.

Whether or not the pictures ever hung in the theatre must remain in doubt, but we may be certain that only above a single level of galleries could there have been enough wall space to accommodate them. In any case it appears that there was only one level of galleries at the Cockpit-in-Court, and this was as true of the refittings in 1660 and 1629 as of the original layout c. 1532. At this earliest date the level ambulatory was lit by the mullioned windows whose existence is witnessed by Webb and Dankerts, but higher up, where the latter shows wooden casements of a

16   John Webb, plan and elevation of the stage at the Cockpit-in-Court, Whitehall

17   John Webb, plan of the Cockpit-in-Court

later seventeenth-century type inserted in the west wall, the interior of the larger octagon must have been uninterrupted plaster, painted blue and potentially at least capable of backing the great panels of Titian and Palma. The reference to the galleries 'over' the cockpit well describes that sense of detachment felt by a spectator on the original ambulatory and even in the topmost degrees of the theatre. The allusion of 1670–1 to the upper gallery 'lookeing downe into ye Cockepit playhowse' conveys much the same idea of separation, and is linked to a reference, not to a lower gallery, but to 'a lower roome next unto the pitt'.

Into the vivid circumference of this galleried house Jones inserted a neo-Palladian theatre of serenely classical appearance. He restored the Tudor decoration but contrived nevertheless to reshape the interior so completely that an audience encapsuled within his new auditorium would scarcely have been conscious of the powerful Tudor shell surrounding it. The old ambulatory was converted into an upper extension of the 'colosseum' by means of additional degrees, the broad new stage was entirely backed by the architectural *frons*, the lantern and elaborate roof were concealed overhead by a sky cloth of calico and canvas. Even the centrality of the old cockpit's design was ignored, the arc of the new *frons* being struck from a centre two or three feet removed from the old. The Palladian disguise was complete.

Our knowledge of Jones's Cockpit-in-Court is based on the useful Works accounts of the conversion, which extend over three years beginning in 1629, and on Webb's drawings.[37] The latter confirm much of what is conveyed in the accounts, but because they actually record a further refitting undertaken in 1660 some care must be taken with them if we are to trace the outline of Jones's work beneath the overlay of the later alterations. The emphasis on the *frons* to the exclusion of the rest of the design, stressed by the provision of a larger scale plan and elevation of the stage to the left of the sheet, probably has more to do with Webb's concerns in 1660 than Jones's in 1629, and should not be taken as proof that the conversion involved the stage area alone. Nevertheless its decorative scheme is a striking piece of design, apparently little changed in the refitting of 1660, and we may profitably turn to it first.

The *frons scenae* appears in all three of the drawings on the sheet. The larger plan and elevation to the left are provided with an inked scale bar representing 30 ft in 169 mm, or approximately 4 ft 6 in to the inch. The scale of the overall plan to the right is scored heavily and carefully pricked out, but because it is not inked it reproduces only faintly in photographs and has been ignored hitherto. It gives 30 ft in 91.5 mm, almost exactly 1:100. Measured to this scale the outer square (174 mm on the sheet) is 57 ft each way externally and the stage (103.5 mm) 34 ft across.[38] The two scales (1:54 and 1:100) are of quite different types, the larger one being conventionally based on an equivalence of feet for inches, and the smaller a comparatively rare decimal ratio perhaps deriving from a measured survey of the whole building.

There are small differences between the two versions of the stage plan. Both show a broad, shallow forestage, but the centre from which the arc of the *frons* is drawn, located at the middle of the stage front in the overall plan, appears about 1 ft upstage of the rail in the larger plan to the left. As a result the small scale drawing to the right shows the greater part of the *frons* drawn within a regular semi-circle whose diameter is located at the front of the stage rail and measures 34 ft. The radius to the rear surface of the *frons* structure is 17 ft. In the larger drawing the radius to the rear of the wall is a little over 16 ft; to the front surface it is a round 15 ft, an indication perhaps that this was Jones's original controlling measure. A sunburst of radii is scored into the surface of the larger plan from the centre of the arc out to its periphery, where each line marks an incident in the detailing: the door frames, the centres and tangents of the attached columns, the sections of the pedestals. Measured with a protractor these lines reveal no obvious geometrical pattern, and it appears that their intervals are dictated entirely by the architectural articulation of the *frons*. The smaller scale plan offers no such radial lines, but a protractor placed over the semi-circle of the stage will show that analogous radii would intercept the arc at intervals dictated by a geometrical construction. From the centre of the *porta regia* it is exactly 30° to the nearer reveal of the first flanking door. The centre of the attached column between the side doors comes at 45°; and at 60° we find the further reveal of the second door. Thus the stage area of the overall survey plan offers a scheme whose geometrical exactness finds no counterpart in the larger plan. We may conclude that it represents Webb's idealization of what Jones designed, or else perhaps a regular scheme underlying what Jones actually built.

The Works accounts for 1629–30 are specific in their record of the orders employed by the Surveyor and erected by John Synsburye and other carpenters:

... for framinge and settinge vpp twoe stories of Collomns in the Cockepitt playhouse beinge X[en] Collomns vppon every Story Corinthia and Composita finishinge the heades with Architrave, freeze and Cornishe vppon each Story and finishinge a backe wrought with crooked tymber behinde them with five doores in the first Story and in the second story one open dore & iiij[er] neeches in the same vpper Storye ... [39]

This description fits the Webb drawing in all the particulars it mentions. The superimposition of Corinthian on Composite was quite normal at Whitehall – it was used, for example, in the contemporary rebuilding of the stairway into the park[40] – yet other details in the design suggest that its adoption in this case was far from a matter of mere local convention. The tenor of the *frons* is Greek with an overlay of Roman; that is, the two classic cultures are brought together in a happy amalgam. At the centre, in the cartouche below the music room opening, is a Roman text, 'Prodesse & delectare', derived from Horace: 'Aut prodesse volunt aut delectare poetae / aut simul et iucunda et idonea dicere vitae.'[41] The passage comes in the *Ars Poetica* just as Horace is regretting the commercialism of Roman society; in contrast to the money-grubbing education of the schools, poetry should make things worthy to be preserved in cedar oil and polished cypress: it will teach and delight, be both pleasing and useful in life. Everything else on the *frons scenae* is Greek: niches for two tragedians (Agathon and Sophocles) and two comedians

(Menander? and Aristophanes) flank busts of Thespis and Epicharmus (the reputed founders of tragedy and comedy) at the upper level, while below are pedestals ready for the figures of Melpomene and Thalia, the muses of tragedy and comedy.[42]

Thus the classicism of the *frons* is Greek in most of its allusion, neatly balanced between the two great dramatic kinds. Its binary reference is summed up by the familiar Horatian tag, with its modulation of the balance: to teach and delight. In 1630–1 the carvers were paid for 'moulding and clensinge of twoe greate Statuaes of Plaster of Paris' at the Cockpit,[43] probably Melpomene and Thalia, and in a note in his copy of Serlio Jones presumably alludes to the bracketed busts of Thespis and Epicharmus when he recalls the 'heads of brass as [I] made in ye scean of ye Theatridion at Whighthall'.[44]

'Theatridion' is a curious Jonesian sort of word; borrowed perhaps from Varro and meaning simply a small auditorium, it is as classical in association as the decorative scheme itself. The precedent for so eager a pursuit of antiquity in the theatre was of course the Teatro Olimpico, which Jones had visited in September 1613, when he recorded some of its details on the flyleaf of his copy of Palladio.[45] By the time he saw it the fixed classical *frons scenae* had been fitted with permanent perspective scenes offering street vistas beyond the five entrance openings, but it is by no means clear that they had been part of the original conception when the theatre was opened in 1585. Rather Palladio had aimed, in the scholarly spirit of the Accademia Olimpica which had commissioned the design, to reconstruct the ancient theatre for modern conditions and to an intimate modern scale. His proscenium alludes to the heroic architecture of the great Roman theatres of antiquity, and his elliptical auditorium recalls, as far as is practicable in a rather shallow room, their vast rounded *caveae*. In accord with the observations of Vitruvius, for whose text he prepared many illustrations, several of theatres, he constructed five stage entrances; it has even been found that the proportions of his auditorium may have been influenced by the Vitruvian account of the method by which a theatre might be laid out according to a geometrical plan derived from the practice of the astrologers and consisting of four equilateral triangles inscribed within a circle.[46]

Jones's theatre is less pedantic than Palladio's, less devoted to the systematic reconstruction in miniature of the appearance of an ancient theatre. It is, nevertheless, like Palladio's a deliberate exploration of the antique theme. It has the conventional five doors, with the central one firmly accented, but it also introduces a central window at the upper level, something not found in the historical atmosphere of Vicenza. Yet where Palladio organized his entire *frons scenae* in the Corinthian order, Jones extended his Graeco-Roman set of allusions by placing a Composite order over a Corinthian one. The Corinthian was famed as the loveliest of the Greek inventions, 'più adorno, e suelto' as Palladio himself remarks; and the Composite is the Roman order, 'il quale vien ancho detto Latino, perchè fu inventione degli Antichi Romani . . .'[47]

The Cockpit also differed from the Teatro Olimpico in the curved plan of its *frons*. There is no obvious source for this unusual arrangement, unless perhaps in Serlio's Third Book where, among the descriptions of ancient theatres, there appears a woodcut of a 'Scene of a Theatre' evidently built on a segmental plan, though whether circular or elliptical it is impossible to say.[48] It shows a single storey with five doorways, the central one fronted by an arched gate. The flanking doorways are separated by arches, so that there are seven possible entrances in all. Serlio reports that he saw the ruins of the theatre as he rode by on horseback between Fondi and Terracina, but the illustration closely resembles an untitled sketch in the *taccuino* of his mentor Peruzzi, now at Siena.[49] In placing the five entrance doors in his own part-circular *frons* Jones may also have been influenced by Vitruvian precedent. The twelve angles in the Vitruvian pattern come at 30° intervals around the circumference of the theatre, five of them pointing to the doors of entrance, and we have seen that in the overall plan to the right of his sheet Webb divides the arc of the *frons* so that the centre of the *porta regia* and the outer reveals of the flanking doors occur at precisely the same 30° spacings. In his adoption of the broad, shallow forestage Jones was assuredly following Serlio, for the overall plan shows it to have measured 34 ft wide by 5 ft deep, proportions which exactly duplicate those of the theatre plan in the original editions of the *Architettura*, where the 'suolo piano' is divided into squares, 34 by 5.

Opposed to the *frons*, with its refined classicism, was an auditorium set up within the bounds of the old cockpit and accepting the main lines of its structure. Yet the steep new degrees in the gallery, a great new cloth in the ceiling and possibly the newly introduced paintings hanging at the rear so completely overlaid the interior that its Tudor character was obscured, and in its place Jones offered a neo-Roman theatre of the Palladian type. So much will become apparent when we turn to the Works accounts covering the conversion, many of which confirm the details recorded in Webb's drawings of the stage and *frons*. But the drawings more immediately register a later refitting, and so do not directly illustrate the condition of the theatre as it was when Jones's conversion was new. Only by making full allowance for the changes introduced at the Restoration, probably by Webb himself, can we adequately reconstruct Jones's work of 1629–30.

That the Cockpit-in-Court was extensively refitted in 1660 we know from the Works accounts for that year, which record alterations to the stage and pit floor, together with the renewal of the gallery seating. Webb's connection with these tasks is nowhere a matter of explicit record, for he had no official post at Court, but in later years he did claim to have contributed to the works at Whitehall in 1660. In a petition of 1668 he listed some of the things he had accomplished for the king:

After having prepared Whitehall for your Majesties happy restauration, your Petitioner withdrew into the country, from whence afterwards in 1663 by your Royall appointment being sent for, to react for your Majestie at Greenwich, hee readily obeyed.[50]

As Jones's natural successor in matters both architectural and theatrical, Webb will almost certainly have overseen the thorough refurbishing of the Cockpit, and it is to this project of 1660 that his drawings will be seen to relate. Their style, with its heavy cross-hatching, indicates beyond doubt that they are in his hand; even the poorly drawn reclining figures on the lower storey pediment show his usual awkwardness with the human form. The sheet is now laid down and its watermark, if there is one, cannot be read, but the draftsmanship is akin to a number of careful drawings made by Webb during the last years of the Commonwealth.

One of the changes made at the Restoration is recorded in the curious steps which Webb shows at the entries to the pit gangways. Most interpreters of the plan have supposed that they lead upwards to the pit from rooms located beneath the gallery.[51] Unhappy though this solution must seem, there is good reason for accepting it: rooms beneath the gallery are mentioned in the accounts several times, proving that there was a considerable interval between the original floor and the upper seating, a height too great to be scaled by the risers of Webb's steps. Consequently they must have connected the lower rooms to an elevated pit floor, or else the elevated pit to the gallery. The former seems more likely, there being an interval of five degree risers between the pit and the gallery front. This design, with its raised floor in the pit, seems too complex to have been an original feature of the building, and indeed we find an explanation for it in the account of November 1660 which, because it describes the work presumably overseen by Webb, must be quoted in full:

Carpenters . . . Makeing of v large boxes with seuerall degrees in them at yᵉ cockpitt and doores in them, taking vp the floore of yᵉ stage and pitt and laying againe the floore of the stage & pitt pendant, making of seuerall seats round and in yᵉ pitt making of two partitions in the gallery there for the Musick and players setting vp a rayle & ballisters vpon the stage making two other seats for yᵉ gentlemen Vshers a [sic] Mʳ Killigrew cutting out a way and making a paire of Stayres cont. [blank] stepps to goe into yᵉ Gallery ouer the stage & incloseing the said stayres with a doore in it Cont. about one square, making of two new doores goeing vnder the degrees and bourding vp one doore vppon the degrees, setting vp xj squares of partitioning vnder the degrees with vj doores in them.[52]

Here almost every item corresponds with Webb's overall plan, from the 'v large boxes with seuerall degrees in them' – the five bays of the gallery, though Webb has failed to ink in the scored lines marking two of the partitions – to the new, or newly extended, winding stair leading to the upper stage level. At this upper level one of the doors marked as communicating with the access way along the rear of the degrees is shown to be open, while its partner, to the right, is closed off, a result of 'bourding vp one doore vppon the degrees'. It seems, then, that the gallery degrees installed in 1629 were completely replaced with new ones, and at the same time the stage and pit floors were taken up and relaid 'pendant'. The refitting of the theatre in 1660 appears therefore to have been extensive, covering almost the whole of the floor plan, but there is no reason to suppose that the *frons* was radically altered.

Eleanore Boswell, who first printed the Works accounts relating to the Cockpit-in-Court at the Restoration, concluded from their use of the word 'pendant' that the house was then fitted with a raked stage and sloping pit of a kind usually associated with scenic theatres. She did not make clear how a raked stage could be married to the fixed proscenium, with its level architectural base, and no subsequent enquirer has addressed the problem. A raked stage would normally house perspective scenery, yet the account makes no suggestion that the *frons* was to be replaced by a frontispiece bordering wings and shutters; furthermore it is most improbable that such a stage would be fitted with a rail, yet one is recorded as part of the new work. The difficulties evaporate, however, if 'pendant' is taken in its architectural sense as meaning 'supported above the ground on arches, columns, etc.'.[53] Clearly the stage floor was raised in this manner from its beginning in 1629, and so would be relaid 'pendant' whenever it was renewed, though the phrasing of the account does suggest an alteration rather than mere repairs. The pit was not raised at all until the reconstruction of 1660, when it was built higher – a little awkwardly, to be sure – and had to be approached by steps leading up from the floor level under the gallery. At the same time this outer area was refitted with partitions and doors, so that in a later account we hear of 'a lower roome next vnto the pitt'.[54] Because the account links the stage along with the pit in this new 'pendant' arrangement, it seems that it too was raised higher, to the 4 ft 6 in level shown in Webb's elevation. Previously, then, it had been somewhat lower, and the elevation contains some curious details consistent with such a history. At the centre the large arch has been drawn twice, first 7 ft clear space above the stage, and then again 1 ft higher. Thus one rather low entry has been replaced by another, evidently the favoured version, which is two squares high (or twice as high as it is wide). The flanking doors shown in Webb's drawing are 2 ft 6 in wide by only 5 ft tall, and although their proportions are neatly rational they would make for very cramped stage entries. Had Jones's original stage been set, before the alterations of 1660, 1 ft lower than Webb's the central door would have achieved its 8 ft height at the position evidently cancelled in the drawing, while the flanking doors would have been 6 ft tall in the clear, and perfectly practicable. Doubtless the old doorway was also 8 ft tall, but this height being reduced when the stage was raised, a new head was designed for the arch 1 ft higher than the old. The pedestals on which the columns are based were also 12 in taller, and somewhat more canonical, than those shown by Webb, who presents them partly obscured by the newly elevated stage.

We may conclude, because Webb indicates both the old and the new heights of the central arch, that the drawings are connected with the actual alterations of November 1660. It is possible that the four side entrances were left impracticably low because they were little used for Restoration performances in this theatre. The drawings clearly show the stage rail, about 1 ft 3 in tall, whose fitting on the 'pendant' stage is recorded in the accounts: 'setting vp a rayle & ballisters vpon the stage'. This is the first mention of such a rail at the Cockpit-in-Court, and it does not sound like the renewal or repair of an old one dating from 1629.

Armed with the knowledge that Webb's drawings record the state of the theatre in 1660 rather than in 1629–30, we may attempt to interpret the levels they imply. In the original building the pit, whose floor we may suppose to have been at grade level, was surrounded by cockpens with an ambulatory above. The lower window heights as shown by Dankerts in the west wall suggest that the pens would have cleared as much as a low room, some 7 ft, so that the gallery above might be lit by the lower mullion windows. The pit was therefore surrounded by a substantial octagonal wall 7 ft or so high, within which the table was ringed with seats ascending like a little colosseum. At the conversion of 1629 Jones cleared away the table and seats and built a stage 3 ft 6 in high all across the inner octagon, removing the upper parts of three of the interior walls as he did so, though presumably retaining as much as he could of their fabric to support the two posts behind the new *frons*, whose function was in turn to support the pyramidal roof and lantern. At the same time he constructed degrees in four bays of the ambulatory, leaving the fifth as before as a royal box:

. . . framinge & setting vp the Deegres in the galleryes over the Cockpitt Cuttinge fyttinge and naylinge Brackett*es* vppon the same woorkinge and settinge of vpright postes to the Ceelinge for the better strengthninge therof and bourdinge the same Degrees three bourd*es* in highte with a bourde to stay theire feete . . .[55]

The plural 'galleryes', a form not found elsewhere in the Cockpit accounts, refers to the four bays concerned, the remainder being devoted to the stage and royal box. The construction of the degrees appears to have been similar to that used in the Drury Lane Cockpit gallery, where upright posts ran from the back of the rear seats to the ceiling joists above. Such posts appear in the section through the Drury Lane theatre, though not in the plan.[56] At Whitehall they were painted the same colour as the major posts which supported the octagonal roof:

Mathew Goodricke Paynt*er* vizt for pryminge stoppinge and payntinge stone Cullor in oyle divers Cornishes pendaunt*es* and mouldings in the viij[t] Cant*es* of the Cockepitt with the postes both belowe and in the gallery aboue in the in syde . . .[57]

Two of the new bays of degrees must have obscured the windows in the walls behind them. The general scheme is probably reflected in Webb's plan, for although the degrees were renewed in November 1660, and appear as reconstructed in Webb's drawing without the supporting posts at the rear, the design constraints were so narrow that the new work can have differed only little from the old. Each degree is only 1 ft 4 in deep, a dimension so small that it is consistent only with a very steep rake where the seating is no more than a rank of perches, rather like misericords with a rise 'three bourd*es*' high between foot and ledge.

The plan includes two wooden partitions between the gallery and the area backstage which are necessary extensions of the *frons* and must have originated with Jones. Both are penetrated by doorways leading from the gangway at the rear of the degrees, though only the western one (to the left of the plan) remains open, its eastern counterpart being inked across to indicate that it was boarded up. Both partitions appear to be drawn cutting abruptly across contiguous windows, with no allowance made for a satisfactory fixing of the doorcases to the walls. The explanation for this perplexing detail is that the doors and windows were at different levels, with the windows presumably below the doorways so that the botched conjunction would not be seen by anyone seated in the auditorium. The illumination from these lights and others at the same level was now rendered useless because it was confined to the dead space between the degrees and the gallery floor; it may have been dispensed with altogether, for in 1629 the Sergeant Painter was paid for painting 'like glasse' twenty panes 'which had bin Lightes'.[58]

After Jones's conversion access to the rooms next to the pit, where the old cockpens had been, caused no more difficulty than in the original building, there being sufficient headroom for doors reached from the pit floor. But it may be that the pit seemed too low and funnel-like when seen from the steep gallery and even from the royal box. In 1660 its floor was raised on joists so that it had to be approached from beneath the gallery by way of steps with at least four risers. At the same time the stage was raised by 12 in. The new steps were only a part of the refitting of the lowest level of the house: the carpenters also set up 'xj squares [i.e. 1100 ft²] of partitioning vnder the degrees with vj doores in them' and provided 'two new doores goeing vnder the degrees', possibly associated with the new steps.

As originally constructed, the cockpit must have had some access from grade level to that of the ambulatory over the cockpens, and this could have been provided by the nine risers in the winding stair recorded by Webb in the top right corner of the plan, where a landing opens onto what appears to be a blanked-off doorway in the wall behind the scene. At first the ascent will have ended there, the ambulatory being the highest part of the house to which regular access was required, but in 1629 a way to the 15 ft level of the stage gallery was provided by the dog-leg stair shown at top left. This was supplemented in 1660 by an extra 'paire of Stayres cont. [*blank*] stepps to goe into yᵉ Gallery ouer the stage', presumably the eleven additional risers in the winder past its quarter-landing. Only five risers are shown leading to the stage itself, hardly enough for the new 4 ft 6 in height, but adequate for the original lower ascent. Either Webb erroneously failed to add the necessary extra step or two in his drawing or the backstage area remained 12 in lower than the new platform laid 'pendant' in front of the curved *frons*. The winder leading from the ground floor to the 15 ft high gallery passage at bottom left is firmly scored into the paper, but not inked. A separate ascent on the auditorium side of the house must have been necessary from the time of the conversion in 1629, and it is not easy to see why Webb failed to ink it in. At the bottom of the drawing he shows the private royal access to the king's box down a stair of twenty shallow risers from the access gallery leading in from the right. This, together with the dog-leg and winder shown to the left of the plan, will have been newly constructed in 1629–30, when the 15 ft levels to which the latter led were first established in the cockpit. All three sets are shown by Webb to have been lit by windows cut in the outer wall, and in the account for 1629–30 we find that the masons were paid for 'workeing and setting vpp three wyndowes of Stone for yᵉ newe staires leadeing to the Cockepitt . . .'[59]

The extension of the winder to give access to the upper level over the stage was probably connected with the need at the Restoration to accommodate dressing-space for actresses. A Lord Chamberlain's warrant, dated 10 December 1662 but convincingly assigned by Boswell to October 1660,[60] calls for 'the upper tyring roome' to be lined with baize, furnished with twenty stools and chairs, three tables, a looking-glass, candlesticks and 'two peeces of hangings and great curtaine rodds to make partitions betweene the Men & Weomen'. The extra stairs will have eased congestion backstage, but the stage itself could still only be reached from above by way of the older dog-leg staircase.

The Jonesian theatre whose structure we have now contrived to distinguish among the details of Webb's later alterations is hardly more than an outline as yet, but some of its features may be fleshed out with details from the Works accounts. Standing at the centre of the 'piazza' by the stage, an observer of the rehearsals for the opening in 1630 would have been struck by the antique style of the work surrounding him. On the one side his view would be closed by the elegant curved *frons*, a little French in its detailing, like Jones's contemporary screen in the chapel at Somerset House,[61] its proportions happier than those recorded in Webb's elevation because of the extra 12 in visible in the lower storey. The chest-high stage, probably without a rail, led to a central *porta regia* 4 ft wide by 8 ft tall clear space, set between four practicable flanking doors 2 ft 6 in by 6 ft. Above the central entrance stood the balcony or 'window' drawn by Webb, and of course the whole *frons* was painted, gilt and adorned with statuary. The auditorium side consisted of a pit and a gallery all fitted with degrees which rose more steeply at the rear, their incline interrupted by six great posts supporting the pryamidal roof and lantern. Beyond the foundation walls from which these columns sprung were rooms, originally the cockpens, reached by doors at either end of the 'piazza' and perhaps also below the royal box, which occupied the gallery bay opposite the stage and held a halpace and state rather than a range of degrees. The highest level of the degrees connected with the new gallery over the stage by means of narrow doorways to either side of the building, emphasizing the fact that the top of the lower storey entablature in the *frons* matched the level reached by the degrees in the auditorium, exactly on the pattern of the Teatro Olimpico.

Jones owned a Palladian drawing of the Olimpico which showed sections of the seating degrees rising from a low orchestra wall to the height of the lower entablature of the *frons*, and Webb made a careful study of it on a sheet now at Worcester College (see plate 28). The Vicenzan theatre had made a firm impression on Jones when he visited it, and now, some sixteen years later, he successfully evoked its memory within the confines of Henry VIII's cockpit. At the Olimpico the classical intention was everywhere overt, from the decorated *frons* with its five stage entrances disposed according to a Vitruvian scheme to its rounded *cavea* (reduced here to a semi-ellipse) closed off at the rear with a *porticus* of columns and more statuary. Jones had no room for a *porticus* but he contrived the relation of the auditorium to the stage in a manner directly reminiscent of Palladio. He too included five stage entrances in the Vitruvian fashion, though where Palladio had built two balconies over the side doors Jones included only one, over the central opening. At the Olimpico the covering overhead was divided into two parts: above the stage was a compartmented ceiling, elaborately decorated, while over the rest of the house lay a canvas painted to represent the sky, a recollection of the open theatres of antiquity. Inspired by Palladio's precedent, Jones constructed a coved flat ceiling over the curved part of the *frons*, though apparently not over the forestage, and by 1632 he had covered the rest of the pit within the inner octagon with a blue sky cloth, pitted with stars:

John walker Property maker . . . cutting fitting and soweing of Callicoe to couer all the roome ouer head within the Cockpitt cutting a great number of Starres of Assidue [gold-coloured foil] and setting them one the Blew Callicoe to garnish the Cloath there setting one a great number of Copperinges to Drawe the cloth to and fro . . .[62]

It may be that the cloth was to be made retractable in order to allow spectacular descents from a machine mounted above in the octagon roof. The previous item in the accounts records payment to Walker

for hanging the Throne and Chaire in the Cockpit with cloth bound about with whalebone packthred and wyer for the better foulding of the same to come downe from the Cloudes to the stage . . .[63]

Whether 'the Cloudes' are to be identified with the starry calico on its copper rings is open to doubt; it is more likely that a trap in the coved ceiling was painted with clouds and opened to permit the throne to descend upstage in front of the balcony and *porta regia*. The blue cloth, made 'to couer all the roome ouer head within the Cockpitt', must have extended over the pit alone, for only with difficulty could it have run beyond the octagon posts to cover the gallery as well. Although its visible side was of blue calico it was lined with more substantial canvas.[64] At the Teatro Olimpico Jones had noticed that 'the rofe was yᵉ rafters and tiles covered with canuase . . .'[65] and now at the Cockpit he repeated the pattern, though allowing his own canvas-backed sky cloth to be withdrawn when required, perhaps to permit light to enter the house from the old lantern overhead. The outer parts of the auditorium, where the gallery degrees rose to their full height, retained their gilt ceilings, now newly washed, repaired and redecorated. Refurbished blue paint covered the walls behind the degrees, and here it may be was introduced a splendid evocation of ancient imperial power in the shape of Titian's twelve panels of the Emperors, all half-figures, arranged presumably three to each of the four bays of degrees. The two Palmas, each 7 ft by 12 ft, can only have hung at the rear of the royal box, so great was the headroom they required. The paintings, if they hung in the theatre at all, must have closed off the auditorium in a manner analogous to, though substantially removed from, the *porticus* of columns and statuary at the Olimpico, and in this gesture towards ancient models they might have been assisted by the presence of the 'postes both belowe and in the gallery aboue in the in syde' which Goodricke painted the colour of stone.

The auditorium was no more than a Palladian envelope, constructed almost tissue-thin within the Tudor building. Because the degrees in the gallery covered the old stone mullioned lights of the cockpit the stage and seating could receive daylight only from the lantern above, and then only when the opaque sky cloth was drawn back on its supporting wires. For the night performances the theatre was made ready with candles, and the accounts, especially for 1631–2, record the lavish supply of their housing:

Candlestickes of Iron beautified with branch*es* Leau*es* and garnished with other ornament*es* to beare Lights in the Cockpitt x^{en} at xxx^{s} the peece . . .[66]

These and two larger 'Braunch*es*' were disposed 'about and before the Stage': that is, they belonged to the stage rather than the auditorium, and they were made splendid with gilding and oil paint as if they were part of a scene:

John Decreit*es* . . . and other Painters . . . for diuer*es* tim*es* Cullouring in Gould cullo*ur* the Braunch*es* of xv^c Candlesticks in the Cockpitt wherof tenn smaller and twoe greater then thother about and before the Stage and for Hatching and Guilding them with fine gould cullouring the great Branch*es* in the front of the stage and Hatching and Guilding all the *partes* to be seene forwards . . .[67]

In the following year £13-6-8 was spent on '. . . Candlestickes ij with diverse braunches for the Cockpitt at Whitehall'.[68]

It could be argued that Jones's conversion merely put a classical gloss on forms derived from the dramaturgical needs of the public theatre companies who were to use the house, and that the Cockpit-in-Court was therefore like a miniature Elizabethan playhouse, built in what was still the central, if fading, tradition of London playhouse design. The 'apron' stage, the fixed *frons scenae* with its doors of entrance, the central upper window, the partly encircling audience in its degrees and gallery: all these (together with the descent machine of wire and whalebone) point to the kinship of Jones's scheme with such houses as the Globe and the Swan. They are persuasive similarities, but there are also differences so marked that the very kinship must be questioned. The presence of a potential upper acting area and a descent machine does argue that the theatre was fitted out with the specific technical demands of the public companies in mind, but the shallowness of the forestage, so like that of the antique theatre as interpreted by Palladio and especially by Serlio, should alert us to Jones's more profound intentions. His most far-reaching departure from the public playhouse model lay in the relation he established between the stage and the auditorium. In his theatre the audience did not encircle the players; they sat on degrees arranged in rather less than five of the eight bays flanking the octagon, all in front of the *frons* and very nearly all in front of the stage. Jones's original plan of the pit is lost, but if it resembled that of the Drury Lane Cockpit it will have had a central gangway reminiscent of the one previously established in the hall at Christ Church by Simon Basil. Any axial emphasis thus introduced was greatly increased by the visual accent of the *porta regia* in the *frons*, with its pedimented window above, and most of all by the presence of the state on the same central axis at the opposite side of the theatre. Playing on this broad, shallow stage, the actor was faced by a U-shaped auditorium interrupted at its centre by the hiatus of the pit gangway where, elevated in his gallery at the further end, the king sat beneath his canopy.

Nothing could be more different from the arrangements in the Elizabethan public theatres, where the gentlemen's rooms were in the 'suburbs' of the stage, and the lords' room in the balcony close to the music room; all sheltered from the weather and the glare of the sun by the cover over the stage. Even at the Blackfriars and the Cockpit in Drury Lane the players had to perform to an audience located all around them; when they stepped onto the stage of Jones's Cockpit-in-Court they found an axial auditorium with central accents directing their attention to the king in his state. What is notable about the conversion registered in Webb's drawings, therefore, is not so much the continuity with the Elizabethan tradition, but the astonishing way in which it rides against that tradition even in a galleried octagonal building whose very form might have been expected to assert the old ways.

Yet neither was the theatre a proper home for the newer courtly entertainment of scenic drama. From time to time it has been argued that its stage was used for scenery, in spite of its manifest unfitness for the role. Generally such suggestions appear unconvincing when closely examined; Jones's drawing of 1639, for example, inscribed 'for yᵉ cokpitt for my lord Chamberalin' is, as we noticed in chapter 3, to be associated with the Cockpit in Drury Lane rather than the Cockpit-in-Court.[69] Carlell's *Passionate Lovers, Part II* was performed at the Whitehall Cockpit on 20 and 27 December 1638, and because a design for the play by Jones is extant[70] it has been supposed that the theatre must somehow have been capable of housing a substantial backshutter some 11 ft wide by 9 ft tall, together presumably with relieve scenes behind it and tree wings in front to complete the setting of a wood. But evidence newly discovered among the reports of the Florentine agent in London shows that *Part II* was almost certainly performed along with *Part I* at Somerset House in July 1638; the revival at the Cockpit some five months later will have been without benefit of scenery.[71]

Yet there does exist among the Jones drawings at Chatsworth a group of three related designs for scenes whose shape and scale appear to indicate that they were intended as rudimentary settings to be placed behind the central arch of the *frons scenae* at the Cockpit-in-Court. Each is drawn within the shape of a tall arch and one – inscribed in lead, possibly by Webb, as 'A Prison' – is ruled up in squares, six wide by nine tall.[72] If the squares represent intervals of 1 ft the scheme measures 6 ft wide by a little less than 9 ft tall, a satisfactory size to install behind the *frons* (whose opening is 4 ft by 8 ft) far enough to the rear to permit entries to be made between the scene and the arch. These small settings, hardly more than miniature relieves and backcloths, must have appeared as no more than illustrative images within the *frons*, less assertive even than Scamozzi's famous street constructions at the Teatro Olimpico, which Jones had of course seen and noted during his visit in 1613.

The changes wrought at the Cockpit in 1660 were designed to improve the visibility of the stage and possibly to render the feel of the house more attractive, but none had to do with the provision of scenery. The stage and pit floor were raised, as we have seen, and the degrees in the gallery reconstructed, though probably to their existing steep pattern. Small alterations were made in the doors, stairs and rooms beneath the degrees, and late in November a warrant was issued for the lining of the stage with green baize, the provision of twelve gilt 'Branches', each to carry three candles, and the installation of six sconces 'in the passages that are darke'.[73] A new crimson canopy was provided for the state in the royal box. Later accounts, admirably summarized by Eleanore Boswell,[74] record the provision of more 'brass branches for lights' in December. In December 1662 two chimneys were inserted, presumably to serve fireplaces in the new upper tiring room constructed in the gallery over the stage and fitted for use by both men and women actors. In the following October a set of twelve steps was built 'goeing vp from the upper tiering roome into ye leads at the Cockpit playhowse', and it may be that a preliminary scheme for them has been added in lead to Webb's plan of the theatre, located in the angle between the partitions to the left of the stage.

In 1665, with the opening of the much larger Hall Theatre in the great hall of the palace, the Cockpit ceased to serve as a playhouse; it was subsequently converted into lodgings for the Duke of Buckingham and by c. 1676 it had disappeared, its place taken by an undistinguished brick structure which in turn gave way to Kent's Treasury Buildings of 1733–7.

6 The Paved Court Theatre at Somerset House

THE Cockpit-in-Court was the second and last of Jones's non-scenic theatres, almost exactly contemporary with the Salisbury Court, a 'private' playhouse in Dorset Gardens built in the same tradition as the Cockpit in Drury Lane. There is no evidence of such houses being erected in London thereafter, and when a fresh spate of theatre building began after the Restoration the only new auditorium to look backwards to the Jacobean pattern was at Vere Street, where Killigrew's short-lived house briefly exploited a market for old plays done in the old way. Of the survivors, only Jones's Cockpit-in-Court remained a non-scenic playhouse for long, its design too firm and idiosyncratic to accept the changed conditions, beyond some rudimentary relieves set up behind the central arch of the *frons*. In a few years it too was superseded, by the scenic Hall Theatre constructed by Webb in the hall of the palace. All the rest presented scenes and machines, more or less elaborate according to the resources of the management. Even as early as 1639 Davenant had been licenced to erect a vast theatre on a site near Fleet Street, dedicated to the development of the scenic arts. In terms of theatre history alone the time for such a scheme had come, given the increasing splendour of the Court masques and Davenant's ambition to translate their techniques to a more public stage. But political history marched to a more frenzied drum, and the project came to nothing. Nevertheless it was the harbinger of a new sort of theatre, and by the Restoration the old non-scenic stage was generally out of fashion.

After the opening of the Cockpit-in-Court on 5 November 1630 Jones had busied himself with the scenes for *Chloridia*, the queen's Shrovetide masque of 1631. His relations with Ben Jonson were sour and within the year he was engaged with another and lesser poet, Aurelian Townshend, in the 'Invention' of *Albion's Triumph*, the king's Twelfth Night masque, performed in the Banqueting House. For it he designed a frontispiece (O & S 190), derived in part from the title pages of recent editions of Serlio and Scamozzi, which asserted the intellectual dignity of 'THEORICA' and 'PRACTICA', two qualities personated by over-lifesize figures incorporated into the supports. The figures were intended to demonstrate, in the words of the masque text, 'that by these two, all works of Architecture, and Ingining have their perfection'.[1] The designer, as much as the poet, might lay claim to intellectual authority. As if to emphasize the matter – and we must allow for a certain edginess in his response to Jonson's belligerent scoffing – Jones prepared a fine and learned drawing for a scene of a Roman 'atrium' (O & S 191), based on Giulio Parigi's Temple of Peace in *Il Giudizio di Paride*. Parigi had committed the solecism of showing the great Composite columns in his wings with a Doric entablature. Jones adapted his model, replacing its wide spaced perspective with a new and more complex system of his own, and correcting the architecture in what John Newman has shown to be a deliberate act of archaeological reconstruction.[2] In the drawing the order retains its Composite mode, but the frieze in the entablature is given an unusual treatment worked out on the authority of an antique marble which Jones had studied in the Arundel collection. Like the frontispiece which framed it, the Roman atrium design is a considered gesture of architectural science, one in the eye, so to speak, for the scholarly Ben Jonson.

Nevertheless one cannot altogether admire the quality of the writers with whom Jones now became associated. With the exception of Carew's *Coelum Britannicum* the later masques, whether by Townshend or Davenant, lack Jonson's intellectual range, and Walter Montagu's *The Shepherd's Paradise*, for which Jones undertook his next theatre, was an interminable and undistinguished neo-platonic pastoral, reported to have taken seven or eight hours to perform. But if the play is of little value the theatre provided for it survives in so profuse a flow of documents that we are able to reconstruct not only the detail of its fabric but even the mental processes by which its design was developed. The confident inventor of *Albion's Triumph* here turned once more to the staging of the drama proper, drawing numerous sketches for the standing scene, shutters and relieves. The design of the auditorium itself he appears to have left to his new assistant, John Webb, but there can be little doubt that its development was under Jones's own supervision, for it follows directly in the line of his earlier preoccupation with the theatre scheme of Sebastiano Serlio.

The theatre was ordered to be built in the Paved Court at Somerset House in the winter of 1632–3, and the queen herself was to take part in the production, along with the ladies of her household. Jones was commissioned to undertake the construction by a warrant dated 3 November 1632:

. . . there is a Pastorall to be presented at Somersett House for which a roome must be purposely made, And therein yᵉ Timber worke of yᵉ Sceane with yᵉ Stage & degrees to be properly done by yᵉ officers of his Majesties workes.[3]

If the Florentine agent in London, Amerigo Salvetti, was accurately informed, this warrant was issued too late for the original production date to be met. In a dispatch dated 16 November (old style) he observed that the pastoral had been intended for the king's birthday, as a present to grace the occasion; it had been put off in part because the ladies were not ready and in part because the 'apparato della scena' had not been finished either.[4] Then, in December, came a period of mourning for the late Prince Palatine; not until 9 January 1633 did the performance actually take place.

The declared accounts of the Office of the Works give a full description of the house which Jones provided for the occasion:

. . . to Richard Ryder Carpenter for framing and razing a greate house of firtimber and Dealebordes in the paved Court lxxvj fo: long xxxvj fo: wide and xxv fo: high with two outletts at the end where the Sceane was [,] putting vp Degrees in the said house and ioisting and bourding the lower roome hee finding all manner of stuffe and workemanshipp iiii^{xx} xiiij^{li} x^s. making a lardge Scaffold all of his owne stufe over all the lower parte of the said house to put vp the Cloth in the Ceeling and to put vp the State xl^s taking downe the Degrees at the Lower end of the said house after the said pastorall were performed altering them for more Conveniency of the house and inlarding the roome with ioisting and bourding it for a Maske he finding all manner of stuffe and workmanshipp vij^{li} framing and putting vp two Outlett*es* xxxviij fo: long the peece with two floores to them over the Degrees on the sides of the said House finding all material*les* and workmanshipp xiij^{li} vj^s viij^d. fitting and putting vp railes round aboute the Stadge at the foote of the Degrees hee finding stuffe and workmanshipp xij^s . . .^{5}

In 1775, when Somerset House was pulled down to make way for the present building, the architect Sir William Chambers, acutely aware of the loss entailed in the demolition, had a careful survey made of the site, and this drawing is now in the possession of the Ministry of Works.^{6} It shows the old palace in some detail, and the Lower Court (or Paved Court) as a rectangle some 76 ft by 63 ft, its western end diminished by extruded corners which reduce its width there to about 38 ft. Into this space Jones had been required to insert his theatre, its 76 ft length as specified in the Works accounts neatly filling the whole length of the Court, and its 36 ft width fitting snugly between the extruded corners. Thus his building incorporated the east and west walls of the Court, but involved the erection of timber lateral walls to the north and south.

Among the collection of Webb's stage drawings at the British Library, Lansdowne MS 1171, is one which, though not identified with any title, nevertheless contains enough specific internal evidence to prove that it represents the Paved Court Theatre. Fols. 9^b–10^a show a T-shaped room with thick walls at the head and foot and much thinner walls at the sides (plate 18). The internal length, measured against the scale which accompanies the plan, is 76 ft, while the width is just over 50 ft at the head and about 35 ft at the foot, the exterior widths scaling approximately 51 ft 9 in and 36 ft 9 in respectively. There are annotations on the drawing in Webb's hand – 'musickhouse' in the box to the left of the stage, and 'passage behind the backcloth' at the top, together with a few marked dimensions – but none gives the theatre's name or location. Nevertheless the scaled dimensions fit the proportions of the site at Somerset House and precisely agree with those of the theatre described in the Works accounts. The thick walls at the head and foot of the T are evidently of brick or masonry, while the thinner side walls (a little less than a foot thick) represent the 'house of firtimber and Dealebord*es*' put up (and later pulled down again) by Richard Ryder. The wall at the head, though marked on the plan only by a line indicating one surface, was some 1 ft 3 in thick, as is shown by the door reveal to one end of it. The drawing of the 18 in thick wall at the foot is not quite consistent with the reading suggested above, for it shows the thin timber walls intersecting the surface where they should merely abut on it, a discrepancy for which I can offer no satisfactory explanation.^{7}

While the drawing and the Works accounts agree precisely on the length of the house, there is some difficulty about its width. First, the documents mention a

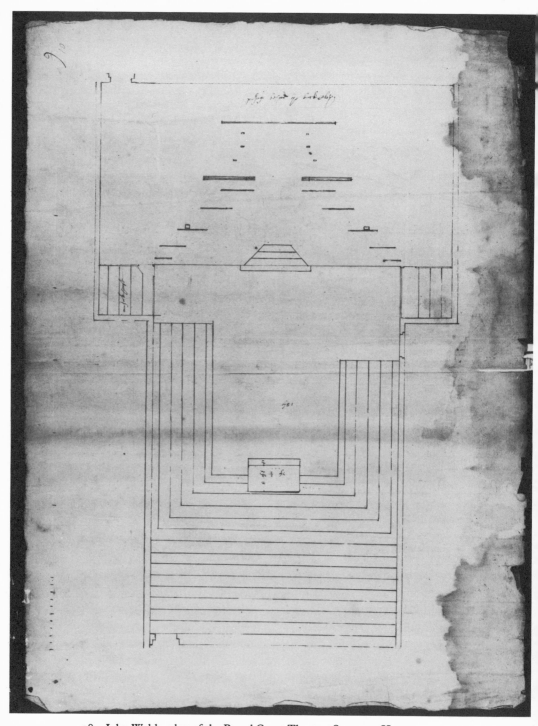

18   John Webb, plan of the Paved Court Theatre, Somerset House

width of 36 ft, while the drawing shows the greater part of the house rather wider than that, about 36 ft 9 in measured externally, or narrower internally at a little short of 35 ft. There is, however, no great discrepancy here. The interior length is given by the accounts and plan alike as 76 ft because that was the given distance as provisionally measured between the extant walls of the Paved Court. The timber side walls are measured differently, carpenter-fashion between their centres. Any framer of timber bays must think of his work thus; a bay cannot usefully be measured between the inner or outer surfaces of its structural members, but only between their centres. Some confirmation of the correctness of this view is perhaps given by Webb's own annotation, on the drawing, of the width of the rectangular 'orchestra' as '18 fo'. At just half the width of the house as given in the Works account this figure bears a simple proportional relation to it, a quite routine example of harmony in design.

While the main body of the theatre shown in the plan is almost exactly 36 ft wide, measured between centres, the stage end similarly measured is just about 51 ft, and this figure does not appear in the Works accounts. They do, however, mention that 'two outletts' were built 'at the end where the Sceane was . . .' Guided only by the *Oxford English Dictionary* one would take these to be exits of some sort, but the use of the word 'outlett' later in the same document suggests that quite another sort of structure may be meant. The theatre was built first for a pastoral and then substantially modified for a masque.[8] The alterations, which are not shown in the drawing, entailed taking down the degrees and 'framing and putting vp two Outlett*es* xxxviij fo: long the peece with two floores to them over the Degrees on the sides of the said House . . .' Evidently outlets could be quite substantial structures.

Fortunately a satisfactory definition of the term lies close to hand. Between 1630 and 1635 the chapel at Somerset House was built to designs by Jones, and among the accounts relating to its construction is one that mentions outlets:

. . . new building a Chappell of Brickes & Stone there ciiij foote longe xxxvj[foo:] brode and lj foote high to the tope of the roofe with twoe Outletts for staires & litle Chappells xij foote one way and xxxvj[foo] th'other way . . .[9]

Comparison of these dimensions with the reconstructed plan published by Sir John Summerson shows that the outlets are what we should call transepts. They are outward extensions from the main body of the building, or what builders more commonly refer to as 'outshuts'.

The 'two outletts at the end where the Sceane was' are clearly shown in the Lansdowne MS drawing. They project a little over 7 ft 6 in beyond the walls of the auditorium, giving a total exterior width at the stage end of 51 ft 9 in. Because this stage end of the theatre is wider than the distance between the extruded corners shown on the Chambers survey at the western end of the Court, it must have been erected against the eastern wall. The west wall therefore formed the rear of the auditorium, communicating at an upper level with the ground floor of the Upper Court, which was two storeys higher than the Paved Court.[10] The drawing shows an access door leading directly to the highest of the degrees in the auditorium, and necessarily coming in at a high level.

Yet despite the close correspondence between the plan and the Works accounts it is unlikely that the theatre was built exactly according to the detailed specifications they contain. When John Webb's house at Butleigh was demolished in the nineteenth century a notebook was found among its timbers, the entries consisting mainly of tables and calculations having to do with builders' cost estimates.[11] The hand in which they are written is reported to be Webb's,[12] and it includes one page devoted to the Paved Court Theatre. There are records of the actual cost of the timber, sawing and working, nails and spikes, together with the 'use' of boards for the degrees and other boards cut out for brackets. The document clearly records what was actually built, and the dimensions it gives are slightly different from those scaled from the plan:

the [house?] being 75 fo: long and 34 fo: brod with 2 outtletts 8 fott out and 33 fo: longe on each side; the depth of it 25 fo: from the ground to the [underside?] of the [beames?] and 42 fo in length at the holle breadth to [have] a flower 18 inches from the ground and to be borded round rufe and all; [only] the two ends are [saved?] with the other housing

In a moment I shall be suggesting that the plan in the Lansdowne MS is a very precise piece of geometrical construction, enshrining a particular system of design on paper; the Butleigh notebook therefore serves as a timely reminder that such schemes were often modified in the execution to the point where the ordering of the original design was lost. Presumably the 76 ft length of the house mentioned in the Works account was found to be 75 ft in the event, and the auditorium was built only 34 ft wide where the plan showed something larger. In fact the Works account retains signs of the plan's ideality, as we shall see, but the more practical notebook probably tells the mundane truth. It also helpfully records the scantlings of the timbers used:

the skanttlings: the posts and enttertises 9 inches and 6: platts 4 & 6 beams 6 & 7 selling joists 4 inches square principall raftters 6 and 4 singell raftters 4 inches square crounpeses and brases 4 & 6: joists for the fflower 4 & 6

Webb had entered Jones's office in or about 1628, and there can be no doubt that the written annotations on the Paved Court Theatre plan are in his hand. It seems likely therefore that he was the author of the drawing as well as the notebook, and there is some indication that he was on this occasion rather more than a mere copyist. Jones was personally responsible for the scenes, for which so many sketches survive from his hand, but there are no similar studies from him for the working plans of the scene and auditorium. Indeed such studies are scarce in the canon of his work, and even the few that we possess are confined to particular details such as a frame for a descent machine (O & S 148), a moving cloud (O & S 407) or – a great rarity – a single plan of a perspective stage (O & S 111 verso). Often his scene designs will give a very good idea of the separate physical elements that went to make up the whole, as when he marks the 'cloudes', 'tentes', 'backcloth' and 'citti of rileve' in the Cockpit scene of 1639 (plate 9). But apart from his drawings for the Cockpit in Drury Lane he left no detailed architectural plans or sections of any of the major theatres with which he was concerned; even the Cockpit-in-Court, for whose design he was certainly responsible, is known to us only through Webb's later drawings. In part this absence of the plans even when so many scenic designs survive is doubtless accidental, for they were probably regarded as mere working drawings of a technical sort, to be discarded once the occasions that prompted them had passed. Webb, on the other hand, devoted himself assiduously to his theatre plans and sections, producing work of a quality worthy to be preserved, and it seems a reasonable if not quite a certain inference that he actually developed some of them from scratch. It is by no means clear that Jones was an enthusiast for the technicalities of theatre design, with their worrisome details concerning the sightlines, the disposition of the audience in relation to the scenic perspective and so on. These he may very well have left to his assistant.

Webb appears to have developed his auditorium design on the paper from the 76 ft given length of the house, dividing it into forty-eight parts in order to arrive at a module of 19 in, the depth of each of the degrees at the back of the auditorium. Eight of these form a distinct group, stretching straight across the room from side to side, 12 ft 8 in and so just eight modules deep altogether. The range of degrees flanking the right wall extends exactly halfway down the house, its rear or topmost bench thus measuring sixteen modules or 25 ft 4 in in length. Although at first sight the front of the scenic stage appears to divide the overall length of the theatre in the ratio 1:2, in fact its line falls just short of the mark, so that a round 25 ft is given to the stage depth, and 51 ft to that of the auditorium. Fifty-one feet is of course also the width of the stage, measured between the centres of its limiting walls.

This is the house where, according to the Florentine resident, Queen Henrietta Maria excelled herself in the acting of Montagu's play:

Last Wednesday her Majesty the Queen performed her pastoral; the scenic apparatus was very lovely, but so was the beauty of the performers, and of the Queen above all the rest, who with her new English and the grace with which she showed it off, together with her regal gestures and actions on the stage, outdid all the other ladies, though they acted their parts too with the greatest variety.[13]

Even before his diplomatic praise of the performers Salvetti mentions the beauty of the scenes, of which some hints are to be found in the play itself. The text of *The Shepherd's Paradise* was not published until 1659 (though some copies were misdated 1629), but several manuscripts survive.[14] From one of these (BL Stowe MS 976) and from the stage designs associated with the play, Orgel and Strong abstracted a series of indications of scene changes, which led them to draw some tentative conclusions about the nature of the stage whose settings so impressed the Italian observer:

One can deduce from the annotations on the drawings that there were at least eight changes of scene, and probably several more. There were apparently three types of setting, presumably similar to the arrangements recorded in the ground plan of *Florimène* . . .:

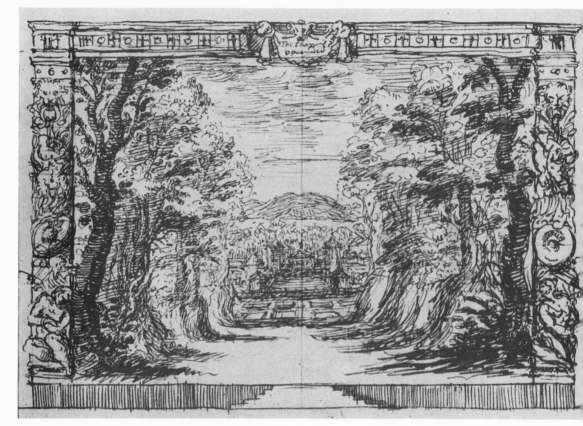

19   Inigo Jones, standing scene for *The Shepherd's Paradise*

1 A standing scene . . .
2 A series of back shutter and wing changes . . .
3 A small number of scenes of relieve placed between the back shutters and backcloth . . .[15]

With the single exception of the wing changes, which entail no more than the thrusting out of a temple between the wings of the standing scene, this arrangement is the one shown in the plan of the Paved Court Theatre. Behind the frontispiece are ranged four pairs of fixed flat wings, grooves for sliding backshutters and three pairs of posts whose function is to support the three layers of the relieve scenes in front of the backcloth.

Among Jones's drawings belonging to the production of *The Shepherd's Paradise* is one of a standing scene of trees with the title of the play inscribed on the skin at the centre of the border (plate 19). The supporting pilasters shown at either side differ from most similar designs in that they are very slender, perhaps to suit the femininity of a play acted by the queen and her ladies. The Paved Court plan also shows slender pilasters in the frontispiece; indeed they read on the scale at about 2 ft 6 in wide, while the gap between them is 30 ft, giving an overall width of 35 ft. This proportion closely approximates that of the design, where the overall width is 199 mm on the paper and each pilaster is 15 mm wide.[16] Given that the gap between the pilasters is 30 ft, as in the plan, the aspect ratio of the border allows one to estimate its height at about 24 ft 10 in overall. The height of the theatre according to the Works account and the Butleigh notebook was 25 ft.

The drawing of the standing scene is squared with a scorer in two ways. First the outline of the proscenium border has been set down, the boundary lines of the supports extending well below the inked lines at either side. Then, probably after the drawing was made within this neatly measured frame, the whole was squared up with a pointer for enlargement, each square one-third of an inch in size and the whole set aligned with the co-ordinates of the base line and the vertical central axis. Neither the top of the border nor the outer edges of the supports match this ruled system, though of course they are defined by the scored lines that were laid down first. The scenic opening is 20 squares wide by 14 high. From the plan we know that its width was 30 ft; it follows that each square represents 18 in, and the scale of the drawing is 1:54 or 4 ft 6 in to the inch. The scenic opening scales at 21 ft high to the quasi-Doric border, which is about 2 ft 4 in deep. The stage is drawn one square high, or 1 ft 6 in (the 'flower 18 inches from the ground' of the notebook), uncommonly low. Steps descend from its front centre to the floor of the auditorium, and although they are shallow there is room for only five risers. Five risers are shown in the plan, but where the elevation places all of them in front of the stage, the plan shows the three upper ones cut into the stage with only the lowest and widest tread projecting onto the floor of the house.

The stage floor is raked continuously from the front to the backcloth, and indeed the plan gives no sign of any levelling-off even at this point, or at that of the backshutters. Yet it is to be doubted whether the queen and her ladies played their parts entirely within the narrow scope of the scenic picture. They must have made their entries between the flat wings, there being no other stage doors, but the steps leading down to the auditorium floor gave them access to their main acting area, the level space between the scene and the auditorium benches. This area is 35 ft wide and some 7 ft 6 in deep, or 34 ft by 8 ft as recorded in the Butleigh notebook, dimensions which resemble those of the forestage at the Cockpit-in-Court (34 ft by 5 ft). The inspiration for this arrangement stems from Serlio, whose unified perspective scene is fronted by a flat forestage running the whole width of the theatre. In Serlio's scheme the vanishing point of the perspective is elevated well above the level of the most notable seats; Webb's notion of dispensing with the elevated forestage and using only a shallow raked scenic stage beyond it means that his vanishing point is much lower than Serlio's and possibly even close to the level of the eyes of the king seated on the halpace at the back centre of the orchestra. That the level floor immediately in front of the proscenium border is intended to be part of the stage is indicated in the phrasing of the Works accounts, which report that Richard Ryder was paid for 'fitting and putting vp railes round aboute the Stadge at the foote of the Degrees'. These rails may be seen in the plan at the front of the small boxes of degrees to either side of the level stage, one of them marked as the 'musickhouse'.

The first performance of *The Shepherd's Paradise* was not well attended, evidently because of administrative over-compensation by those who feared that the sensational sight of the queen acting in a play might cause too great a crush for the auditorium to hold. There were rumours that it would be staged again at Candlemas (2 February), but no actual record of a performance on that date survives. The Revels accounts do show, however, that a play was performed at Somerset House on the day following:

ffebruary 3. for 5 mens worke day & night at a dancing & play — 00.16.08 [17]

Possibly this was the second performance of the pastoral. Soon afterwards the theatre was considerably altered for the performance of the lost queen's masque on Shrove Tuesday. We have no drawings of these changes, and the masque for which they were made has not come down to us, but the declared account does give some indication of what they entailed. Strangely enough it does not appear that Ryder was called upon to alter the stage itself, or even to make new scenic devices. Rather he had to alter the auditorium by 'taking downe the Degrees at the Lower end, . . . altering them for more Conveniency of the house and inlarding [sic] the roome with ioisting and bourding it for a Maske . . .' In addition there were to be the 'two Outlettes xxxviij fo: long the peece with two floores to them over the Degrees on the sides of the said House . . .'

Interpretation of these changes is made more difficult by the ambiguity of the word 'lower' in relation to the axis of the building. Usually it means the end opposite the state or high table, perhaps on this occasion therefore the scene end. In that case the 'ioisting and bourding the lower roome' of the house as originally erected must have meant the construction of the stage. But in that case also the 'Cloth in the Ceeling' must have been over the stage, since it was to be put up on a scaffold 'over all the lower parte of the said house'. The cloth is doubtless a velarium of the kind which Jones had provided at the Cockpit-in-Court (and which had earlier appeared at the old Whitehall Banqueting House in 1604 [18]). If so, then 'lower' must mean the end opposite the scene, away from the queen and her ladies. On the whole this seems the likelier interpretation, particularly since the Works account mentions the state in the same breath as the velarium, and the state was certainly in the auditorium. This being the case, the house was altered for the masque with the removal of the range of degrees at the base of the stem of the T; the extension of the floor thus made available was newly joisted and boarded for dancing; and on either side of the house extensions were made ('Outlettes') to permit new rows of benches constructed as galleries to look over the tops of the degrees already there, somewhat on the model of the gallery at the recently-converted Cockpit-in-Court. Although in the plan the right-hand range of degrees reached halfway down the length of the house, or 38 ft, the new 38 ft long outletts could not have been intended exactly to match it because the extruded corners of the Paved Court flanked either side of the western end of the house and left no room for extensions. These doubtless occupied the space between the extruded corners and the front of the raked stage, and their construction must have entailed the incorporation of the existing music boxes.

The Paved Court scheme is remarkable among the theatres designed by Jones and Webb for the completeness of their control over its development, for in earlier documented examples their work had always been swayed by some powerful external constraint. In Drury Lane it was the original cockpit, whose structure Jones had to incorporate into his playhouse. At the Cockpit-in-Court his work was restricted to the conversion of a pre-existing building of assertive character. Here at Somerset House only the dimensions of the Paved Court appear to have limited the scope of the designers, and we may be confident that the finished drawing expresses Webb's considered ideas about the accommodation of a scenic play, developed under Jones's influence to be sure, but also marking an independent and potentially fruitful interest in the details of auditorium design. His solution is a sensible – and relatively cheap – adaptation of Serlio's theatre scheme, like the Paved Court a house set up in a palace courtyard. The Italian's expensive semi-circular *cavea* is here reduced to three sides of a rectangle, with the state at the centre of the periphery of the orchestra. Jones's complementary standing scene is of the general type of Serlio's Satyric Scene, but greatly modified in the execution. The formation of the tree wings owes much to Giulio Parigi's Mount Ida in *Il Giudizio di Paride*; where Serlio's trees spring directly from the raked surface of the stage, Parigi, followed by Jones, softens their rigidly orthogonal line by giving each wing a profiled and often rather tangled bank at its foot.[19] The Serlian scene is constructed as a series of book-wings with diminishing orthogonal sides leading to a fixed backscene, but Jones's flat wings converge towards a backshutter assembly beyond which are scenes of relieve and a backcloth. Such a disposition of the scenic elements had been Jones's practice in masque design since at least the early 1620s, and the Paved Court design therefore broke no new ground for him. Nevertheless it is the earliest play scene to use flat wings enclosing a shallow perspective stage, and it is remarkable that the raked stage shown in the plan is so diminished by the steps cut into it that it offers hardly more than a kind of low platform or halpace for the display of the actresses, and scarcely a place for action at all. It is in the shape of a shallow inverted V, its arms no more than seven or eight feet wide between the steps and the wings. Its very structure would propel the performers down onto the level floor of the house, in close contact with the audience and particularly with the state, leaving Jones's scenic picture as a decoration in three dimensions, neatly framed within its border.

The Paved Court documents provide an unusual opportunity to distinguish the quality of Webb's interest in theatre design from that of Jones. The plan is a model of precision, and even – in its modular layout – of a kind of architectural pedantry. Everything about it is shaped by systems of proportional relations, and on the paper the drawing is exact and rigorous. By contrast the design for the standing scene and border is freely handled, though architectonically firm and disciplined by a ruled frame. Where Webb's plan is a technical document, Jones's elevation is an expressive work of art.

Yet it would be a mistake to think of Webb as a mere plodder, giving executive reality to Jones's inspired directions. His contribution to the design is a creative one, and it appears to take its departure from a weakness in Jones's own conception of his task. A close examination of his drawings for *The Shepherd's Paradise* shows that Jones paid little attention to the careful proportioning of their perspective construction. The raked stage and tree-formed side wings shown in the designs (O & S 245 and 246) make few demands on his technical proficiency, for there are no firm lines to mark the orthogonals of the view (in contrast, say, to Serlio's Tragic Scene). The exact proportioning of the elements of the scene which would be required in an architectural setting is here unnecessary, although to be sure a general foreshortening is required. Only when the scenes are completed by the backshutters or relieves do they present an identifiable vanishing point and so require for their execution at least a nominal acquaintance with the principles of linear perspective. The standing scene of trees should, strictly considered, imply a horizon and vanishing point which are retained as constants throughout all the changes of the backshutters and relieves; each shutter or relieve design should therefore show the vanishing point at the same height above its bottom edge. It can hardly be doubted that Jones was capable of constructing a rigorously proportioned scene, but in the *Shepherd's Paradise* sketches he shows little evident interest in the matter. In the three standing scene drawings the squares of the backshutters can be discerned between the furthest wings, the tops marked by cloud rows. In the complete frontispiece design (plate 19) the vanishing point is high, more than halfway up the shutters, while in the palace design for Act I (O & S 246) it is low, less than a third of the way up, though its exact location is made uncertain by the loose handling of the architectural perspective of the buildings. A third version of the standing scene, in which it is closed with woodland (O & S 136),[20] appears to locate the horizon about halfway up the backshutters. The two sets of relieve designs for the play ought in theory to be consistent with one or other of these depictions of the standing scene, but they are not, nor are they consistent with each other. O & S 249 and 250 are both roughly square overall in elevation, and are ruled up into smaller squares, ten by ten. The vanishing point and horizon appear some four squares above the foot of O & S 249, and in O & S 250 they are ambiguously presented. In the background the horizon is six squares high, while in the foreground the orthogonals of the arch through which the scene is viewed converge at a point only some two and a half squares above the foot of the shutter, with the result that the design is irrational if judged as a piece of methodical perspective. The relieves, that is to say, provide horizons at quite different levels, indicating that on this occasion Jones did not aim to create a rigorously constructed foreshortened vista in which the horizon was consistently dictated by the proportions of the standing scene. A backshutter design of a garden, O & S 252, is divided into squares nine by nine, and yields a horizon halfway up from the grooves; but while in this it resembles O & S 136, a comparison with two other shutter sketches assigned to the play by Orgel and Strong reveals a confusing variability. In O & S 251 – 'The seuenth sceane a Prospect of Trees & howses a shutter' – the horizon is little more than a quarter of the way up the shutter surfaces, and in O & S 253 it is about a third.[21] Jones's backshutters and relieves are not, in short, carefully assimilated to the perspective of his standing scene, but are proportioned independently. From no point in the auditorium would they consistently appear to be continuous with the raked stage and its rows of diminishing wings.

Webb's plan of the auditorium is by comparison a paragon of precise method. As will become apparent in a moment, the design is based on a geometric construction, but the absence of compass pricks in the paper indicates that the preparatory work was roughed in on another sheet; the present drawing is inked on a groundwork of scored lines whose positions have evidently been transferred from such a preliminary draft. I have said that the source of the design is the theatre scheme in Serlio's Second Book, but Webb adopts more from the *Architettura* than the general disposition of the parts of the auditorium. He embraces also the intellectual scheme by which they are ordered, a system of constructive geometry. Serlio's plan is drawn up, as we saw in chapter 3, according to an *ad quadratum* method, the width of the orchestra being related to that of the whole house in the ratio $1 : \sqrt{2}$, or 24:34 measured by the reticulation of the forestage. Such proportioning is a quite logical consequence of the accommodation of a segmental or semi-circular *cavea* within the boundaries of a rectangular site, whether it be a courtyard or a hall. At the Cockpit in Drury Lane Jones made a related use of the *ad quadratum* scheme when he extended the circle of the original building to include a rectangular stage whose front he placed along the side of a square inscribed within the circle of the pit. Again, as in the Serlian source, the occasion for this resort to the quadrate method lay in the need to assimilate a rectangular to a circular principle of design. At the Paved Court no such motive existed, for the house was entirely rectangular, and built within the limits of a rectangular courtyard. In the drawing the degrees are set quite simply along the sides of the auditorium, offering what seems to be a direct and straightforward arrangement. Yet for all its rectilinearity, Webb's design does contain a remarkably thorough expression of the *ad quadratum* programme as it appears in Serlio.

The scheme begins with the orchestra, labelled as 18 ft wide. Like Serlio's 6-unit scaled measure marked at the centre of his forestage, this 18 ft unit is the premise from which the logic of the remainder of Webb's plan is developed. That this is so is in part confirmed by the scale bar, which gives 60 ft in 253 mm, or 1 mm less than 10 in, indicating that an original scale of 6 feet to the inch has been altered by a very slight shrinkage of the paper. The orchestra is within 0.25 mm of 3 in wide on the sheet, and is labelled at 18 ft. On the paper, then, the *ad quadratum* scheme was developed from a unit 3 in long. Its constructive centre is to be found at the point where the angles of the degree corners converge in the auditorium. This point is just 9 ft from the line of the front degree where it is obscured by the state. The orchestra is thus laid out about a square 18 ft across, the front degrees following three of its sides, leaving the fourth open towards the stage. A square constructed *ad quadratum* around the initial one would be 25.46 ft across (18 ft x $\sqrt{2}$), and does not appear directly in Webb's drawing, though its upper side exactly coincides with the boundary of the 'piazza della scena' as defined by the interior end walls of the outshuts to either side. This square in the *ad quadratum* scheme therefore marks the boundary between the rectangle of the auditorium and that of the 'scena' as a whole. The next larger square has sides of 36 ft, defining the width of the theatre as stated in the Works account and as measured between the centres of the timber flanking walls. Finally a square measuring 36 ft × √2, or 50.91 ft, defines the width of the scenic end of the house, again as measured between the centres of its timber walls.[22]

Unlike many mediaeval applications of *ad quadratum* construction, Webb's scheme appears to have had little practical value for the carpenters working on the site. The establishment of the width of the scenic end as the same as the diagonal of a 36 ft square seems more a paper exercise than a practical method of value in setting out the footings of the house, for it makes no use even of such readily available measuring instruments as the surveyor's line, which was customarily marked off in pole divisions of 16½ ft. Rather the design shows Webb, at twenty-two years old only at the outset of his lengthy career, theorizing in the light of Serlio's example. His house is of course smaller and simpler of construction than its model, but it uses the same constructive geometry even while it reduces the expensive segmental ranks of the Italian's seating to straight sided benches. In one respect Webb takes the scheme a step further when he proportions the auditorium 1:√2 (36 ft wide by 51 ft long to the front of the stage), hardly an exceptional way of proportioning a room, of course, but in this case surely attuned to the larger *ad quadratum* programme.

One further measure is again not strictly a part of the scheme but appears to be related to it. The distance from the centre of the construction to the rear corners of the house, measured to the centres of the lateral walls there, is just 36 ft, so that the centre lies at the apex of an equilateral triangle raised on the line marking the rear (or lower) wall of the theatre. It seems likely that Webb began his plan with this construction, using it to establish the centre for his subsequent, and very Serlian, *ad quadratum* proportioning of the house.[23] The method exactly repeats that of the 1551 edition of the *Architettura*, where the centre is located at the apex of a 34-unit equilateral triangle based on the backline of the auditorium.

The Paved Court stage offered a much lower, more horizontal, vista to its audience than did Serlio at his Vicenzan palazzo. Jones does not appear to have provided changing sky effects, though he did use cloudrows, which are visible in his designs for the standing scene. The height of the house was 25 ft, and in his characteristically schematic way Webb allowed just 25 ft for the depth of the whole of the stage to its back wall. Indeed, at only two or three inches over 50 ft wide internally this scenic end of the house is designed almost exactly as a double cube. Lacking a section of the house as meticulously prepared as the plan, we are unable to judge the rake of the stage and the height of the vanishing point in relation to the spectators. It may be, however, that Webb intended the scenic horizon to be set precisely at the level of the king's eye, for the state is a low one, mounted only by two risers, as if to suit the shallow stage. If so, he must have been disappointed with the variable horizons of Jones's backshutter designs.

Webb's plan is a sophisticated reinterpretation of Serlio's seminal theatre scheme. What, then, are we to make of what I have called the 'mundane reality' of the dimensions recorded in the Butleigh notebook? They show that in the event the careful *ad quadratum* proportioning of the theatre was rejected in favour of something altogether simpler and more direct, yet if anything even more schematic. The house as built was 75 ft long and at the wider stage end was 50 ft across (the sum of the 34 ft wide main structure together with its two 8 ft outshuts). We have only the plan to assert that the stage was 25 ft deep, but if this dimension was retained the whole stage area as realized was a perfect double cube, 50 ft × 25 ft × 25 ft. The remaining part of the wider section of the house was 8 ft deep (33 ft less 25 ft for the stage), so that the whole auditorium was 50 ft deep, the sum of the 8 ft 'piazza' and the notebook's '42 fo in length'. The stage front therefore exactly divided the length of the house in a ratio of 1:2, and its 21 ft high scenic opening was half the depth of the seated area. Whether the 34 ft width of the house had anything to do with Serlio's scheme, where the auditorium is 34 units wide, it is impossible to say. Certainly the simple proportions of the notebook dimensions owe nothing directly to the plan in the *Architettura*, and when the house was expanded for the Shrovetide masque its auditorium will have covered an area just 50 ft square, diminished only by the extruded corners at the rear. Nevertheless in Webb's original plan there are regularities of proportion in the placing of the state, the stage front, the backshutters and backcloth which do recall a similar schematism in Serlio. There the distance between the vanishing point and the front of the scene is divided by the backcloth in the ratio 3:2. Webb does not mark the vanishing point (and Jones's sketches leave doubts about whether it was ever securely determined) but his backshutter assembly, positioned on a scored line across its front, divides the distance from the backcloth to the stage front in the ratio 2:3; furthermore the stage, at 20 ft deep to the backcloth, is similarly proportioned in relation to the 30 ft depth to the presumed location of the king's seat on the state. Lacking further evidence of the sort that might have been provided by a detailed section of the theatre, or even by some precisely drawn scenic elevations, we cannot say what end, if any, was served by these simple niceties of proportion. They provide yet another indication of Webb's methodical way of co-ordinating the parts of his theatre and contrast acutely with Jones's more relaxed treatment of the scene designs. They are quite independent of the *ad quadratum* scheme of the auditorium layout, and point rather in the direction of a problem to which Webb was soon to turn with equal thoroughness, the question of the detailed handling of perspective design in the theatre, and of its influence on the arrangement of the auditorium.

7 The 'Florimène' Theatre at Whitehall

BOUND UP together with the Paved Court Theatre plan in Lansdowne MS 1171 is a group of drawings showing the great hall at Whitehall fitted out for the performance of a French pastoral, *Florimène*, by the queen's ladies in December 1635. The text of the play is not extant, but a detailed English scenario was published,[1] doubtless to provide a guide for courtiers whose French left something to be desired, and from it we can derive a satisfactory, if hardly complete, idea of what the work was like. Its style must have been that of the courtly *précieuses*, for contemporaries praised it more for its grace and richness than for its good sense. The scene designs survive in an almost complete series among Jones's drawings at Chatsworth, and the architectural plans and sections in the Lansdowne MS, all by Webb, attest to his particular interest in the production as illustrating that type of scenic stage where the angled wings are fixed and only the backscene is capable of changes. In the Paved Court Theatre the raked stage was shallow and the wings, fixed like those of *Florimène*, were simple flats; for *Florimène* they were constructed in two parts in the Serlian fashion, with one face parallel to the stage front and the other foreshortened along an orthogonal. The raked part of the stage was considerably deeper than it had been at the Paved Court, and the drawings are detailed enough to give a fairly complete idea of the proportioning of the perspective vista. The stage was less an advance than a variation upon the theme of the Paved Court Theatre, but the auditorium shown in the largest of the architectural plans is rather more elaborate than the one provided for *The Shepherd's Paradise*, and quite as substantial as many of those erected in the hall and the Banqueting House for even the most impressive of the masques. Indeed this well-organized auditorium, with its two levels of galleries, its broad orchestra for the danced intermedii, its handsome frontispiece and useful forestage, was the most fully developed of all the temporary Court theatres intended for the drama, and it is fortunate that so many records of it survive.

Earlier conversions of the building to theatrical uses are less well documented, but they are the specific antecedents of the *Florimène* scheme and should be noticed here. The great hall was the scene of royal festive and ceremonial occasions from the time when Henry VIII took it from the disgraced Cardinal Wolsey until it burned to the ground some 170 years later. The cardinal had built it in the years of his pride, a large house of glory, made of white ashlar stone, raised on a vaulted basement, its walls buttressed and three feet thick, its central axis planted almost due north and south. In this capacious room, nearly 90 ft long by some 40 ft wide inside, the

Tudor monarchs held their plays and masques beneath what must have been an
elaborate hammerbeam roof of the type still to be seen at Hampton Court and
Christ Church, Oxford, both of them halls of a similar span. But where Christ
Church was built in eight bays Whitehall had six, each about 15 ft 4 in wide. On the
eastern wall the second bay from the south was built outwards as a great window
which overlooked the chapel and the river, while opposite on the western wall the
royal entrance led from the monarch's apartments. In his *Long View* of London
(plate 1) Hollar shows something of the four-centred mullioned windows which
occupied the higher parts of each remaining bay, and states also that the lateral
walls were battlemented, like those at Hampton Court. At or near the centre of the
gabled roof was raised a notable louvre, intended to convey the smoke from a hearth
below; at the northern end of the interior, by Caroline times and probably from the
start, was a screen of timber, some 13 ft high and set 10 ft from the wall. Above it,
balustraded with a railing 3 ft 6 in tall, was a musicians' gallery. The hall was, in
short, a typical Tudor institution: beyond the screens passage lay the pantry and the
kitchens, while to the south, divided from them by the hearth and its louvre, stood
the royal dais with its separate entry and its large bay window.

During a life of almost two centuries the hall saw the productions of a host of
plays and masques, and from the accounts of the Revels, the Chamber and
especially of the Works we may gain some idea, though unfortunately a most
inadequate one, of how it was fitted up on such occasions. Its floor was of tiles,
repaired by the bricklayers in 1568:

Bricklayers occupied in newe pavinge of the hall in diuerse and sundrye places . . . To Iames
Ancell for v^c of pavinge tyles of viij ynches broade at v^s the Hundrethe – xxv^s.[2]

Sometimes – probably rarely, for the record is unusual – the tiles were covered by a
wooden dancing floor: '. . . making a stage three foote highe from the grounde
vpon the Trestles all the length and breadth of the hall . . .'[3] Presumably it was such
a wooden floor that was covered with green cloth in 1613 for a masque, for Richard
Ansell the matlayer was paid not only for supplying the cloth but also for 'naylinge
the same downe at two seuerall tymes vpon the floore in the bankettinge house and
once in the Hall for the Maskes performed before his *Majestie* at Shrovetyde'.[4]
When the hall was fitted up for plays the accounts of the 1570s spoke of '. . . setting
vp the frame in the halle for Playes maskes and Tragedies at diuers tymes . . .',[5] and
in the Revels accounts we read of carpenters being paid to renew this structure:

Carpenters occupied not onelye in repayring of the old frame and Settinge of it vpp But alsoe in
makeinge of Certayne particions and dors with diuerse other necessaries . . .[6]

Precisely what this frame consisted of, and how it might have been supplemented
with doors and partitions, we may only guess, but for many years such formulae as
these were used to describe the preparations of the hall for plays. Thus in the 1560s
we read of '. . . newe making and setting vpp of scaffoldes partitions and dores and
other necessaries for the Maundayes Plays Tragedyes maskes Revelles and Tryvm-
phes . . .'[7] and similar terms were still employed in the last years of Elizabeth's

reign. Degrees were erected for the accommodation of the audience, as in 1594/5:

> . . . fyttinge of degrees for both sides of the Hall, Cuttinge and nayleinge of brackett*es* and Deale boordes on them in the Hall, for the Earle of Sussex and gent*lemen* of Grayes Inne to make there shewes . . .[8]

While degrees seem to have been constructed for plays at all periods, only in Jacobean times do the records sometimes allude to galleries built over them, and these generally not for plays, as in 1612/13:

> . . . in makeing ready the Hall with degrees and galleries for a Maske to be p*er*formed before the kinge by the gentlemen of the Temple . . .[9]

and again in 1637/8:

> . . . preparing the Hall for the Maundy and putting upp a Gallery at th'end therof for the Gentlemen of the Chapple . . .[10]

Sometimes the erection of degrees entailed the disturbance of the tiled floor, which then had to be repaired:

> . . . paving with brickes, & paving tyles in the haull and entryes bothe, before and after Shrovetide being broken vp in placeinge of degrees for y*e* plaies . . .[11]

> . . . paveinge a great p*ar*te of the hall w*hi*ch was taken vpp to place the degrees stages and devises againste the marryage of the L*or*d *Hay* . . .[12]

The location of the stage, when one was used, is given only on a few occasions between 1601 and 1603, when it was specifically – and therefore perhaps atypically – recorded as being set in the middle of the hall. The entry for 1601–2 was cited above in chapter 1; two years or so later a similar form was followed:

> . . . making readie the hall with degrees and footepaces vnder the state with a Stage in the middle and making of soundrie p*ar*tic*i*ons with bourdes in the entries and passages for plaies . . .[13]

On this occasion the special placing of the stage appears to have been influenced by James himself, for the carpenters were paid for 'altering of a Stage in the hall to bring it nearer the king . . .'[14] We may recall that at Christ Church less than two years later Simon Basil placed the royal 'Isle' only 12 ft or 15 ft from the scenic stage, and that when he was forced to move it further away the king complained of not being able to hear the actors.

In all these accounts the royal state is often mentioned, and usually involves the construction of an elevated platform or halpace for the monarch's seat. Occasionally there is mention, as in the passage quoted on p. 3, of places for the musicians. And finally it appears that at all periods the hall might be darkened for the performance of plays and masques, for there are several records of its windows being boarded up, partly no doubt for the protection of their lights amid all the activity of construction:

> . . . Boarding vpp all the wyndowes in the Hall, setting vpp rayles, and boardes vppon the Degrees and fitting the Hall for Playes . . .[15]

One last example of these administrative records, taken from the period just before Jones's arrival at Whitehall, will serve to summarize the kind of theatrical arrangements he found being made there and which he saw little reason to alter for a good many years, at least for the performance of plays:

. . . making ready yᵉ haull, and great chamber with seates or standinges, & particions in soundrye places, Joisting, and bourding with deales, yᵉ haull florre all over bourding vp soundry lightes in yᵉ stonne windowes there making of degrees soundry one vpon another for the Queens Majestie vnder yᵉ clothe of estate in the haull, all for yᵉ plaies at Shrovetide . . .[16]

Most of the plays performed in the hall were acted by the public companies, who brought with them the rhetorical traditions of the London stage. Masques were another matter, and scenes of various sorts were usually employed in them, ranging from the emblematic mansions of Campion's *Lord Hay's Masque* (1607) to the great rock designed by Jones for Chapman's *Middle Temple and Lincoln's Inn Masque* (1613) and the two-level perspective stages he erected there for the lost masques of 1619 and 1621 (O & S 101, 110 and 111).[17] Indeed if the rough plan of a scene which appears in O & S 111 (i) (on the verso of O & S 111) does refer to the Twelfth Night masque of 1621 it must show the arrangements made in the hall, for the Banqueting House was at that date still under construction, its predecessor having burnt in 1619. Here the stage is much shallower than those implied in the vista designs for St George's Portico or *The Vision of Delight*. At the rear is a backshutter assembly with a scene of relieve behind it. The main stage has three pairs of flat wings (one set of them almost cropped away) and a small rectangle may represent one of the posts whose function was to support pulleys for a descent machine. The location of the proscenium border is not made clear, but at the front of the stage there are two sets of steps leading down to the dancing floor. Only one of these is complete and uncropped, and because it contains sixteen risers it implies a high stage: in the related frontispiece design (O & S 110) the stage appears to be some six or seven feet high. At the deepest part of the scene, immediately in front of the backcloth, a row of circles apparently shows the masquers ranged in tableau, and the logic of the scene's construction requires them to move forward through its foreshortened space to reach the steps by which they can descend to the dancing floor and possibly approach the state. For all its lack of physical depth the scene was still intended to function as the route for a triumphal entry, much like those of the earlier masques.

The first clear record of a scenic play in the hall at Whitehall is for *Florimène* in 1635, and for this the translation into a theatre was as complete as any that had been effected hitherto, even for the masques. It set the form, indeed, for John Webb's final refitting of the room as a permanent theatre in 1665, a post-Restoration conversion which will be the subject of a later chapter. Jones designed the scenes for *Florimène*, but as with the production of *The Shepherd's Paradise* the plan of the auditorium appears to have been drawn up by Webb. Here, in contrast to the spare allusions of the Court accountants, we find a wonderful richness of documentation, set down by the designers themselves.

The architectural drawings connected with *Florimène* were not all made at the

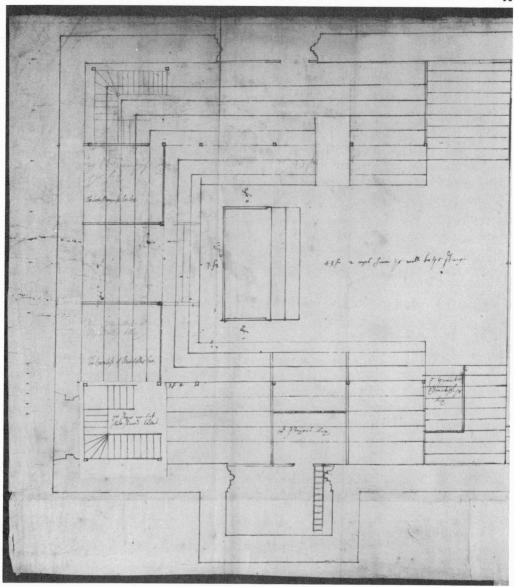

20   John Webb, plan of the auditorium prepared in the hall at Whitehall for *Florimène*,
1635

time of its performance. All are evidently in Webb's hand, but they appear to date
from different periods in his life, some being contemporary with the production
and others later reassessments of it. Jones's scene designs are all working drawings
concerned with the actual staging of the play, for they are squared up for
enlargement by the scene painters, and are splashed with their distemper. It is
necessary to distinguish between the drawings actually used for the construction of
the theatre and those which seek to interpret the work, for the latter can hardly be

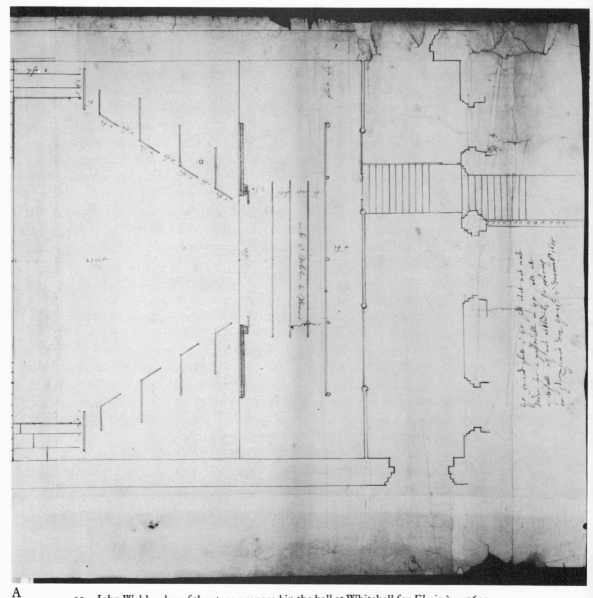

21   John Webb, plan of the stage prepared in the hall at Whitehall for *Florimène*, 1635

relied on as evidence of what was built. The most important of the architectural drawings is a large working plan (336 mm × 675 mm) of the hall showing the auditorium and the scene in some detail (plates 20 and 21).[18] It is endorsed by Webb, though it is possible that he has added the long title in the right margin at a date later than that of the drawing itself, for here his hand is rather looser than in the detailed annotations. Most of these measurements and identifications are in ink, as is the title, and are probably contemporary with the drawing, though they appear to have been preceded by a few lead inscriptions. At the top of the drawing some of the auditorium degrees are cancelled by means of a blank paste-on indicating a vomitory, and this partly covers a lead annotation: '43 fo[ot 2 inche]s', a measure which is rendered more fully in ink below: '43 fo 2 inches from the wall to the stage'. Similarly some lead notes designate the boxes to the left of the plan as 'the Cowntese of Arundelles box' and 'the lady marquis her box'. These have also been duplicated in ink, but not in Webb's hand. A scheme for a staircase leading to the front of the gallery from the floor of the hall appears in lead at the upper left corner, apparently superimposed on the ink lines of the degrees; it is restated more emphatically on a flap attached to the corner opposite, where it is inked and given an explanatory label: 'this stayers are but flatt staued laders'. The paste-ons, which seem largely concerned with the problem of audience circulation, postdate the inking of the main part of the plan, and are perhaps contemporary with the inked measurements, since both duplicate preparatory notations done in lead. Three other, smaller, paste-ons cancel inked lines which mistakenly carry the box partitions across the plan of the end wall of the hall at the left of the drawing.

The palimpsestical quality of the drawing, with its lead, ink and pasted-on corrections, indicates that it was a working plan, not a finished theoretical or illustrative piece. The impression of workaday utility is further strengthened by the nature of the paper, which consists of several pieces pasted together, doubtless for reasons of economy, before the underscoring was ruled. There are two major parts on which the whole body of the hall is drawn, joined approximately down the middle of the forestage. Below these is a strip on which the bay window is drawn and which consists of four smaller pieces pasted together. Each of the two larger pieces has a watermark, but although both are pots they are quite different from one another, indicating that the fragments of paper came from distinct sources.

A companion drawing in the Lansdowne MS (plate 22)[19] seems likely to be contemporary with the production, for although it has no annotation and indeed was not indentified as belonging to the *Florimène* set at all until 1973, it has the same pot watermark as the lefthand or southern part of the plan, which it closely resembles in both style and scale. The draftsmanship is meticulous, and is certainly by Webb. The drawing renders in some detail a section of the stage and scene, together with the area backstage, and gives a clear account of how the two-level scene was constructed. Backshutter assemblies are shown both below and above, with two pairs of shutters in the lower set and one in the upper. Interesting details are given of the hall's original screen, minstrels' gallery and four-centred arch to the screens passage door. The raked stage is carried by quartering centred at 2 ft intervals, while the back stage has more closely spaced timbers, on 18 in centres, evidently because it has to take the weight not only of the shutter and relieve assemblies but also of the entire upper stage, for which no separate supports are marked, capable of conveying the load directly to the floor of the hall. No wings are indicated, but their positions as well as that of the frontispiece are implied by the sections of five cloud borders and the frontispiece entablature. The height of the

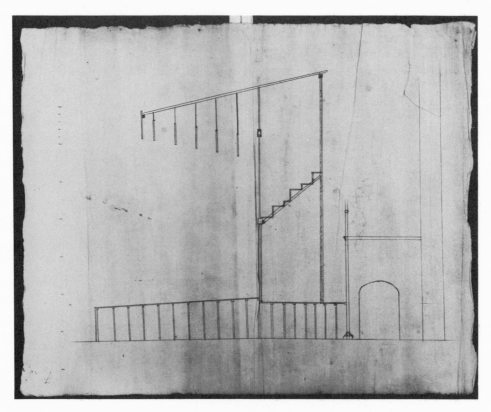

22   John Webb, section of the stage prepared in the hall at Whitehall for *Florimène*, 1635

stage is 4 ft 6 in at the front, rising to 5 ft 6 in immediately before the backshutters, behind which it is stepped down to almost 5 ft. The rake is continuous from the front of the forestage to the backshutters; behind them the stage is level. All this is consistent with the hall plan, and it is clear that the section, though untitled by Webb, was correctly identified by Orgel and Strong as belonging to the *Florimène* series.[20]

Among the information not duplicated from the plan is the height of the frontispiece, which scales at 30 ft 8 in above the hall floor, with an opening 22 ft high above the stage. The lower backshutters are 10 ft high and the upper ones a little taller at 11 ft, their top just in line with the top of the frontispiece opening. No indication is given of the visual foreshortening of the scene, unless indeed the rake of the stage and the diminishing elevations of the cloud borders might be conceived as doing so. But these are only of general import: if Webb thought of the visual geometry of the scene as in any way continuous with his proportioning of the auditorium he has not included the relevant information in this section of the stage.

Two other drawings for *Florimène* which are also bound up in the Lansdowne MS are of a very different quality. One is a plan of the stage alone (fols 15[b]–16; plate 23),

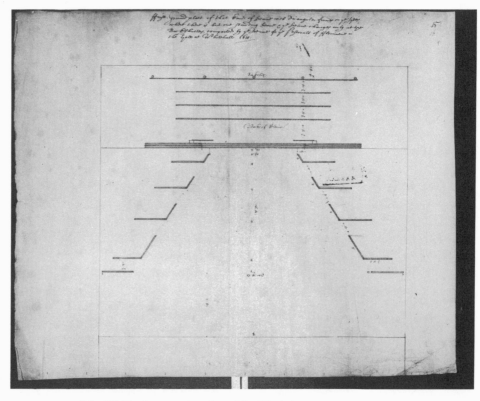

23   John Webb, interpretive plan of the *Florimène* stage

and the other a schematic diagram of the scene indicating the proportions of its
foreshortened wings as well as a geometrical section of the stage (fols 13[b]–14, plate
24). The plan is on a sheet 328 mm × 426 mm, and the analytical study is 333 mm ×
449 mm. They have the same watermark and both are titled and annotated in
Webb's later hand, which has a more pronounced rightward slant than his writing
of the 1630s. The endorsements indicate that it was his intention to use the
Florimène scheme as an illustration of the scene designer's geometrical methods.
Fols 15[b]–16 are titled:

First Ground platt of that kind of sceane with Triangular frames on y[e] sydes [i.e. 'book-wings']
where there is but one standing sceane & y[e] sceane changes only at the Backshutters, comparted
by y[e] sceane for y[e] Pastorall of fflorimene in the hall at Whitehall *1635*.

The titles on the more evidently schematic drawing (fols 13[b]–14) are just as
pedagogical in style: 'Second Ground platt for y[e]/standing\sceane with Triangular
frames'; and, above the section

Profyle of y[e] stage for y[e] proportioning y[e] shortning sydes of sceanes with Triangular frames when
there is but one standing sceane, comparted by the Ρ [*sic*] sceane of y[e] Pastorall of fflorimene in y[e]
hall at Whitehall *1635*.

24   John Webb, interpretive diagram of the *Florimène* stage

Such endorsements imply that there were to be other studies of scenes in which the
side wings as well as the backshutters changed, and these we do indeed find in the
Lansdowne MS (fols 1^b–2 and 3^b–4) 'comparted by ye sceane of . . . Salmacida
Spolia', which was performed in 1640. All four sheets have similar watermarks, and
because the titles of the *Salmacida Spolia* drawings are so clearly a match for the
Florimène ones it is unlikely that the latter were prepared before 1640; indeed it is
possible that all these demonstration drawings date from the Commonwealth years
or even as late as the Restoration, when Webb was eager to publicize his skill as a
scene designer. In his later drawings Webb habitually indicates the points between
which his annotations of measurements are taken with diminutive chevrons, and
this is the style also of the *Florimène* drawings, with the exception of the working
plan of the hall, where the measures are indicated by dots. They are indicated by
dots also in the Paved Court design of 1632, so that once again there is reason to

suppose that the large hall plan is contemporary with the production of *Florimène* in 1635, while the more schematic drawings were prepared later on.

Evidently Webb found in the *Florimène* scheme a satisfactorily complete example of one kind of semi-changeable scene. It was of course Jones who was warranted, on 24 October 1635,[21] to design and construct the theatre and its scenes in the hall, and from his hand there survive a number of the original designs, including two of the frontispiece with the standing scene of angle wings, one of the backshutters suitable to the standing scene and a series of four relieve designs showing the seasons, with a fifth of the temple of Diana. *Florimène* was a pastoral set on the Isle of Delos, close to the temple of Diana and sometimes actually before it. The play's conventions doubtless lent something of their force to Jones's decorative scheme, and on his frontispiece he shows *putti* cavorting with sheep and goats, others offering garlands and idyllic figures playing the pipe and tabor. The relieve of the temple of Diana is a deliberate study in the Ionic order, for according to Vitruvius[22] the order had been invented by the builders of a temple dedicated to the huntress, its column shafts eight diameters high, more slender and more feminine than the Doric. Accordingly the statue of Diana is shown in Jones's drawing surrounded by eight Ionic columns, their shafts eight diameters tall, the further ones fluted perhaps in imitation – as Vitruvius said they should be – of the folds of a matron's gown. The temple made a second appearance in the last act of the play, this time as a shutter and presented more explicitly as an exterior view, but again in the Ionic mode, though without the fluting in the columns.

The acts of the play were separated by intermedii during which the backshutters, showing the shoreline and the sea, parted to reveal the cut-out scenes of the seasons, based on etchings by Tempesta. All of the relieve drawings are by Jones, and most are ruled up for enlargement in a similar way, giving a height of ten ruled squares in six inches on the paper. The second temple shutter design differs markedly from the rest in this respect, being ruled seven squares high and as many wide. Most of the relieve drawings, besides being in Jones's hand, are titled by him; but they belong to the group of documents relating principally to the scenic drama which Webb appears to have gathered together and reclassified (see chapter 1, pp. 18–20 above). Webb added his own, more generic, titles in chalk, and renumbered the relieve designs by striking out Jones's figures and replacing them with new ones. Thus the first relieve of the production (O & S 328) is not one of the seasons series, but the temple of Diana, part of the play's emblematic Introduction. Jones labelled it simply 'Tempell of Diana for yᵉ pastorall of Florimene 1635' and did not number it; his numbered sequence began with the 'Scene of winter' (O & S 329), perhaps included an unlabelled design for spring based on Tempesta (O & S 330), and continued with '3 somer' and '4 Autome' (O & S 331 and 332). All these titles are in Jones's hand, in ink, and identify the subjects of the drawings. Webb renumbered them, striking out 1, 3 and 4 and replacing the figures with 2, 4 and 5, so including in his sequence the introductory temple of Diana. In the margin of this design he added in chalk 'The first Releiue', placing the words carefully around the original title so that we may now be quite sure that his note was made after Jones's title had been written on the sheet. In a similar fashion he entered, in chalk, a generic title beneath each of Jones's subject titles, adding the word 'Releiue' to each. On O & S 327, untitled by Jones, he wrote 'The shutter [o]f ye Isle of [D]elos being for [y]e standing sceane', and on O & S 333, not in Jones's hand but showing the temple of Diana, he wrote '6th sceane the 2.d Temple of Diana a shutter'. Thus Webb reordered Jones's drawings, and by adding O & S 333 to the set aimed to include the entire series in his sequence.

The group of drawings relating to the production of *Florimène* thus constitutes a major part of two separate collections whose provenance can be traced back to Webb: the scene designs at Chatsworth are classified and endorsed by him, and the four architectural drawings form the largest section of his folio of theatre plans in the Lansdowne MS. Together they reveal his abiding interest in what he saw as a peculiarly instructive production, one worth going over again and again in later years as the fount of much practical information. The two demonstration diagrams and the detailed plan of the stage provide the commentary, but the plan of the hall and the section of the stage are the text, and if Webb himself found them worthy of analysis we should in our turn be prepared to weigh them with some care.

The large *Florimène* plan is evidently a working drawing of the same type as the design for the Paved Court Theatre. It provides a scale, but also helpfully gives many of the key dimensions on the drawing itself, so that it is not necessary to mediate most of the measurements through the scale bar. At first glance the plan appears to show an *ad hoc* proportioning of the parts of a neo-Serlian theatre fitted up within the well used Tudor building whose dimensions it so conveniently records for us. The arrangement of galleried auditorium, forestage and two part scenic stage which it shows is rigidly subordinated to the given proportions of the hall, in the manner of the Christ Church theatre of 1605, though with an opposite orientation. Here the elevated stage is placed in front of the existing and presumably Tudor hall screen, and access is provided from the minstrels' gallery above by way of a set of steps with eleven risers to the topmost parts of an upper stage where, according to the 'Argument' of the play, a number of deities were revealed among the clouds in the last act. The stage floor is divided into two parts by a backshutter assembly with grooves for two pairs of shutters. Between this and the backcloth the deepest part of the scene is equipped with supports for scenes of relieve. The main stage is 23 ft deep in front of the shutters, and set with fixed angle wings of the Serlian type. The frontispiece is reared 7 ft 2 in from its front, its supports marked as '3 fo 8' wide. At either end of the broad strip of the forestage is a small box, probably for the music, containing three degrees whose height above the stage is evidently indicated by lines marked across them in the easterly set which show the degree closest to the wall to be 4 ft high above the forestage. In the plan, no access is marked from the forestage to the area of the hall floor immediately at its foot, called the 'piazza' by Serlio and Simon Basil. This is 20 ft wide and 8 ft 2 in deep, and is flanked to either side by a range of nine degrees, the easterly set containing a separate box. The auditorium proper consists of a rectangular orchestra at the level of the hall floor, flanked on three sides by ranges of eight degrees. Above the back five degrees of each range a gallery is raised, presumably containing a further five degrees. Boxes are marked in some of the bays defined by the gallery posts, and in the western range close to the hall entrance from the royal apartments a vomitory 3 ft 4 in wide is marked as cutting through the five lower degrees in the bottom range. It seems likely therefore that the risers of the degrees were at least 1 ft 2 in, yielding a minimum headroom of 7 ft beneath the sixth row. Some of the box partitions extend from the back wall as far as the gallery posts, while others are carried forward even into two of the three degrees on the orchestra side of the posts. Stairs are marked in lead, and – on a flap – in ink, leading up into the galleries, each set containing twenty-three risers, though these are variously arranged. There is a ladder in the bay window, presumably for the same purpose. Partitions are marked at the stage end of the galleries. The halpace for the state, 11 ft wide by 7 ft 8 in deep, occupies the south end of the orchestra and is approached at the front by steps with three risers; at its back and sides it is bounded by a railing.

All these complex features are brought together within the fixed limits provided by the sturdy walls of Wolsey's hall, their arrangement broadly following that of Serlio's scheme, though sophisticated at the stage end by the two-level changeable backscene, in the auditorium by the upraised galleries reminiscent of the Elizabethan and Jacobean private theatres and between the two by a proscenium border or frontispiece. Yet there is nothing approximate or *ad hoc* about the *Florimène* theatre. Webb here, as in nearly all his architectural designs, plays the geometer, developing the plan and section according to principles not merely of utility or pleasure but of rational measurement too, so that the parts of the whole relate to each other in specific harmony. For all the practical difficulties that must have been encountered in the design, this theatre is at least as coherently ordered as that of the Paved Court three years earlier, its parts meticulously proportioned in a series of simple ratios which take their departure, as humanist theatres had done since the time of Vitruvius, from the width of the orchestra. And in his few written dimensions Webb offers the exact minimum necessary to indicate the thorough-going proportionality of his design.

The width of the orchestra is given in the *Florimène* plan by the addition of that of the state, marked as '11 foott', and the two parts of the orchestra flanking it, '2 fo 2' and '2 f 2', for a total of 15 ft 4 in. The depth of the stage is marked as '23 foott', and it will be observed that this measure is exactly half as much again as the width of the orchestra. This same measure of 23 ft (or 143.5 mm on the sheet)[23] is repeated as the width of the auditorium between the gallery fronts as indicated by their supporting posts, but in this case the dimension is not specifically noted by Webb. Similarly the depth of the orchestra from the front degree behind the state to the edge of the piazza is 143.5 mm on the paper, or 23 ft by the scale. Thus the orchestra floor is a rectangle 15 ft 4 in by 23 ft, proportioned 2:3. The depth of the piazza scales at 8 ft 2 in, while the forestage is marked as 7 ft 2 in deep for a total once more of 15 ft 4 in between the orchestra and the frontispiece. In the section the overall height of the frontispiece above the hall floor scales at 30 ft 8 in (no written dimensions are given on this drawing), or twice the width of the orchestra. The smallest expression in the drawings of a fraction of the orchestra width appears to be the depth of the three degrees between the orchestra and the gallery posts, 3 ft 10 in or one-quarter of 15 ft 4 in. If, for the sake of convenience, we call this measure U, the standard width of the orchestra will be 4U, its depth 6U. The width of the auditorium between the galleries is also 6U, and the depth of the orchestra from the piazza to the rear gallery is 7U. The distance between the galleries and the frontispiece (i.e. the depth of the piazza and forestage taken together) is 4U. The stage is 6U from its front to the backshutters and the frontispiece is 8U high.[24] Some smaller details are incorporated into the scheme. The gallery bay divisions, marked by the posts, are approximately 2U wide, but in fact vary a little from bay to bay: nevertheless, in expressing the gallery fronts as $3\frac{1}{2}$ bays from end to end and 3 bays across the auditorium they signify the actual proportionality of this part of the theatre.[25] Both alternative staircases are erected within corner posts set out in a square 2U each way. And finally, although the halpace for the state is 11 ft across, it measures 7 ft 8 in (2U) from front to rear, including the steps by which it is mounted.

The width of the bays of the Tudor hall is not precisely known, but because there were six of them distributed along the 92 ft length of the building, measured between the centres of its end walls, we have already estimated them at 15 ft 4 in. It is possible therefore that Webb took his measure for the theatre scheme from the fabric of the hall itself; if so the depth of the stage at 23 ft was equal to $1\frac{1}{2}$ bays, and the standard interval, used for the width of the orchestra, was taken from the width of a single bay.

Two further measures are repeated in the plan, though they seem not to be proportioned to the orchestra width: the depth of the orchestra measured from the rear gallery rail to the front of the forestage is 218 mm on the sheet, which is also the length of the scale bar and indicates 35 ft; and the depth of the galleries on all three sides of the auditorium is 51 mm, or 8 ft 2 in. Added together as the full depth of the auditorium they come to 43 ft 2 in, as Webb observes in the most prominent of his annotations: '43 fo 2 inches from the wall to the stage'. Since the piazza is also 51 mm (8 ft 2 in) deep the length of the range of degrees between it and the back wall is likewise 218 mm (35 ft). Webb's written dimensions are scanty, but they are enough to enable us to deduce the rational organization of his design without recourse to detailed scaling. The plan declares its proportionality through the marked measures, supplemented only by the overall size of the scale bar. We merely have to note that the depth of the galleries from the back wall to the piazza is the same as the length of the scale bar to conclude by subtraction that the piazza is 8 ft 2 in deep. We then add the marked '7 fo 2' of the forestage to discover that the frontispiece is 15 ft 4 in from the galleries, the same as the marked total width of the orchestra. Likewise we note that the distance from the rear gallery front to the stage equals that of the scale bar, and conclude that the galleries are, like the piazza, 8 ft 2 in deep. Observing that the width of the orchestra between the gallery fronts is the same as the marked '23 foott' of the depth of the stage, we can calculate the width of the hall as 39 ft 4 in (23 ft + 2(8 ft 2 in)). From this it would appear that the width of the scenic opening in the frontispiece is intended to be just 30 ft (39 ft 4 in less twice the '4 fo 8' marked for the distance between the opening and the wall), though in fact the dimension as drawn scales at a few inches less.[26] On the whole, because distortions in the paper may have altered the drawing in the three and a half centuries since it was made, it is better to trust the written dimensions than those scaled exactly from the sheet, and Webb provides just enough of them to make such an approach possible.

In fact the rectilinearity of the auditorium end of the plan is now no longer quite true, and the orchestra itself is a little wider at the south end than the north, scaling accurately at the marked dimension of 15 ft 4 in only across its centre. Yet if this distortion is caused by the instability of the paper, it is clear that the drawing of the outer walls of the hall was deliberately rendered out of true by the draftsman, for a departure from the scored underdrawing may be seen at both ends of the piazza, tracing the walls as they turn a little westerly as they approach the northern (scene) end of the building. Accordingly the area behind the shutters is not quite a true rectangle, and although it is just 143.5 mm deep at its eastern side (scaling at 23 ft, the same as the depth of the main stage), it is somewhat shorter than that measured along the western wall. The internal length of the hall is therefore 89 ft 2 in at the east side (or 43 ft 2 in + 23 ft + 23 ft), and a little less at the west. The width of the piazza cannot be calculated from the annotations, but scales at exactly 20 ft.

The scale bar of the plan represents 35 ft by 218 mm, or almost exactly 1:49. This is a most unusual ratio, though not perhaps quite out of the question. Draftsmen sometimes scaled their drawings after a geometrical procedure on the paper had established the size of an important dimension, with a resultant appearance of irrationality. Nevertheless it seems likely that in this case the cause of the irregularity is nothing more mysterious than paper shrinkage. If the sheet on which Webb made his drawing has shrunk by about 2 per cent – a common occurrence in old documents – the apparent scale will have decreased from an original, and far more usual, 1:48, or four feet to the inch. There are several indications that this is so. First, it is what we should expect from the type of scale (1:72, or six feet to the inch) in the analogous Paved Court Theatre plan. Next, the companion section of the *Florimène* scene has a scale bar representing 35 ft in 219.5 mm, or 1:48.6. It appears that this sheet also has shrunk, but not quite so much as the plan. Again, Jones's complete elevation of the stage and standing scene is drawn within carefully ruled lead lines which show its scale to be approximately 1:36, three feet to the inch, a ratio of the same common type. Moreover in Webb's plan the degrees on all three sides of the auditorium scale at 12 ft deep from the wall to the orchestra, and while this interval is only 74.5 mm on the sheet as it now exists, it would have been exactly 3 in if the original were scaled at 1:48.

The depth of the auditorium from its back wall to the front edge of the piazza is 218 mm on the sheet, or exactly 35 ft, a distance which may be expressed as 12 ft for the depth of the degrees at the back of the house, plus 23 ft for the depth of the orchestra. Likewise the internal width of the hall, which scales at 39 ft 4 in, may be expressed as the sum of the depth of both sets of lateral degrees (2 × 12 ft) plus the width of the orchestra between them (15 ft 4 in). But a further repeated measurement is found in the depth of the piazza and of the galleries on all three sides of the auditorium. Each is 51 mm on the sheet, scaling at 8 ft 2 in, an interval which is related to the 23 ft width of the auditorium between the galleries by a simple *ad quadratum* construction. If a circle 23 ft in diameter (or 11 ft 6 in radius) is drawn with its centre in line with the stage ends of the galleries, its circumference touching the gallery fronts, and a square is inscribed within it, the side of the square closest to the scene defines the location of the stage front, 8 ft 2 in from the centre (11 ft 6 in ÷ √2 = 8 ft 2 in). This construction is similar in principle to that used by Jones at the Cockpit in Drury Lane (plate 8), and represents a modification of the system used by Serlio, where the piazza is as deep as the radius of the orchestra and the width of the orchestra is proportioned *ad quadratum* to the width of the whole theatre. The remainder of the *Florimène* plan is constructed from a repetition of these dimensions which might have been achieved in a variety of ways through geometrical development on the paper, though the precise ones used are now probably beyond recovery. In our earlier analysis we found it useful to christen with the letter U a module of one-sixth of the repeated 23 ft measure; to this we may now add P for the related piazza or gallery depth of 8 ft 2 in. The width of the hall, which scales at 39 ft 4 in, may therefore be expressed as P + 6U + P, the auditorium being 6U wide between the gallery fronts. The orchestra floor is 6U deep, and from the rear gallery front to the piazza is 7U. The distance from the back wall to the stage is therefore P + 7U + P (43 ft 2 in by the scale and Webb's annotation). The stage is 6U deep to the shutters, and a further 6U to the back wall of the hall beyond the screens, so that the interior length of the building may be expressed as P + 19U + P (or 89 ft 2 in by the scale). The piazza and forestage combined are 4U (15 ft 4 in) and the distance from the frontispiece to the shutters is 2U + P (15 ft 10 in). All these proportional relations, derived though they are from an original *ad quadratum* construction on the paper, may be read from the drawing, as we have seen, directly from Webb's written annotations supplemented only by an occasional reference to the whole length of the scale bar.

None of this perhaps rather laborious demonstration would be necessary if it were obvious from the start that the *Florimène* plan was a theoretical rather than a practical scheme. Designers have always delighted in the use of the foot-rule and the dividers, and if the drafting procedure I have indicated is not all visibly recorded on the present sheet – the actual constructions, with their pricked centres and guiding lines having been made on a preparatory study and not transferred – the drawing is only like a thousand others in the modular and geometrical quality of its development. But there can be little doubt that the *Florimène* plan is indeed a practical drawing, with its workmanlike cancellations, revisions and notations, and its firm geometrical basis is therefore of special interest, for it indicates that Webb proceeded from a theoretical base towards his practical goal, rather than vice versa.

25 Inigo Jones, standing scene for *Florimène*

He desired, that is, to relate the gallery depths to the width of the auditorium in an *ad quadratum* proportion akin to the system he had planned for the Paved Court, though a little sophisticated in response to the special constraints of the comparatively long and narrow Tudor hall within which he had to work. That he chose this geometric construction, with its incommensurate $\sqrt{2}$ proportions, rather than a more strictly Vitruvian modular system of planning is a fact of some interest, for it shows that his thinking was deeply influenced by the Serlian model, where a related *ad quadratum* method is followed. For all its superficial air of improvisation, the *Florimène* plan is as painstakingly developed a design as any in the Jones/Webb canon.

Where the Paved Court stage offered a shallow raked area for the scene, with fixed flat wings and no elevated forestage, the *Florimène* plan shows something deeper, with angled 'book' wings like those in the Somerset House designs, and room for more dramatic action than the mere entry and exit of the players. The inner faces of the wings form orthogonals which, when projected to their vanishing point, meet exactly on the surface of the backcloth, some 8 ft 8 in beyond the shutters. When they are projected forwards beyond the frontispiece these orthogonal lines meet the walls of the auditorium exactly at their junction with the front of the forestage. Thus the angled wings are located on the sides of a triangle whose base is the full width of the stage front and whose apex is at the centre of the backcloth. This deep scene was given practicable access to the piazza and orchestra, for although none of the plans includes them, the stage was apparently cut away at the centre to make room for two sets of steps leading down to the floor of the hall. These are shown in Jones's major proscenium design (plate 25) as having six risers apiece; Webb's section of the stage shows it to have been 4 ft 6 in high at the front, so that each riser of the steps would have been 9 in high.[27]

It seems likely that most of the action of the play took place within the area between the wings, on that part of the stage which lay behind the frontispiece. Few scenes involved more than three or four actresses at a time, save for those which showed a crowd of shepherds and shepherdesses clustering about the temple of Diana, which we know to have been upstage, located beyond the backshutters. None of the action of the pastoral proper requires a descent into the orchestra, an approach to the state or even the use of the piazza. The intermedii, on the other hand, all contain dances performed by various groups of figures, old men, lovers, reapers and satyrs, and these will certainly have been performed at floor level, probably in the orchestra. The play dramatized the customary neo-Platonic pastoral theme of the illusory confusions through which lovers must pass on their way towards achieving their desires, and most of it, like *Artenice*, appears to have been contained within the illusionistic world of the scene itself; but the intermedii of the seasons, which illustrated the progression from love's cruelty to its fruition by moving from images of winter to ones of autumn, broke out of that world in two directions: upstage through the backshutters to the scenic relieves, and downstage to the dancing place at the foot of the degrees in the auditorium. The whole construction had an air of deliberate artifice, for the contained, illusionist stage of the pastoral itself expanded at certain moments of ritual, once into the relieve area with the first representation of Diana's temple, and twice into the upper stage: in the second act for Diana's descent in a chariot, and again at the end of the play when the upper cloud shutters parted to reveal an assembly of deities gathered to bless the Delian marriages about to take place below.

A few of Jones's designs for the *Florimène* settings and especially his drawing of the standing scene and the frontispiece (plate 25) contribute directly to our understanding of the auditorium and the way in which the dimensions of the scene were integrated with those of the theatre. The most telling clue to the visual ordering of any perspective scene is the height of its horizon, and therefore of the vanishing point of its orthogonals. At some time in the 1620s Jones appears to have adopted, at least for plays, a two-horizon system in which the rake of the stage was shallow and implied a low vanishing point, while on the backshutters and relieves an altogether higher horizon was painted, pitched at the height of an actor or actress as measured at the front of the forestage. In this way the stage was given a rake sufficiently shallow to permit it to be used as a practicable acting space, but its low horizon, though repeated in the foreshortening of the wings, was modified at the shutters and relieves, whose treatment closed the scene in a more painterly fashion. *Florimène* closely follows this dual scheme, which is of course irrational if judged by the strict standards of perspective scenography, but permits a compromise to be effected between the theatrical criterion of a horizon pitched at the level of the chief onlooker's eye and the painterly criterion, taught by Alberti, of a horizon pitched at the height of a figure in the foreground of the scene. The shallow rake to the stage shown in Webb's section for *Florimène* (plate 22) is 1 in 23; in the plan the wing feet, which we may assume to be orthogonal, converge towards a vanishing point 8 ft 8 in beyond the shutters. This point must therefore be 8.67 ÷ 23 ft above the foot of the shutters, or about 4½ in. At a total of 5 ft 10½ in above the hall floor this horizon and its vanishing point appear to have been pitched at the same level as the king's eye as he sat enthroned in his state at the further end of the orchestra. The state stood on a halpace mounted by steps with three risers to the front; if these were 8 in each and the platform 2 ft high, the seated king would have been elevated just high enough to look horizontally towards the vanishing point of the raked stage and its wings.

The low horizon of the stage is however nothing like what Jones caused to be painted on his backshutters. In the standing scene design the groove assembly dividing the two levels of backshutters is lightly indicated in the sky to the left of the centre of the drawing, while the foot of the lower shutters may be estimated to lie immediately behind the furthest cottage wings. Exactly bisecting the height of the backshutters, so defined, the horizon of the sea surrounding the Isle of Delos establishes, in as literal and direct a fashion as may be, the visual horizon of the backscene itself. *The Argvment of the Pastorall of 'Florimene'* goes some way towards confirming this relation between the geographical horizon and that of the perspective when it describes the scene: '. . . and a farr off, to terminate the sight, was the mayne *Sea*, expressing this place to be the Isle of *Delos*'. In one sense it is the backshutters which 'terminate the sight'; but in the vista they represent, that function belongs to the clearly established horizon of 'the mayne *Sea*'. If the frontispiece design be thought insufficiently precise to indicate the exact elevation of this marine horizon on the backshutters, Jones's detailed shutter design (O & S 327) reinforces the point: the horizon is shown exactly halfway up the drawing. In his section of the scene, Webb shows the backshutters as 10 ft high, and mounted on grooves which elevate them a little above the height of the backstage to just 5 ft above the floor of the hall. Halfway up these shutters, the horizon lay 5 ft 6 in above the stage front, or 10 ft above the hall floor.

The relieve designs, though not entirely consistent with one another, are broadly compatible with those for the shutters in establishing a horizon halfway up the shutter opening. The drawings for the temple of Diana and for the four seasons are all ruled up for enlargement, and the four of them titled by Jones and further annotated by Webb are ruled into ten squares high, answering to the 10 ft height of the opening. O & S 329 and 332 are 13 squares wide, while 331 is 12½ squares wide. In the hall plan the backshutter opening is noted as '13 fo:' across. One relieve – O & S 328, of the temple of Diana – is only 12 squares wide, and this is scaled with foot divisions showing that each ruled square is one foot across. It must have been modified a little in the execution to fit the 13 ft opening. In two of these clearly identified studies the horizon is shown halfway up the composition (O & S 329 and 331), and in a third (O & S 328) the orthogonals converge towards a vanishing point at the same elevation. In the fourth (O & S 332) it is only four squares up. Of the two remaining studies, one (O & S 330) is untitled and divided into six by thirteen squares in the lower half only. The relieve is constructed in two parts, with low pavilions in the foreground leading the eye towards a villa at the rear. The 'orthogonals' of the pavilions overlap but share the same horizon as the villa and its immediate surroundings, pitched about five squares high. The other drawing (O & S 333) though annotated by Webb is without a title by Jones and is not from his hand; it is ruled up 7 squares high by 7 squares wide, and its carefully maintained vanishing point is 2½ squares up. It may have been intended only as a subordinate part of a larger shutter design.

The evidence of the relieves, with the exception of O & S 332 and discounting the possibly anomalous O & S 333, generally supports that of the designs for the standing scene, which place the back horizon exactly halfway up the shutters, and therefore 5 ft (represented by five ruled squares in some cases) above the grooves, or 5 ft 6 in above the stage front. Such a height, 10 ft above the floor of the hall, bears no relation to the elevation of the king's eye as he sat in his place on the relatively shallow state at the opposite end of the orchestra. Thus there is nothing in the relieve designs to show that Jones sought to integrate the back horizon with a fixed station point in the auditorium, though of course, as we have seen, the wings and stage floor, with their separate and lower horizon, very probably did align in this fashion with the monarch's eye. Nevertheless the height of the shutter horizon is not without some proportionate relation to the rest of the theatre, at least to the frontispiece. The height of the scenic opening at 22 ft above the stage front is just four times the height of the horizon, and the width of the border, given as '3 ft 8' in the hall plan and scaling the same through its entablature in the section, is two-thirds of that height. Alberti, in counselling the painter to establish his horizon at the height of a human figure placed in the foreground of his composition, divided that height into three braccia;[28] in Alberti's terms, therefore, the *Florimène* frontispiece has an opening twelve braccia high; its border is two braccia wide; and its back horizon is three braccia above the level of the forestage.

Webb's section of the scene gives other indications that its proportions were related to those of the theatre as a whole. The overall height of the frontispiece above the floor of the hall is 30 ft 8 in, or just twice the width of the orchestra, whose measure we have found to be the standard used in the plan. This is however no more than a straightforward commensurate link between the frontispiece and the auditorium, and does not affect the scene proper. But the schematic section of the stage (plate 24) shows Webb carefully noting a horizon rather lower than that indicated by Jones's sketches, and yet similarly related to the proportionality of the auditorium. He modifies the continuously raked stage of the working drawings, replacing its front part with a flat forestage in the Serlian manner, 4 ft 6 in high like the front of the original, and raked only in the part behind the frontispiece. He also rules what is clearly intended to be a horizon line, extending it from a station point in the auditorium 27 ft from the frontispiece and pitched at a level which he marks as '3:fo:2:ʸ' above the '4:fo:½' of the forestage, for a total elevation of 7 ft 8 in above the floor of the hall. This elevation is one-quarter that of the top of the frontispiece, and is related to the standard width of the orchestra (of which it is one-half) and therefore also to the 23 ft depth of the whole stage to the shutters (of which it is one-third).

The proportionality of the *Florimène* hall design is not restricted to the physical structure of the auditorium alone, though this is developed like the Paved Court Theatre as a series of extensions of the width of the orchestra, itself quite possibly a measure taken from the bay divisions of the Tudor building. The frontispiece is absorbed into the system, as is the elevation of the back horizon, so that scene and auditorium alike are unified by the same architectural harmony. The *Florimène* scheme is the most complete example in our early stage history of a theatre designed on principles derived from the humanist architects of Renaissance Italy.

8   The Masquing House at Whitehall

ARLY in 1635 Davenant's *The Temple of Love* was performed in the
Banqueting House at Whitehall. It proved to be the last of the Stuart
masques to be staged in the building, ending a series which had begun with
The Masque of Augurs in 1622, survived the withdrawal of Jonson after *Chloridia*
(1631) and flourished with grand if frequently less potent works by Townshend,
Shirley, Carew and Davenant.

In September 1637 a warrant was issued for a vast new Masquing House to be
erected between the Banqueting House and the great chamber of the palace.[1] Its
announced purpose was to relieve the Rubens panels in the ceiling of the
Banqueting House from the attacks of smoke and condensation caused by the
torches of the masques and doubtless by their crowded audiences, but it is possible
also that it was intended to offer a better, because wooden, alternative to the
echoing acoustics of Inigo Jones's noble room. Such at any rate was the opinion of
Balthazar Gerbier, writing in Restoration times about such *salles des fetes*:

Neither can all great Rooms of Princely Palaces serve for this use, except they be after the
Moddell of such as the Italians have built, as there is a good one at *Florence* in *Italy*, with
conveyances for Smoak, and capacities for Ecchoes, which *Inigo Jones* (the late Surveyor)
experimentally found at *Whitehall*, and by his built Banquetting House, so as having found his
own fault, he was constrained to Build a Woodden House overthwart the Court of *Whitehall*.[2]

The name of the Masquing House describes its purpose, as does its less respectful
nickname, 'the Queen's Dancing Barn'. It was never used for the production of the
drama proper, and strictly speaking lies beyond the scope of this book. But Webb
made two detailed drawings of its stage (plates 26 and 27) which, besides recording
something of the layout of the building, comprehensively illustrate the sliding-wing
system of changeable scenery which Jones was beginning to introduce into his
dramatic as well as his masquing stages. In addition, the drawings throw some light
on the particular quality of Webb's interest in theatre design at a time when Jones
was at the height of his influence both as scenographer and as architect, and his
pupil had yet to undertake the first independent commissions of which we have any
certain notice.[3] No subsequent theatre design appears to have come from Jones's
hand, so that the Masquing House represents his last if not his deliberately final
recorded thoughts on the matter. In 1638–9, at the instigation of the Lord
Chamberlain, he was to return to the Cockpit in Drury Lane to provide it with
scenes, probably for the new company of the King's and Queen's Boys, but there is
no evidence that he then redesigned the auditorium.[4] Webb, on the other hand, was

at the beginning of what was to prove a long theatrical career, ranging from his work on *Cleodora* in 1640 to his conversion of the Hall Theatre at Whitehall twenty-five years later. His drawings of the Masquing House stage ought therefore to be considered if we are to assess his contribution to the theatre projects undertaken by the Works before both his and his master's careers were interrupted by the Parliamentarians. Webb's work as an architect of the Paved Court and *Florimène* auditoria may now be recognized, but neither his facility with the machines and pulleys by which the spectacle of the masques was realized, nor his confidence in composing assured perspective scenes was yet established at the time when the new 'Woodden House' was opened.

From the start the building seems to have been more than a temporary expedient, for it gave scope for the development of scenic machines more elaborate than any that had been used in London: the last entry in *Luminalia*, for example, staged in 1638, consisted of a transparent cloud which 'came forth farre into the Scene' bearing masquers: 'Which Apparition for the newnesse of the Invention, greatnesse of the Machine, and difficulty of Engining, was much admir'd, being a thing not before attempted in the Aire.'[5] Such expensive imagery had its political uses, and the very first scene presented in the Masquing House, the first entry of *Britannia Triumphans*, showed 'a farre off a prospect of the Citie of London, and the River of Thames, which being a principall part, might bee taken for all great Britaine'.[6] At the centre of this perspective synecdoche, taken from the south to the north, lay the great pile of St Paul's, on whose fabric Inigo Jones was currently at his restorative work. Webb prepared a more practical version of Jones's original fluent scene design, more closely in accord with the description given in Davenant's text and therefore probably the one that was actually used, and in it the Globe Theatre appears, neatly aligned with St Paul's west end. Thus the scene with which the Masquing House opened confronted the audience with two pillars of Stuart cultural policy: the Laudian reformation associated with the renewal of St Paul's, and the humbler but hardly less attractive institution of the King's Men at the Globe.

Not even so auspicious an opening could however obscure the fact that the house was built in a difficult, indeed a disastrous, period. It served for a series of three spectacular masques – *Britannia Triumphans*, *Luminalia* and *Salmacida Spolia* – before all such activity ceased under the Commonwealth, and it was torn down for its valuable materials in 1645, less than eight years after it had been built. In its time it must have been an imposing presence, for it was both large and prominently sited. In November 1637 Sir John Finett wrote to Viscount Scudamore:

This fabrick is placed . . . wythin some ten foot of the bancetting howse, extending in lenght toward the hall and gard chamber about a hundred and ten foot, in bredth: ten or twelue foot into the fyrst court; and about fyve and forty into that of the preaching place.[7]

As to size, the Works accounts for the building, first published by Glynne Wickham, give more precise information:

. . . for building of a greate new *Masking roome att Whitehall* being Cxij foote long lvij[en] foote wide lix foote high to the raising plate . . .[8]

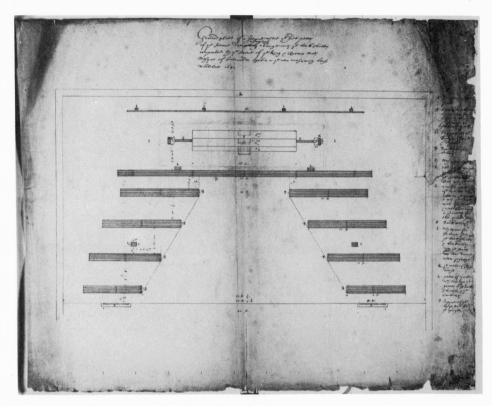

26   John Webb, plan of the Masquing House stage

Since, as the accounts make clear, the building was of timber, we may allow about a foot for the thickness of its walls, and it appears that the interior was to be a room approximately 55 ft by 110 ft, just the size of the Banqueting House itself. Webb's two drawings, in BL Lansdowne MS 1171, are a plan and section of the stage set up in the Masquing House for *Salmacida Spolia* in 1640 (plates 26 and 27). Their chief interest is of course their depiction of the scenic machinery, which included winches, ropes and pulleys for ascents and descents, but Webb also gives some dimensions relevant to the structure of the frame of the house. Its width he registers at 55 ft 9 in internally, and he shows a 'roofe' over his scene – a kind of grid – rising at the rear to 47 ft above the floor. The stage is 7 ft high at its front, high enough to accommodate one set of winches beneath it, and 31 ft deep from front to rear. No hint is given of the arrangement of the auditorium.

Not only was the plan of this timber house uncommonly large, its height was so great as almost to beggar belief. According to the Works account it measured 'lix foote high to the raising plate . . .' (i.e. to the top of the walls by the eaves). Webb's section of the scene alludes to a 'vault' beneath the floor of the main room tall enough to house winches for the ascent machinery upstage; if the 47 ft high scenic 'roofe' took up the whole interior height of the room, and the floor and joists

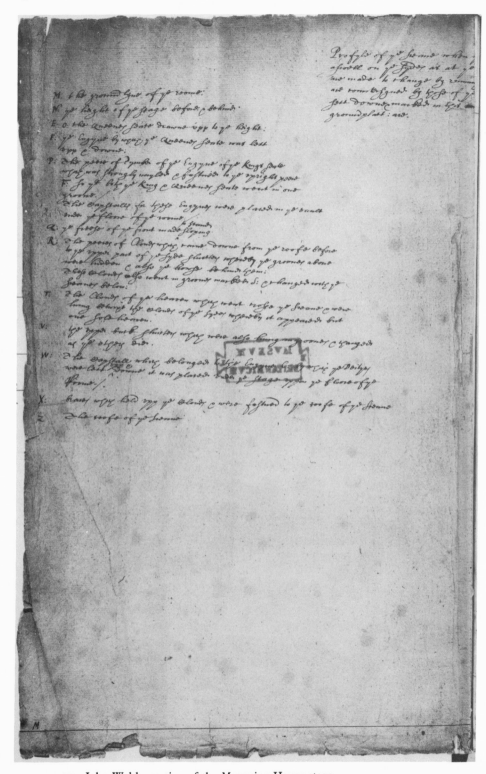

27   John Webb, section of the Masquing House stage

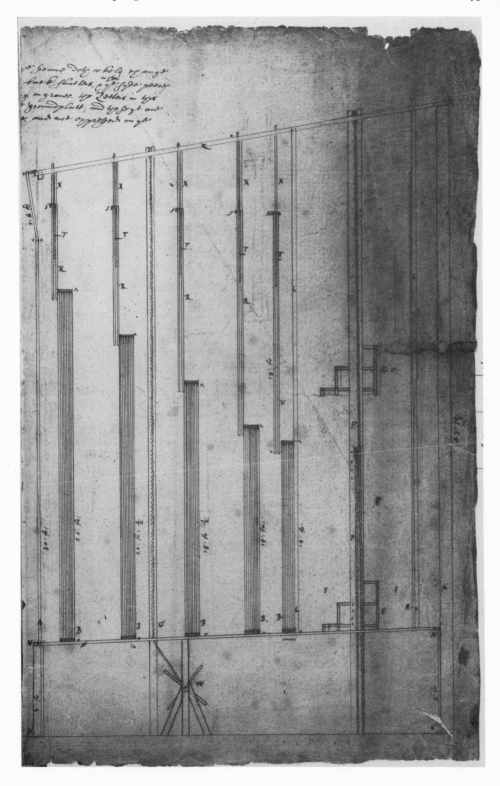

between them were a foot thick, the basement might have afforded 11 ft of headroom even without excavation. Nevertheless the height of the building as recorded in the Works account, and largely confirmed by Webb's section, is little less than astonishing: with a pantiled roof above the plates pitched as low as 35° the altitude of the ridge would have well over 80 ft, a dizzy rise for a timber structure.

A building as large as this would surely have been noticed by an artist making a detailed prospect of Whitehall during the eight years it stood in its prominent place. Yet Hollar's neat, if not altogether accurate, etching of Whitehall seen from across the river gives no sign of it,[9] and of course later views like those of Jacob Esselens[10] show its site as a void space. But in the depiction of Whitehall in Hollar's great etching, the *Long View of London*, we do see something of the Masquing House (plate 1). It is shown to the far side of the great hall, its long axis running roughly southeast and northwest, its further end located between the Banqueting House to the left and the guard chamber to the right. It is a tall, single ridged roof with gable ends, taller than the great hall itself, above the top of whose roof we see it, yet not so tall as the Banqueting House. Its ridge reaches just to the height of the lower part of the cornice of the Banqueting House, or about 60 ft as judged against the building as it now stands.[11] It appears that Hollar deliberately reduced its size to avoid outscaling its handsomer neighbours. Certainly it is intended for the Masquing House, for no other building stood on this site during the years (1636–44) when the artist was making his preparatory drawings for the *Long View*.

Besides looming vast the Masquing House was, in Finett's deliberately chosen word, 'stately':

Wee haue a stately buylding toward in Whytehall (but more stately for forme and use then for matter or substance being all of wood) . . .[12]

If was expensive: Garrard reported its cost as £2,500, and the Works accounts authoritatively (if inaccurately, for the sums do not all add up) give it as £2,142-15-10, though this amount did not include the specific production costs of *Britannia Triumphans*. Unfortunately Hollar's viewpoint allowed him to give no hint of the location and type of the twenty windows mentioned in the accounts:

. . . for working framing and setting vpp of Tenn windowes of firtymber in the lower part of the said roome at vij^s the peece and Tenn windowes likewise in the vpper part of the said roome at xj^s the peece . . .[13]

Inside the house there was a deal floor divided into two parts: the cheaper work beneath the stage was $9\frac{1}{2}$ squares (or 950 ft^2), while the remainder amounted to $53\frac{1}{2}$ squares (5,350 ft^2), the total falling just a little short of the external area covered by the whole house, 6,384 ft^2. The stage must have been originally a good deal smaller than that shown by Webb in his drawings for *Salmacida Spolia*: there it ran all across the room and was some 31 ft deep, with an area of 1,728.25 ft^2, more than 80 per cent larger than that mentioned in the Works account of 1637–8. The interior walls were lined with whole deal boards, their joints battened with slit deal, and overhead was stretched a blue cloth velarium amounting to 411 ells, or about 4,624 ft², enough to cover the whole of the auditorium, assuming that 30 ft of the length of the room was devoted to the stage and scenes.

On the verso of one of Jones's drawings for *Britannia Triumphans* there is a fragmentary list, spoiled by cropping, of workmen engaged on building the Masquing House and fitting it out for its first production.[14] It gives a wonderful sense of the teeming business of the project: twenty men on the roof, twenty more on the quartering (the construction of the walls), twelve on the windows, twelve boarding the floor, with eight assistants readying the boards for them, twenty constructing the degrees and galleries, ten men at the 'passages att the endes' and eight tilers. On the stage, besides the Master Carpenter, there were twelve men for the shutters and clouds, seven of them named individually. This great cohort – 122 men altogether – was paid, according to the 'Wages and Entertayment' section of the declared account, a total of £603-13-2 at rates ranging from 1s to 2s 6d *per diem*, a sum consistent with Davenant's claim that the building was completed within two months. The list also gives a few details about the structure of the house. It appears that there were access passages or lobbies at the ends which were reached, according to the Works account, by 'ffouer paire of staires to goe vpp into the same roome . . .' That the auditorium had galleries is hardly surprising, but although degrees were called for in the original warrant of 29 September neither they nor the galleries are mentioned in the Works account. It is possible that, as in the Banqueting House and great hall, they were fitted up as a separate task, independent from the main project. They would hardly have been struck and re-erected especially for each production. One part of this fortuitously preserved list of artisans is puzzling, for it calls explicitly for 'the sceane to bee all tiled ouer'. Since the whole building had a tiled roof of nearly 14,000 pantiles and 6,000 Flemish tiles it is not clear why this specific provision was necessary, unless perhaps at the time of the opening the roof was still unfinished. In that case Jones's note would represent a necessary precaution for the protection of his scenes and machines from the mid-winter weather.

The great span of the tiled roof evidently called for special structural measures, for it was 'supported with xij greate Butteresses of ffirtymber'. Although the account specifically reports that the *roof* was thus supported it seems unlikely that the term 'Butteress' would be employed of interior posts, though such a usage is by no means impossible (*OED buttress* 2); rather the thrust of the great open span was taken to either side by a rank of six flying shores of timber, which accordingly divided the house into five large bays, each of which apparently had two windows, for a total altogether of twenty. The interior was thus left clear of structural encumbrances, and the sky cloth could cover the entire auditorium without interruptions.

The Masquing House was the last of the theatres to be designed by Jones, and it served the Caroline Court well in the closing years of the Personal Rule, realizing in urbane and sometimes esoteric imagery the neoplatonic aspirations of the monarch, his policies and his increasingly testy passions. The first scene to be staged in the room represented the unruly follies of a British people abandoned to cheap ballads, mountebanks and incoherent behaviour, and the last was characteristically an ascent of deities singing of exemplary love and harmony to the king and queen left behind to preside over the *terra firma* of the dancing floor. In these masques Jones achieved an artistry of scenic transformation and movement which was both more active and more spectacular than his work of the previous decade. But again it was Webb who made the detailed schematic drawings of the machinery, and it is perhaps tempting to conclude that it was he who put into material execution the dynamic ideas of the Surveyor. The 'invention' was certainly Jones's, but the ropes, the pulleys and the capstans might conceivably have been Webb's.

The matter cannot easily be decided. Webb's two drawings of the stage must be understood in relation to his strange depiction of the scene for *Salmacida Spolia* in O & S 409, where the perspective is handled incompetently. All three sheets contain similar columns of explanatory notes keyed to the drawings (though in the scene design itself the key letters are missing) and chiefly devoted to the mechanics of the stage. The plan and section, both drawn to a scale of 1:48 (four feet to the inch), are minutely exact in almost every detail, while the scene design appears to have shrunk from an original scale of 1:30[15] and is notoriously ill drawn. Between them the plan and section give much information pertinent to the design of the stage. They show that the frontispiece was square overall: 42 ft wide and 42 ft high from the floor to the top of the border. At 7 ft the front of the stage was pitched at one-sixth of the overall height. The width of the scene design is established by ink framing lines drawn over ruled scorings which scale at 38 ft apart, corresponding to the midpoints of the front wing assemblies in the plan, also 38 ft apart. To these points the outer edges of the front wings would come when the flats were thrust inwards to their engaged positions. On the plan Webb marks orthogonal lines connecting the front inner corner of each wing assembly; when projected towards the back of the scene these lines converge a little short of the surface of the backcloth. Similar lines connecting the corners of the second or third wing in each set would converge almost exactly at the backcloth, and it seems likely that the assemblies were arranged so that on average they conformed to an orthogonal system akin to that of the *Florimène* stage.

The wings were of the sliding kind, as Webb notes: 'B The side shutters which runne in groues & change ye sceane 4: severall tymes.' A full explanation of the working of the stage belongs to the history of the masque rather than the drama, and has been given by Orgel and Strong; it was an expensive method, and perhaps for that reason not much employed for the dramatic stage. Neither *The Shepherd's Paradise* nor *Florimène* made use of it, but Jones does appear to have adopted it occasionally for plays, perhaps as early as a performance of Thomas Heywood's *Love's Mistress* at Somerset House in 1634. In his address to the reader Heywood makes a courteous acknowledgment of Jones's contribution, which has otherwise escaped the record:

I cannot pretermit to give a due Charracter to that admirable Artist, Mr. *Inego Jones*, Master-surveyor of the *Kings* work, &c. Who to every Act, nay almost to every Sceane, by his excellent Inventions, gave such an extraordinary Lustre; upon every occasion changing the stage, to the admiration of all the Spectators: that, as I must ingeniously confess, it was above my apprehension to conceive, so to their sacred *Majesties*, and the rest of the Auditory . . .[16]

In claiming that the 'stage' was changed Heywood implies that something more than backshutter and relieve movements were involved; his statement is not at all clear on the matter, but any more comprehensive changes will almost certainly have been effected by means of sliding wings like those in the *Salmacida Spolia* drawings.

Almost two years later such movable wings were used for a performance of Strode's *Floating Island* before the king in the hall at Christ Church, Oxford, and it appears that Jones designed them, perhaps with Webb's assistance. They are described in a contemporary account attributed to Brian Twyne, an Oxford antiquary who had been among those appointed to welcome the king to the city,[17] and was doubtless an eyewitness of the productions he reviews:

A goodly stage made at Christchurch from ye vpper-ende of ye hall allmost to ye hearth, after ye newe fashion with 3 or 4 openinges at ech side thereof, and partitions much resemblinge ye deskes in a library, out of which ye Actors issued forth on ech side, and these partitions they could drawe in at their pleasure vppon a sudden, and thrust out newe in their places accordinge to ye nature of ye scene, like churches, dwellinge houses, pallaces or ye like, which bred great varietie & admiration: and ouer all, delicate payntinge resemblinge ye Cloudes & Sky cullur &c At ye vpper ende, a great fayre shutt of two leaues painted curiously on ye outside that opened and shutt together againe without any visible helpe; within which was set forth ye emblemm of ye whole playe in sumptuous manner to behold: therein was ye perfect resemblance of ye billowes of ye sea rollinge vp & downe, and an artificial Iland with churches & houses, wauinge vp & downe really & floatinge in ye same in one whole peice, ye rockes & trees & hilles, in & about ye shores thereof, in ye playe of ye passions calmed: and, after that many other fine peices of work and landscips at sundry openinges thereof, did appeare; & there was a chayre came glidinge in vppon ye stage without any visible helpe &c. but in ye other playe called ye Royall Slaue where within these shutts as a curious temple and ye sun shininge on it there was much more varietie of ye scene, and curious prospects of forests & ye like, within those great shutts spoken of before, with villages, & men visibly appearinge in them goinge vp & downe here & there, about their businesse &c.[18]

The text of *The Royal Slave*, published in 1639, lists eight 'Appearances' evidently involving five separate backshutter or relieve scenes, set according to Twyne's narrative 'within these shutts . . . within those great shutts spoken of before . . .' For this play Jones[19] seems to have concentrated most of his scenic invention in the area of the relieves, providing 'much more varietie of ye scene' there than was found in the same deep part of the stage as set up for the presentation of the previous day. The side wings prepared for *The Floating Island* were changeable, as well as the backshutters, and evidently the whole scene was frequently changed during the course of the production, precisely in the manner of the later drawings for *Salmacida Spolia*.

It may be, then, that by 1640 Webb was ready to undertake the technical design of a system which to Jones must have become largely a matter of routine, but his two architectural drawings of the stage were made for pedagogical purposes, not for the team of carpenters from the Works. There are no corrections, no *pentimenti*. The comments are explanatory, not exploratory. The dimensions have no lead revisions and both plan and section are as cleanly presented as the demonstration diagrams of the *Florimène* stage (plates 23 and 24), drawings which they closely resemble in technique, and with which they share the same 'grapes' watermark. The title inscribed by Webb on the plan is therefore probably contemporary with the drawing itself and explains its purpose as a memorandum or more likely a teaching device:

Ground platt of a sceane where ye side peeces of ye sceane doe altogether change with ye backshutters comparted by ye sceane of ye King and Queens M*ajesties* Masque of Salmacida Spolia in ye new masquing howse Whitehall 1640.

The title of the section is in a similar pedagogic vein, and confirms the view that these are fair copy drawings, far removed from such original working designs as those for the Paved Court and *Florimène* theatres. They merely record the stage at the Masquing House; they are not designs for it, and may indeed have been drawn years later.

For some years before 1640 Jones had been composing frontispieces for masques whose scenic openings were squared up 34 units wide by 30 high. It is a reasonable assumption that each unit represented one foot, but quite why he should have settled on these precise figures is obscure.[20] Nevertheless he persisted with them. The series began with *Albion's Triumph* in the Banqueting House in 1632, and continued at the same house with *The Triumph of Peace, Coelum Britannicum*[21] (both 1634) and *The Temple of Love* (1635). He appears to have carried on working to the same dimensions in the Masquing House, for although no proscenium design for either *Britannia Triumphans* or *Luminalia* can be adequately scaled, Webb's drawings show that *Salmacida Spolia* was presented within a scenic opening 34 ft wide by 30 ft tall. This exact conformity to the established pattern suggests that the stage was made either immediately to Jones's direction or under his very precise guidance, and the design cannot be claimed as Webb's even though the drawings are from his hand.

Yet if Webb was here concerned to memorialize the achievements of the Caroline spectacle, he was also actively engaged in its production. Some of his sketches at this period are working pieces, such as the relieve scene of the City of Sleep for *Luminalia* (O & S 386), which is unfinished and cursorily titled. It is likely that his design for the opening scene of *Britannia Triumphans* is the one that was actually used, for it agrees with Davenant's text in showing trees among the suburban houses of London. But nowhere at this date do we find a Webb drawing of that probing, experimental kind represented by Jones's sketch of the great cloud in *Salmacida Spolia* (O & S 407), to which the artist added the marginal note:

The great cloude which comes fourth and opens and discovers ye Queens seeatte in a bright cloude To trye yf this great cloude may come do[u]ne betwene the groufes and then bee drawne open, and whether ye shutters and this great cloude may not bee drawne away boath togeather.

Here Jones is thinking first of the image he requires, and secondly of the technical means he might use to achieve it, and the second concern, though subordinated to the first, is clearly capable of modifying it. Webb's comments, on the plan, the section and all the other drawings connected with productions in the Masquing House show none of this exploratory mood, nor are they for the most part prescriptive. Generally their purpose seems to be analytic, and there is little evidence that at this stage in his career Webb was actively contributing to the 'Invention, Ornament, Sceans and Apparitions' which 'were made by Inigo Jones, Surveyor Generall of his Majesties Workes'.[22]

9   An unidentified theatre project

IT IS THE FATE of many architectural schemes never to rise from the paper on which they are drawn. Moreover those that are realized in wood and brick are the ones that will be kept on file, for nothing succeeds like success, and even as paper the failures are the more likely to perish. Each of the projects we have examined so far in this book was actually built, if not quite in the form represented by the extant drawings, but there will have beeen others, theoretical or even merely speculative projects perhaps, which flourished only in the imagination of their authors and now are entirely lost. Many will never have been more than rough sketches on light paper. The drawings that survive are for the most part quite the opposite: painstakingly prepared on heavy and expensive rag, they were always likely candidates for preservation. Just occasionally a more fanciful sort of drawing might receive a similarly thorough treatment and survive because of its high quality. One such is John Webb's scheme for an apparently unrealized scenic theatre based on Palladio's Teatro Olimpico.

At first the design was thought to be by Jones. In 1917 William Grant Keith published one version of the drawings, which he had found inserted between folios 56 and 57 of Jones's copy of Palladio housed in the collection at Worcester College Library.[1] The sheet had been folded and trimmed to fit the pages of the book, forming two folios. On the recto of the first was an inscription, probably in the hand of Dr George Clarke, identifying the drawing as 'The Theatre at Vicenza – designed by Palladio and described at the beginning of his book by Inigo Jones.' The verso contained an elevation and plan of a scenic theatre facing the recto of the second folio on which appeared two half-sections of the Teatro Olimpico in Vicenza, each based on a Palladio drawing in the possession of Jones and now at the RIBA.[2] The final verso was blank.

Keith assumed that the drawings were by Jones, but in fact the watermark is a 'Royal' crest and crown with a pendent B; the counter mark is a crowned AR, indicating that the paper was manufactured in the reign of Queen Anne (1702–14).[3] Howard Colvin has concluded that the whole sheet is a copy by Henry Aldrich of a second set of drawings whose existence was first noticed in print by Simpson and Bell in 1924,[4] though by that date the two sheets had been mounted together at Worcester College Library.

This second group of drawings (plate 28) was recognized by Simpson and Bell as the earlier in date and indeed the object of the Aldrich copy. Where the copy is neatly performed with little underscoring and modelled with wash, the original is extensively underscored and is modelled with ink hatching evidently by John Webb, whose handwriting appears in marginal and other notations. The water-mark of this sheet gives no clue to its date, consisting merely of a nondescript crowned 'Pot' without further identifications. Like the copy it is inscribed, but here the words are in ink over lead, and although the lead is barely visible it resembles Webb's hand: 'The Theater at Vicenza – designed by Palladio – described by Inigo Jones at yᵉ beginning of Palladio.' Then, in ink only and probably in the hand that inked over these words, an attribution: 'This drawing was Mʳ Webbs.'

The two sets of drawings have been adequately distinguished by Harris and Tait in their catalogue of the Worcester College collection, where they are numbered 16A–D (the Aldrich copy) and 15 and 249 (Webb).[5] Unfortunately the catalogue reproduces only the Aldrich copy, not the Webb original, and thus presents to the reader yet again the eighteenth-century reproduction which had been printed by Keith in 1917, by Lily B. Campbell in 1923 and by Richard Leacroft in 1973.[6]

The drawings to the right side of Webb's sheet are clearly copies, with a few minor alterations, of Palladio's drawing of the two alternative schemes for the *frons scenae* at the Teatro Olimpico. This design, which presents the alternatives as two half-elevations pasted together down the middle, includes a cross-section of the seating of the Vicenzan theatre, together with the 'portico' of columns and statuary. The *frons* itself consists of superimposed Corinthian orders, but the third, attic, storey is drawn taller in the left half than in the right, while the backing of the portico is adjusted to match the top of the *frons* to either side.[7] In Webb's version the alternatives are presented as two separate drawings, the right side at the top of the sheet and the left at the bottom. These copies are about one-quarter the scale of their Palladian original, to which their fidelity is close. It extends to many of the inscribed dimensions which Webb takes directly from the source, and includes also the details of the statuary; even the bracing beneath the degrees is faithfully reproduced. The lower elevation does however omit the figures with which the third-storey columns are adorned in Palladio; all the capitals are presented without their carving; the degrees whose profile appears in the original are doubled up as treads and risers of stairs by Webb; and some details of the springing of the central arch are less happy in the copy than in the original.

Palladio's drawing was among those acquired by Jones during his Italian tour of 1613–14.[8] All who have commented hitherto on the Aldrich and Webb sheets have assumed that one or other of them was either directly in Jones's hand or else by Webb but copied from a lost Jones original possibly dating from as early as 1615. It seems more likely, however, that the whole set has nothing to do with Jones at all. Aldrich's copy superficially resembles Jones's draftsmanship in its use of wash and line, but its importance is merely fortuitous (in that it has been repeatedly published as Jones's work) and it may be set aside. Webb's sheet is annotated with two memoranda in the plan and section of a theatre which fill its left side:

Memorandum in ye designe this Arch is in height most two squares: whereby yᵉ length of yᵉ stage comes to bee lesse then is heer drawne

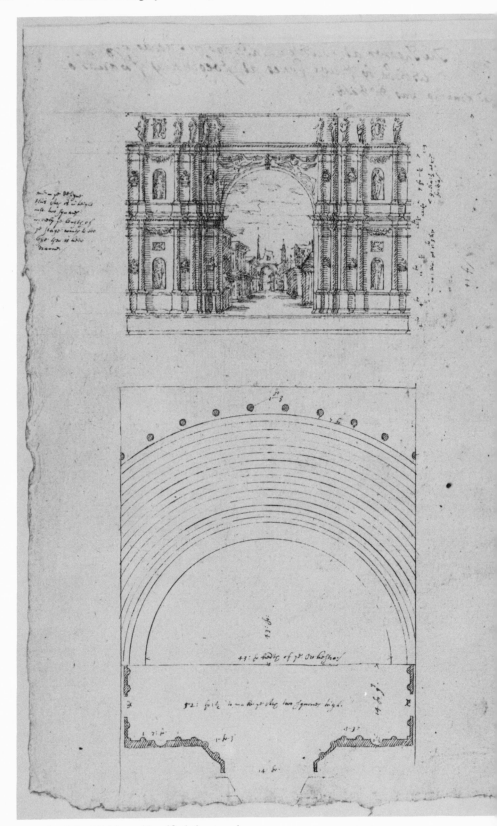

28   John Webb, unidentified theatre plan

and, across the stage in the plan:

52: fo: ½ to make ye Arch two squares high.

If Webb's drawing were a copy of an original design by Jones it would not have contained these signs of work in progress. Many of Webb's drawings do indeed render copies of Jones's studies tidied up for posterity, and perhaps for the engraver and press: examples are the design for the Barber-Surgeons' theatre and that for the Star Chamber and its ceiling. But the memoranda attached to the present theatre design resemble rather the notes attached by Webb to his own work, such comments, for example, as appear on the frontispiece elevations for *The Siege of Rhodes* (plate 11) and the Hall Theatre at Whitehall (plate 31), as well as the plan for the latter (plate 29). Aldrich must have had reasons for copying almost every word and detail from Webb's sheet, but Webb himself was never so meticulously faithful to Jones's drawings as to reproduce even their marginal notes. The notes, then, are Webb's and they allude to his own drawings, recording an attempt to develop what is plainly an impressive if rather frigid theatre design from the premises of Palladio's Olimpico scheme. Unfortunately neither the paper nor the style of Webb's hand in the drawing may be accurately dated, though the method of indicating dimensions between chevrons suggests that it may have been made after 1635, when Webb appears to have adopted the habit.

The occasion for the design remains unknown. Webb was much given to speculative architectural thought, particularly during the last year or two of the Commonwealth when commissions were few and the memory of Jones's example strong, yet the period seems less than propitious for a theatre scheme, even for one of a merely hypothetical sort. No exterior walls are shown in the plan, indicating perhaps that it was intended for a theatre to be set up in an existing hall, like that at Christ Church (plate 2). As we shall see in a moment, Webb's project is drawn to a scale which would render it too large to fit even the Banqueting House or the Masquing House at Whitehall, and while some of the measurements are reduced in the written notations sufficiently to make the fit possible, there is no positive evidence that the design was intended for either building. It is even possible that it was meant for a courtyard such as the Paved Court at Somerset House, but in that case one might have expected the walls to be shown, as they are in the plan of 1632 (see plate 18). There is at present no good reason for believing the project to be anything other than a theoretical exploration by Webb based on Palladio's drawing of the Olimpico.

The chief interest of Webb's scheme lies in its development of the hint of the triumphal arch contained already in Palladio's permanent *frons scenae* with its greatly accented *porta regia*. At Vicenza Scamozzi had fitted this central opening, as well as the four smaller flanking ones, with perspective street vistas, and although these are not recorded in the Palladian drawing Webb has applied the theme to the central arch alone, building it wider in his scheme until it is capable of containing a full, if miniature, Tragic Scene constructed on Serlian lines with fixed angle wings, a backscene and presumably a backcloth, though the deeper parts of the set are not recorded in the plan. As in the Olimpico design the *frons* is articulated in three storeys and its height, given in a marginal note as 43 ft, is close to that of the lower alternative for the Vicenzan theatre, marked by Palladio as 43 ft 6 in. Perhaps because the central opening has been rendered much wider than Palladio's, the entrance doors flanking it have been omitted; only those in the return walls at either end of the stage are included, presumably on the Vicenzan model, although they are registered neither in Palladio's elevation nor in Webb's copies of it.[9] Webb's decorative style is much more restrained than Palladio's, and appears to owe something to Jones's work at the Cockpit-in-Court. Where Palladio has pedimented windows filled with statuary in both lower storeys, Webb provides only niches and swags in the wider bays where the missing doors might have been. The remaining bays are far narrower, shrunk almost to coupled columns, with room between them only for busts mounted on brackets, a device borrowed from the *frons scenae* at the Cockpit-in-Court (plate 16). None of the second-storey columns are enlivened with statuary, and where the attic storey in the Palladian drawing is articulated with pilasters and panels into bays corresponding to those below, Webb treats this top level as a large uncompartmented frieze decorated presumably with bas-reliefs, its central part left blank where it covers the arch.

Webb gives the height of the great *frons* as 43 ft overall, or 39 ft above a 4 ft stage which rakes downward to 3 ft 6 in at its front. His theatre is specifically a scenic one, but Palladio's *frons* design makes no concessions to scenery, even of the limited sort that was eventually to be installed beyond its stage entrances, and shows instead a level platform stage. Webb's Tragic Scene adopts the high-horizon convention of its Serlian source, and although we should not take literally the abrupt incline implied by the elevation it is clear that he intended the stage to be raked from its front all the way to the backscene. In a series of annotations Webb relates the articulation of the orders on the *frons* in the usual way to the diameter of a column; thus the lower Corinthian columns are ten diameters high ('10:dia: at 1:^{fo} 3$^{di:}$') for 12 ft 6 in and the upper order is '9 - dia: $\frac{1}{2}$ at 1:\fo:dia' for a total of 9 ft 6 in. These measures, together with the entablature and attic storey, accurately tally with the overall dimension of 43 ft, which is clearly a considered total and agrees with the scale inked in below the lower section of the Teatro Olimpico. Although not all of the noted dimensions agree with it, many do and it appears that the one scale is intended to apply to all four drawings on the sheet. The width of the stage to this scale is 56 ft between the faces of the return walls of the *frons*, or just 59 ft overall as measured between the outer boundary lines marked in the plan. Some of the measures inscribed on the plan are consistent with the scale: the '7: fo' bay with its niche is correctly scaled, as is the '3 – 3' narrower one to the right and the '14 fo 9.^{y}' depth of the stage to the surface of the *frons* wall. The degrees are not quite evenly drawn, but the whole rank of fifteen appears to take up about 22 ft 6 in, in line with the customary allowance of 18 in each. Four important measures differ from the scale: the '52:fo: $\frac{1}{2}$' width written on the stage appears to be a preference rather than a scaled dimension; the clear-space width of the arch is given as 14 ft but scales at 18 ft; the width of the orchestra is noted at 43 ft but scales at 49 ft; and the depth of the auditorium, also noted at 43 ft, likewise scales six feet larger.

The plan of the auditorium at the Olimpico is not described in the Palladian section, nor in Webb's copies of it, but he will have known that it was a half ellipse shaped to present the rounded form of an ancient Roman *cavea* in a room where the space available for it was wider than it was deep. The auditorium in Webb's scheme derives rather from the semi-circular orchestra and degrees published by Serlio in the Second Book of the *Architettura*. Here the orchestra is ringed with seats for the noblest among the spectators, and the diameter of the ring they form is just 43 ft, scaled against the squaring of the forestage in accord with Serlio's note that each square represents 2 ft.[10] Webb's *cavea* has seventeen risers in all, where Serlio's has only fifteen, and the latter introduces gangways and stairs where the former does not, but the similarities both general and particular argue that it was Webb's intention to marry a scenic version of Palladio's monumental *frons scenae* to an antique auditorium based on Serlio's pattern.

Some of the details of proportionality found in the drawings confirm this view. The marginal note to the elevation of the projected theatre links the width of the stage to the height of the arch in the *frons*, a simple correspondence found in Palladio's drawing for the Olimpico, where the central opening is marked as 24 ft 6 in tall clear space, the *frons* is drawn three times as wide (73 ft 6 in) and the orchestra twice as wide (49 ft).[11] Webb's split drawings of the Olimpico are difficult to measure as a single entity, but they approximate the proportionality of their original. In the elevation and plan of his theatre project certain dimensions are related to a similar, though not identical, scheme. The width of the orchestra, noted as 43 ft, approximates that in the copies from Palladio and scales at 49 ft.[12] The great arch in the *frons* scales at 28 ft high, clear space, and this measure is half the width of the stage measured between the interior faces of the return walls. The front angles of the splay leading to the arch are likewise 28 ft apart, most readily measured in the attic storey which curves away from the auditorium along an arc continued across the opening by lines incised into the plan with a scorer.[13] The columns in the portico are marked as 7 ft apart between centres, and this is the width also of the prime bays in the *frons* wall, marked in the plan to the left of the arch and scaling the same in the centre bay of each return wall. The plan as drawn therefore repeats a module of 3 ft 6 in in the bay structure (2 units), the width of the orchestra (14U), the depth of the auditorium to the rear riser (14U from the stage), the width of the stage between the opposed return walls (16U), the height of the stage front (1U) and the height of the centre arch (8U). The modular scheme probably derives from Palladio's drawing, where the stage is 3 ft 6 in high and the arch above it 24 ft 6 in (or, in terms of the units used by Webb, 7U).

Two further measures belong to the system although they are not true to scale. The width of the arch is given in the plan as 14 ft (or 4U) but actually scales at 18 ft, while the stage, which scales at 56 ft (16U), is noted as '52: fo: ½ to make ye Arch two squares high'; 52 ft 6 in is 15U. Plainly the scale to which the project is drawn was dictated by that of the copies of Palladio on the right side of the sheet, but after the whole had been planned, scored and inked Webb changed his mind and suggested in a series of additional notes how the great arch, drawn about $1\frac{1}{2}$ times as high as it is wide, might be recast in the double-square proportions approximated by the Teatro Olimpico's *porta regia*. It seems that the width of the stage was to be reduced to 52 ft 6 in and that of the arch to the 14 ft inscribed across it in the plan. Provided its height were left as it is at 28 ft the arch would then have possessed the proportions of a double square. If the narrowing of the arch were achieved by a corresponding reduction in the width of the stage, as seems to be indicated by the words '52: fo: $\frac{1}{2}$ to make ye Arch two squares high', the orchestra would need to be reduced too, and Webb added the note that appears on it, superseding the scale: '43: fo bredth of ye Orchestra'. The new dimensions for the *frons* are all within the commensurate system of 3 ft 6 in modules, but this latest orchestra width (and auditorium depth) is not, perhaps because Webb chose to acknowledge his debt to Serlio's 43 ft orchestra more directly in the modification than in the original scheme. Neither are the new dimensions to be thought of as consistent with each other in scale, for in fact they differ considerably. Were the plan to be redrawn using the inscribed figures it would look different from the original scheme; but that it was Webb's practice sometimes to make a drawing to one set of dimensions and then mark it with another may be seen from his plan for the stage of the Hall Theatre, Whitehall (plate 29).[14]

In settling on a 43 ft width for his orchestra Webb not only imitates Serlio but seizes the opportunity to bring the auditorium into a simple proportion with the *frons*, which he has already established as 43 ft high at the original scale of the drawing. By reducing the orchestra and the depth of the *cavea* to this same dimension, he brings to the auditorium something of the geometry of the cube, without altogether surrendering to its imperious symmetry.

That Webb was able, with what looks like insouciance or at least indifference to practical realities, to contemplate changes in the proportions of his theatre so radical as these suggests that it was not intended to fit within the bounds of an existing hall or courtyard. In most of its characteristics the theatre project remains more literary and theoretical than practical; the drawings make few concessions to such matters as audience circulation or the conduct of the players' business on stage. It is, indeed, difficult to think of any real English theatre, whether at Court or in the parishes of London, that could have made much use of this rigidly formulated *frons* with its necessary but permanent and unmoving Tragic Scene. At the Ducal Court of Sabbioneta such a theatre had its particular uses, but they were not of a kind to appeal to a Stuart king and the actors by whom he was likely to be entertained.

10 The Hall Theatre at Whitehall

THE RENEWAL of the drama which accompanied the restoration of Charles II was not a simple recovery of its state at the closing of the theatres nearly twenty years before. In the interim a metamorphosis had quietly occurred, and playgoers' expectations in 1660 differed from those of their theatre-loving fathers. It remains a matter of debate how much the drama continued by developing along its old lines and how much was new and influenced from abroad. In exile in France, Charles and his Court had seen the plays and players of Paris; they had been present at the Petit Bourbon and the Palais Royal, and had doubtless observed the construction of the loges and stages at the Hotel de Bourgogne and the Marais. During shorter sojourns in Bruges and Brussels they saw how professional scenic theatres might be set up in tennis courts and other enclosed halls. Soon after the Restoration the Comédiens de Mademoiselle d'Orléans were welcomed at the Cockpit in Drury Lane, where the king saw them perform their 'machine' plays,[1] and before long Charles sent his favoured Betterton off to Paris to bring back technical information about the French players' methods.[2] The old, non-scenic type of theatre, perhaps represented by Killigrew's hastily opened Vere Street playhouse, was to give way to another kind of house, designed to contain scenes and even the sort of machines, though somewhat reduced in scale, made popular in Paris by Torelli.

At first, of course, Jones's Cockpit had to serve, and for a time the visiting French troupe made it the London centre of the visual drama, their way prepared by the fruitful collaboration of William Davenant and John Webb. The stage was now more closely controlled by the government than it had been earlier in the century, and only two managements were issued official grants or patents. The King's Theatre under the leadership of Thomas Killigrew opened in Vere Street and Davenant's Duke's Theatre in Lincoln's Inn Fields. The latter was in use by June 1661 before Betterton had been sent on his Parisian mission; like the Vere Street playhouse it was constructed in an enclosed tennis court, but it impressed its royal patron enough for him to show off its designs to the Florentine agent in London:

[The Duke of York] showed me the design of a large room he has begun to build in the Italian style in which they intend to put on shows as they do there [in Italy], with scenes and machines.[3]

When it opened the Duke's Theatre was clearly an impressive house, its scenes lively and lithe in movement, its auditorium, for all the narrow rectangle of its site, sufficiently rounded in plan to convey to the observer the idea that it was based on a circular plan:

The theatre is practically round in plan, surrounded within by separate compartments in which there are several degrees of seating for the greater comfort of the ladies and gentlemen who, according to the liberal custom of the country, share the same boxes. Down below there remains a broad space for other members of the audience. The scenery is entirely changeable, with various transformations and lovely perspectives.[4]

It is not known who designed this theatre, or rather conversion, but Webb had repeatedly worked with Davenant before, in the Caroline masques and at the Cockpit in Drury Lane, and he is as likely a candidate for the role as any. Two years later Killigrew moved from Vere Street to the new Theatre Royal in Bridges Street, and this house too may have possessed a rounded auditorium as well as ingenious scenes and machines, for the French traveller Balthazar de Monconys described it as the best formed ('le plus propre') and the most beautiful he had ever seen, its boxes lined with gilt leather, and the benches in the pit disposed so that each was higher than the one in front, in the form of an amphitheatre.[5] By 1665 London possessed, according to the French visitor Chappuzeau, three active scenic houses: Davenant's at Lincoln's Inn Fields, Killigrew's at Bridges Street and, in addition, 'vne troisième en Drury-lane qui a grand abord' – doubtless George Jolly's troupe at the Cockpit.[6] All three were superb at decor and scene changing, and in their use of music and lighting. And of course – though Chappuzeau does not say so – at least two of them possessed rounded auditoria in what the Florentine agent Salvetti had called 'the Italian manner'.

In the same year as Chappuzeau's visit to London the masons and the carpenters of the Works were busy at Whitehall converting the Tudor hall into a permanent court theatre designed to replace the Cockpit-in-Court, whose curious Palladian design rendered it unsuitable for the scenic drama. In the spring of the year, from February to April, extensive alterations took place in the hall, and although the warrant for the work is missing from the public records there can be no doubt that John Webb was the designer, under the nominal supervision of the Surveyor, Sir John Denham. Webb's plan and section of the stage are extant among the drawings at Chatsworth, as is his design for the frontispiece, identified among the same collection by Eleanore Boswell in 1932.[7] The collection also contains, as we shall see, Webb's preliminary design for the frontispiece as well as three designs for scenery, at least two of which are of the traditional Vitruvian or Serlian generic type. While none of these drawings offers information about the auditorium itself, the Works accounts published by Boswell do give a good deal of information, though unfortunately not quite enough for us to be sure about how Webb exercised his considerable talent and authority in theatre design on this occasion. Here, in this well-documented case, so much more clearly present to us in the records than either Lincoln's Inn Fields or Bridges Street, we ought to be able to assess the relative strength of English tradition and French example as shaping forces in the development of the Restoration theatre. Yet even in her definitive study of the Hall Theatre, when Eleanore Boswell was able to draw on the extensive public records related to it, as well as Webb's drawings, no clear picture of the auditorium emerged, nor can I now advance on her conclusions. What follows is therefore a brief summary of her observations about the theatre as it stood in 1665–6.[8]

However eager the new king was to introduce the modern theatrical practices of the Continent to his Court at Whitehall, his funds lagged sadly behind his desires. John Webb, who in palmier days had assisted Jones in the costly construction of the vast, but temporary, Masquing House in 1637, was now constrained to prepare a permanent theatre in the Tudor hall using a good deal of the old material he found there. According to the detailed Works accounts, published *in extenso* by Boswell,[9] an old stage or dais at the south end of the hall was incorporated into the structure, having been raised higher and cut shorter. On it a footpace was constructed for the state, with a rail set round about it. Twelve boxes and several degrees were put up 'round ye said stage, boarded underneath with slitt deale'. Above all this a slender gallery was raised along the south wall, all the width of the room and only 7 ft deep. At the northern end a new 'Stage for the Sceens' was built, '39 foot long 33 foot wide and v foot high', equipped with a frontispiece which was boarded above, all the way up to the roof of the hall. Beyond this were 'severall frames shutting vpon ye said stage', evidently for the sliding wings and shutters. As we shall see, the stage stood up against the screens 10 feet from the end wall, so that its front was located 43 ft from the wall, and at 39 ft practically spanned the whole width of the building. We may deduce that a space 46 ft 2 in long was left for the auditorium, but while we have Webb's drawings to inform us about the construction of the stage much of the auditorium remains an enigma. It is not clear, for example, whether the twelve boxes constructed 'round' the old stage or dais were actually on it or were merely placed on the floor of the hall on three sides in the manner of the degrees for *Florimène*. It is tempting to suppose the former, because between this southern part of the house and the main stage was a pit for which a special floor was constructed: 'making a pendant floor in ye pitt with degrees at each end with 16 seates in it'. The degrees could hardly have been placed fore and aft, but must have flanked the lateral walls of the hall. If, as Miss Boswell supposed,[10] the 'pendant' pit floor sloped upwards away from the stage it will have reached a height towards the rear perhaps equivalent to that of the old stage on which the state was placed; if so the twelve boxes must have been elevated too, in order to see over the back of the pit.

There is, however, some doubt about this 'pendant' floor. Very early in the history of the Hall Theatre there begins in the records a series of entries recording the temporary flooring over of the pit for balls and 'ballets'. At first the task seems to have been done from scratch each time, with new materials, but from about 1675 a ready-made floor was always kept in the theatre, stored under the stage when not in use. The entries referring to it sometimes (especially in the later years) record that it had degrees at either end, complete with rails to them, and these, together with the floor of joists and boards, constituted the major removable components by which the conversion was routinely accomplished. If the theatre possessed a permanent sloping pit with degrees 'at each end' it is possible that the temporary floor might be installed over it, but difficult to visualize how the degrees might have been arranged on its raked surface. Beyond the allusion to degrees at each end of the pendent floor the accounts for carpenters' work in the 1665 conversion make no mention of degrees at the sides of the hall, but the matlayers were paid for matting 'all the Degrees and seates in the Pitt'. In June 1675 existing degrees 'on each side ye pitt' were enclosed at the front,[11] and it may be that they had been a permanent part of the auditorium from the beginning. By the 1680s the dance floor over the pit was itself certainly equipped with degrees and rails probably intended to meet with and extend the permanent ranges.

When she wrote her account of the Hall Theatre Eleanore Boswell consulted Professor A. E. Richardson, the architectural historian, on the meaning of the word 'pendant' in the present context, and was advised that it probably described a flat floor raised on joists.[12] She rejected this opinion, believing rather that the pit was raked, yet the most natural way to interpret the record of 1665 is surely to accept that it refers to the elevated dance floor, raised possibly to the height of the stage,[13] or perhaps lower, but in any case providing a level surface more suitable for dancing than the flags and tiles of the hall. According to Webb's notations on his plan and section of the stage, the theatre was orginally prepared for the queen's 'ballet', and although this event has otherwise escaped the records there is no doubt that the theatre was conceived from the start as a dual-purpose room somewhat in the tradition of the Paved Court Theatre at Somerset House.[14] When set up as a playhouse it had a pit which extended between elevated lateral degrees and consisted merely of the original floor fitted with benches. For the dances the benches were presumably removed and the pit bridged over with the removable 'pendant' sections usually stored under the stage.

The size of this temporary floor is often given in the records, but it changes from time to time, from about 600 ft^2 in October 1666 to about 500 ft^2, the most usual size. Late in the life of the theatre, after many alterations had been made to the stage, pit and auditory, its size was specified as 28 ft by 18 ft (i.e. 504 ft^2).[15] Unfortunately none of this is explicit enough to make certain the extent of the pit when the theatre opened, and without some clear idea of its shape it is hardly possible to characterize the remainder of the auditorium with any authority. That there was a seated pit, that behind it the state stood raised on a stage, that 'round' the state were placed twelve boxes and that above them ran a shallow gallery: so much we may be sure of. The disposition of the '4 stepps of staires goeing down to ye stage where ye footpace was made for ye K & Queen to sit in' may only be guessed at.

At the northern end of the house four tiring rooms were constructed in and above the screens passage. They were equipped with two fireplaces whose chimney openings were cut through the old stone wall; and because '4 pair of staires' were constructed 'leading vp to ye great Stage and ye said Tiring Rooms' it appears likely that two of the rooms were built in the musicians' gallery above the screens, behind, that is, the new musicians' seat in the upper stage. Otherwise it is difficult to see how there could have been space for all the tiring rooms and stairs in the area behind the stage.

The Works accounts for the conversion of 1665 do not include payments to the painters, so that it remains unclear how the theatre was finished. It was extensively matted, on the backs and seats in all the boxes, the degrees in the southern gallery and all the seats in the pit. The music room above the stage was covered in matting, on floor and walls alike, as were the tiring rooms at the northern end. Even the walls and floors in the invisible parts of the scene backstage were covered like the rest in bullrush matting. The result will have been to deaden unwanted sounds, and perhaps to insulate the players a little from the chill winds off the Thames.

Despite these precautions the Hall Theatre apparently possessed poor acoustics. After his first visit there Pepys complained that the house was, 'though very fine, yet bad for the voice, for hearing . . .'[16] Webb made no attempt to counter the loss of the actors' voices among the open beams of the hall's Tudor roof. He boarded up the windows, but this measure will only have increased the cross-echoes in the auditorium. Not until 1671 was a ceiling cloth or velarium introduced, made of sky-coloured calico stretched on painted ropes. Miss Boswell assumed that the device was borrowed from the Palais Royal,[17] but it had long been a tradition in the London Court theatres, even from the time of the Elizabethan Banqueting House at Whitehall; similar cloths were erected in the Jacobean Banqueting House, the Cockpit-in-Court and the Paved Court Theatre at Somerset House, among others.[18] Two years before the velarium was fitted up in the Hall Theatre, Robert Streeter, the Sergeant Painter, had painted an elaborate one on canvas for the Sheldonian in Oxford; set on a network of gilt, moulded 'ropes' it represented a great red drapery 'furled up by the *Genii* round about the House towards the Walls', exposing the sky with clouds and a baroque assembly of allegorical figures.[19] It was Streeter who, while the calico cloth was being installed in the ceiling of the Hall Theatre, painted four pairs of wings 'of boscage' for the stage, together with a new pair of backshutters. At this time too he coloured the cord to support the ceiling cloth and altered the figure of Fame on the stage frontispiece.[20] It is to be doubted whether Webb had anything to do with these latest alterations; his name appears in none of the records connected with them, his relation with the Office of Works was tenuous by this time, and within a year or so he would be dead.

The very fulness of the Works accounts which tempts interpretation also defeats it. Chiefly because of the uncertainty over the shape of the pit, no adequate idea of the appearance of the auditorium emerges. It is clear that over the years the stage was gradually extended into the pit, but we cannot confidently interpret the terse phrases of the accounts in which this development is recorded. We have Pepys's word for it that the theatre was 'very fine', but the readiness with which it could be adapted from year to year with new boxes, degrees and benches, alterations to the pit, stage and frontispiece, the introduction of new entrances and the closing of old ones, suggests that it could hardly have been an impressively coherent piece of design in the first place. Because the Hall Theatre was Webb's most substantial contribution to the development of the Restoration playhouse, it is disappointing that the auditorium cannot be more completely visualized. If the pit floor was indeed raked, as Miss Boswell supposed, the rear boxes and the state must have been elevated above it, and the general layout would thus have resembled that which recent research[21] has revealed at the Hotel de Bourgogne, though without the loges on the side walls. But if, as seems more likely, the 'pendant' floor of 1665 was merely the movable dance floor designed to cover a level pit consisting of the original tiles of the hall, the arrangement would rather have resembled Webb's own work for *Florimène* in the same building thirty years before.

Fortunately the stage end of the theatre is known from the less ambiguous evidence of Webb's drawings. The plan (plate 29) immediately recalls the *Florimène* stage; from the Works accounts we know that the scene was built at the northern, or screen, end of the hall, and since the screen does not appear in the drawing it follows that the stage must have been set against it, just as it was for *Florimène*. The Hall Theatre design differs most from its predecessor when it replaces the angle wings of Serlian ancestry with clusters of changeable flat wings in the manner of the *Salmacida Spolia* scheme. Here the clusters are represented as mere rectangles, with none of the details of the grooves marked, but the intention of the drawing is clear enough. Like the wings, the backshutters also are represented as undifferentiated rectangles in plan, but behind them the relieves and backcloth are ranged in the familiar way. All this is confirmed in the companion section (plate 30), which provides in addition an indication of the rake of the stage, a view of the stage 'roof' and the interlocking system of wings and cloud borders. An upper stage contains degrees for the 'Musick' where the *Florimène* stage had seats for deities, but in both there was room for shutters in front.

There is no immediate sign in these drawings of an apron stage or proscenium doors and balconies, features which had almost certainly been introduced at both Lincoln's Inn Fields and Bridges Street. Webb evidently intended at first that the actors should play within the pictorial world of the scene, there being no indication in the drawings of access stairs leading to an orchestra, nor in the Works accounts of an orchestra in the pit, both of which had been important parts of the *Florimène* scheme. In these matters the model for the Hall Theatre was rather the stage devised for *The Siege of Rhodes* at Rutland House and the Cockpit.

The drawings however are not quite what they seem at first sight. They are well supplied with annotations of dimensions, and on the plan a scale bar is scored along its left edge, pricked out at intervals of 5 ft, for a total of 20 ft. Most of the marked dimensions have been entered first in lead, then either revised or confirmed in ink; a few have then been changed again in lead, so that where for example the third set of wings is marked in ink over lead as '6-fo 8^{yn}.' wide, an additional lead note reads '6 fo'. The scale represents 20 ft in 185 mm, or 33:1, a ratio probably derived from the use of a surveyor's line in measuring the interior of the hall in preparation for its conversion, 33:1 representing two rods to the foot. By the scale most of the inked dimensions are correct, but some – notably those concerned with the frontispiece – are contradictory and confusing. The overall width scales at exactly 40 ft, but Webb notes it as '39 fo–6^{yn}. between wall & wall'. The frontispiece support at the right is

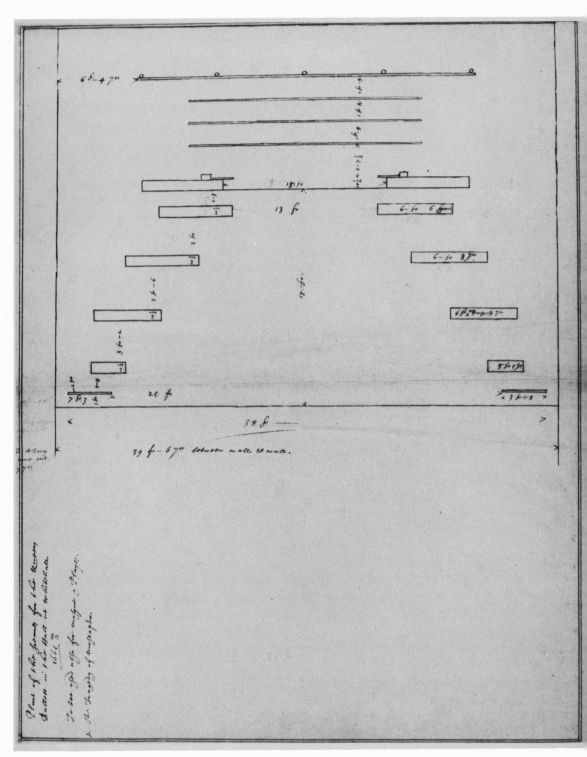

29   John Webb, plan of the stage at the Hall Theatre, Whitehall

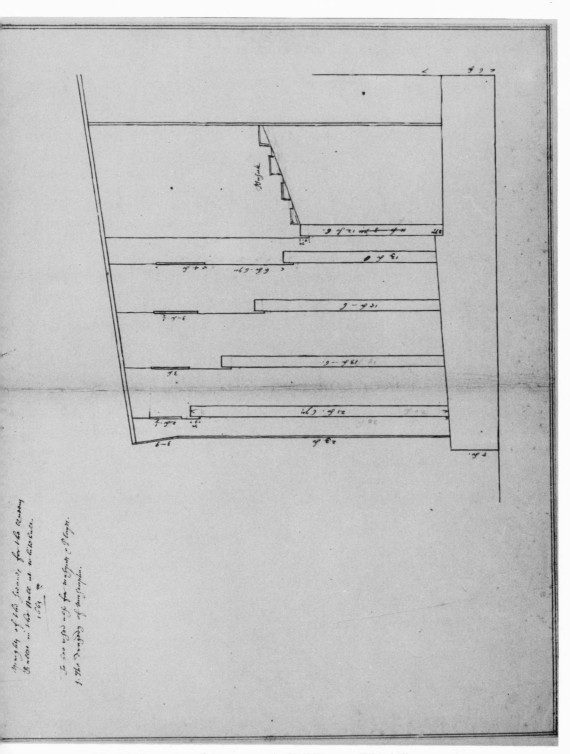

30   John Webb, section of the stage at the Hall Theatre, Whitehall

marked '3 fo–8', but scales at 3 ft 6 in, while the distance between the outer edges of the supports, given as '38 fo–', actually measures 38 ft 2 in. While these notations roughly agree with the scale, others are much wider of the mark: the scenic opening, drawn 31 ft 2 in wide, is noted as '25 fo', and the distance from the left wall to the inner edge of the support next to it is given as '7 fo 3', much more than the drawn dimension.

It seems clear, then, that for the frontispiece at least the plan offers alternatives: one is drawn, and shows a structure scaling at 40 ft across, with supports 3 ft 6 in wide and an opening of 31 ft 2 in. This drawn plan is then slightly modified with one set of notations, giving the frontispiece as 38 ft across, its supports 3 ft 8 in each, and the opening between them, though its dimension is unmarked, implied at 30 ft 8 in (the whole being 3 ft 8 in + 30 ft 8 in + 3 ft 8 in = 38 ft wide). A further alternative set of measurements, marked on the plan but not even approximately drawn on it, reduces the opening to 25 ft by moving the supports inwards to the point where their inner edges are 7 ft 3 in from the walls, for a total of 7 ft 3 in + 25 ft + 7 ft 3 in = 39 ft 6 in, precisely the span noted 'between wall & wall'. Thus the written alternatives are as consistent as the original drawing, but evidently represent Webb's later thoughts on the matter.

When Eleanore Boswell noticed that the 25 ft opening matched that of a frontispiece design at Chatsworth she dismissed the actual proportions of Webb's plan as 'inaccurate',[22] a judgment which was, as we shall see, misleading. Nevertheless her identification of the proscenium design was entirely sound. The drawing (plate 31) shows a strong rusticated frontispiece consisting of an architrave supported by massive blocked Doric columns, somewhat reminiscent of those used for *The Siege of Rhodes*. At the centre is a broken segmental pediment adorned with a cartouche inscribed, 'Hi sunt de pace triumphi Bella dabunt alios'. Above this is the seated figure of Fame blowing a trumpet, and it has not been observed hitherto that Webb here borrowed from Remigio Cantagallina's etching of Giulio Parigi's first intermezzo of the Palace of Fame, for *Il Giudizio di Paride*. The choice of this source, so often Inigo Jones's point of departure in his Whitehall masque designs,[23] together with the imperious motto, indicates how completely Webb was captive to the old Caroline traditions of courtly magnificence. That the design was indeed made for the Hall Theatre is proved by Miss Boswell's discovery among the Works accounts of payments made to Robert Streeter 'ffor new painting the figure of fame and Altering the posture'; taken together with the dimensions of the drawing, which are given explicitly in its squaring-up, this entry of January 1671 confirmed her identification.[24] She might also have observed that the elevation is made to the same 1:33 scale as the plan and section.

The frontispiece design is notable for its inclusion, to either side of the columns, of further structures consisting of podiums of rusticated masonry with blank arches, and above them small balconies with doorways behind, above which are trophies of arms. A note in Webb's hand reads, 'This dores were left out a way being made in ye Belconies A.A. for the Players to gett vpp into them vpon

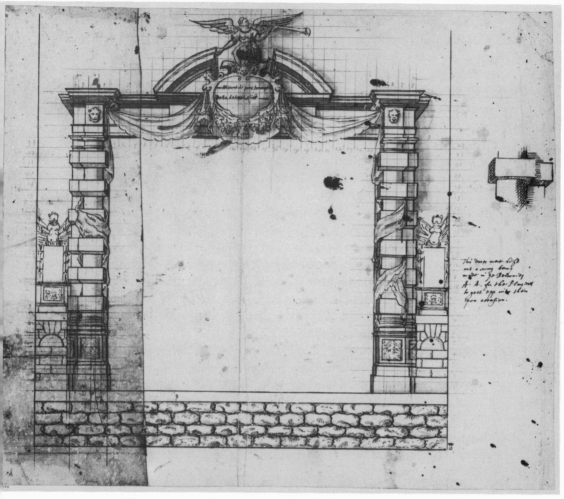

31   John Webb, the 'Fame' frontispiece for the Hall Theatre

occasion.' The whole height of these structures is somewhat less than two-thirds that of their contingent supports, and they have about them the air of improvised additions to the scheme. A note on the plan, unrecorded by Miss Boswell, not only confirms the relation between the plan and the frontispiece design, but indicates something of its evolution. The note is written across the ruled margin at the top of the drawing (i.e. stage right); it begins in lead with the words, 'The passage 2 fo. The thicknesse of the pee[re?] 7 yn.' Then it continues in ink: 'So the belcony will come out 3–7^{yn}.' This is all rather puzzling. What does Webb mean when he writes that the balcony 'will come out' by a specified distance? In the 'Fame' design there is some indication that he meant that each balcony and its podium was to project forwards from the plane of the frontispiece supports. The convention of a left light is observed, and Webb lays in a shadow where the left balcony structure casts it across the pedestal of the adjacent support, while to the right there is no shadow because the podium represents the foremost part of the work. In the plan the edge of the stage is shown and noted '1 fo' in front of the plane of the frontispiece; the marginal note records that a further 2 ft are required for a 'passage', together with 7 in for the thickness of the 'pee[re?]', presumably the front face of the podium. The balcony structure will then project, or 'come out', 3 ft 7 in in front of the main frontispiece. In order to accommodate the projecting structures the stage must have been brought at least 2 ft 7 in further forward, and indeed the Works accounts do record that it was 33 ft deep, 3 ft more than is shown in Webb's plan.

The balconies were raised on podia 7 ft high, and provided with 2 ft 6 in parapets. The doorways behind them, surmounted by trophies and intended to be constructed in the plane of the frontispiece, were to have been 6 ft tall and 2 ft wide, but in the event they were omitted. An actor standing in one of the balconies could address the audience directly, or, turning to one side, could face the shallow forestage between the two projecting structures. In this way something of the patent theatres' apron and stage balconies was introduced, though Webb seems to have been less than enthusiastic about the idea, his design resembling the opposed rostra for the academic exercises at the Sheldonian rather than the useful balconies of the public stage. Nevertheless it is possible that the forward projection of the podia was employed to provide doors of entrance to the forestage in their inside flanking walls. These walls are unfortunately not visible in the elevation, but the reference to a 'passage' in the note on the plan seems to indicate that the forward extension of the structures included room for entrances.

The evidence is not without its ambiguities, but it appears that Webb's first designs for the Hall Theatre presented a plane frontispiece with no forestage, doors of entrance or balconies. Before the actual construction of the stage in 1665 he redesigned this part of the theatre, providing a shallow forestage flanked by podia supporting balconies to either side, together perhaps with doors of entrance in them. When this arrangement was under construction he omitted the balcony access doors, some other way being found for getting the actors up into the pulpit-like structures. It seems also that the area of the stage allowed for them was square in plan. The frontispiece supports in the 'Fame' design are included in the measured system of squaring-up, and are noted at the top as 3 ft 8 in wide. The annotation on the plan allows 7 ft 3 in for the support and balcony structure combined, leaving 3 ft 7 in (unnoted) for the latter, precisely the same as the forward extension recorded in Webb's note.

No note appears on either plan or section to acknowledge the increased depth of the stage as given in the Works account, where the 'Stage for the Sceens' is specified as '39 foot long 33 foot wide and v foot high'.[25] Evidently it was made a few inches narrower than the hall itself, measured by Webb at 39 ft 6 in. In the section the stage scales at only 4 ft high at its front, but is raised by means of an annotation to the 5 ft given in the Works document. Webb's first thoughts about the Hall Theatre stage are recorded in the plan and section as they are drawn, with the lower stage and wider scenic opening. As slightly modified in the first set of annotations the frontispiece was of much the same size as that constructed for *Florimène*: 38 ft wide

32 John Webb, the 'Festive' frontispiece for the Hall Theatre

overall, with an opening 30 ft 8 in by 23 ft tall, and an overall height, including that of the stage, also of 30 ft 8 in.[26] That the opening was to have measured just 30 ft 8 in suggests that Webb intended to use the same 15 ft 4 in module in his Hall Theatre design as he had made the basis of the earlier conversion: the projected opening's height, at 23 ft, derives from the same measure (23 ft = 15 ft 4 in $\times \frac{3}{2}$), with the result that the opening is proportioned 3:4.

With its narrower, 25 ft, opening the 'Fame' frontispiece fits one set of dimensions noted by Webb on his stage plan, but it remains to discover the design that fits the others. The 'Fame' drawing is notable among Webb's canon for being finished with a wash that has faded to a light golden brown, where his custom was generally to shade with hatching or a grey wash. In the collection at Chatsworth is a group of designs for a proscenium border, a woodland setting and a street scene, all rendered in the same golden brown wash over black ink (plates 32, 34 and 35). They are highly-finished drawings, perhaps presentation pieces, and all three are

33   John Webb, Tragic Scene

developed over a precisely ruled underdrawing made with the scorer. Orgel and Strong grouped them together as the work of Webb, apparently basing their judgment on style alone.[27] That the drawings do belong together there can be no doubt, for all render the stage height at 45 mm on the sheet and the stage opening as 200 mm high. The two scenes are 313.5 mm wide overall, wider than the opening in the proscenium drawing (277 mm) by an amount suitable for the overlap we should expect to find where the border supports cover the front wings. The two scene designs indicate the shape and size of the wings in the scored underdrawing, their inner corners aligning on straight 'orthogonals' of which the upper set converge to a vanishing point 59 mm above the line which indicates the stage front.

That Webb was indeed the author of these painstaking studies is confirmed by yet another drawing, one much more obviously in his characteristic hand, and representing an architectural setting contained within the same border that appears in the presentation frontispiece design. The drawing (plate 33) shows the left half of the scene and border only, the former in ink and the latter in black chalk. The ink drawing is unmistakeably Webb's, with heavy cross-hatching, and is based on Jones's design for the first scene in *Albion's Triumph* (1632), though further

34 John Webb, Satyric Scene

developed by reference back to the original source in Parigi's *Il Giudizio di Paride*.[28] While only half the scene is drawn, the whole is represented in a scored underdrawing of exactly the same type, size and proportions as those of the street and wood scenes, but contained within the proscenium border. Here again the stage is 45 mm high, the opening 200 mm by 277 mm, the border 34 mm wide all round and the top of the backshutters 96 mm above the stage. The diminishing of the wings is however sharper than in the two wash drawings, the ruled top orthogonals converging to a lower vanishing point only 38 mm above the stage front. Nevertheless the lateral spacing of the wings is identical with that in the other two scenes, and the scored lines indicating the dimensions of the border are exactly the same size as those in the proscenium design. All four drawings belong in the same set, and are linked to the Hall Theatre not only by the faded golden brown wash which three of them have in common with the 'Fame' design, but also by their proportions, which exactly fit the remaining set of dimensions marked by Webb on his stage plan.

None of the group boasts a scale bar, but at 45 mm their representation of the stage height is sufficiently close to the 46 mm of the 'Fame' drawing to suggest that

35   John Webb, Comic Scene

it too represents 5 ft. At this scale the borders are 3 ft 8 in wide and the scenic opening 30 ft 8 in for a total of 38 ft, all to the nearest inch. To the conclusions that the drawings are by Webb, and that they date from the period of his 'Fame' frontispiece design, we may now add the further observation that they precisely fit one set of dimensions marked by him on the Hall Theatre plan. The whole group represents, not Webb's very first intentions, which evidently included the 4 ft stage drawn in the section, but his first revisions of them made before the subsequent recasting of the design in the more upright proportions of the 'Fame' frontispiece. The overall height in both of the wider frontispiece drawings corresponds to that given in the section of the top edge of the border, but at 22 ft their scenic opening is one foot lower, the same as Jones and Webb had used for *Florimène*. In raising the height of the stage from 4 ft to the 5 ft of the Works account and the scene designs, Webb reduced the height of the opening correspondingly by 1 ft, keeping the overall elevation the same. The repeated measure of 30 ft 8 in again indicates that the drawings belong in the hall at Whitehall, for it is a simple multiple of the 15 ft

4 in module used for the *Florimène* scheme and apparently derived from the bay structure of the building. The increase in the height of the stage, together with the corresponding decrease in the height of the opening, appears to have entered Webb's thinking after he had drawn the section of the scene, for a set of lead annotations on the wings reduces the height of the downstage pairs (from '21 fo.6^{yn}.' to '20 ^{fo}', and from '18 fo–6' to '18 ^{f}') to accommodate the reduction in the height of the opening. Doubtless their original proportions were restored when the 'Fame' frontispiece was constructed to the taller 23 ft dimension.

The 'Fame' design is a working drawing, for not only is it ruled up for enlargement, its squares carefully numbered, but it is splashed with the scene painters' distemper. The wider frontispiece design is by contrast unreticulated and unmarked, and it seems likely that it represents a scheme 'not taken', even though it is part of a project sufficiently advanced to have been noted in the dimensions of the plan and section and to be offered as a well-developed set of related drawings. Something must have made Webb change his mind, and the marginal comments on the plan suggest that it was the need – conceived for whatever reason – to include the proscenium balconies. But it may be too that he saw that his wide scenic opening would have led to numerous difficulties in the management of the sliding flat wings. It is not clear from his drawing as it stands how he proposed to find room for their retraction, especially the forward pairs. The lead annotations in both plan and section apparently reducing the size of some of the wings, their width as well as their height, perhaps recognize that the original scheme was oversized in relation to the available width of the hall. The reduction of the scenic opening to 25 ft would have improved the sightlines into the scene somewhat, the original wider angles having permitted spectators sitting at the sides of the house to see between the wings to the walls beyond.

The wider frontispiece (plate 32) shows how deeply Webb's thinking was still rooted in the Jonesian successes of thirty years before. Its proportions are almost exactly the same as those of the *Florimène* scheme, and are conceived in the same modular mould. Its imagery is derived quite directly from Jones's magnificent design for *The Triumph of Peace* (1634), and indeed Simpson and Bell, unaware that it was by Webb, thought that it might have been Italian in origin and therefore used by Jones as his inspiration for the masque.[29] A comparison of the design with Jones's is enough to convince the observer that all the inspiration lies with the latter; our present, more meticulous piece is clearly the copy, smothering the fire of its original. The precise allusiveness of Jones's scheme has been shorn of its particularity: the 'Hieroglliphicks of Peace Iustice and Law' described in Shirley's text of *The Triumph of Peace* are here omitted, and where the original border showed 'a ground of Arbor-worke entermixt with loose branches and leaues',[30] Webb's version is plain. It retains much of the merely festive symbolism of its source: the masking vizards, the crossed torches, the knotted draperies, the *putti* with trumpets. But where Jones particularized his theme in the great figures of Minos and Numa which decorated the supports, Webb places in their niches the more generalized figures of Tragedy, with a crown, and Comedy, with masks; in pursuit of this generalized theatrical theme he shapes the vizards on the frieze into tragic and comic masks. The particular references of the original are made universal and a little blunted; Webb's frontispiece is a jack of all trades.

The inscription on the plan has a similarly all-purpose air: 'Plant of the sceanes for the Queens Ballett in the Hall at Whitehall 1665 / To bee vsed also for masques & Playes. 1. The Tragedy of Mustapha.' Nothing is known of the queen's ballet in 1665, but Orrery's *Mustapha* is extant, as are Webb's backshutter and relieve designs for it, drawn to match the dimensions given in the plan and section, onto which a similarly universal title is inscribed.[31] At Chatsworth there are other backshutter designs of the same dimensions, probably for other plays. The Hall Theatre was to be used for 'Ballett' as well as drama, and the Works accounts show how frequent were its conversions into a ballroom of sorts. The festive, torchlit and vizarded subject matter of the frontispiece design suited the universal theme very well, and in offering what were evidently his versions of the Vitruvian or Serlian Comic and Satyric Scenes to go along with it Webb was thinking as a late Renaissance architect rather than a contemporary man of the theatre. The setting representing a street is in the tradition of Serlio's Comic Scene, and its treatment of the architecture craves comparison with Jones's Tragic Scene probably of 1629 (plate 14). There substantial and sophisticated urban buildings, whose design derives from a multitude of continental Renaissance sources, are brought together in a way that John Peacock has argued is both 'scenographic' and yet devoted to the principles of 'sollid Architecture'.[32] In Webb's scene, apart from the domed temple at the right, the buildings have neither scenographic nor architectural authority; their open perspective, reminiscent of both Jones's and Webb's own scenes of London in *Britannia Triumphans*, presents the backshutter cityscape as a panorama, but the opportunity is not grasped to render it particular and vital. With the notable exception of the Pantheon-like temple, most of the buildings derive directly from Callot's *commedia dell'arte* engravings, published in France in 1618 and occasionally used also by Jones. The open-topped house to the left is from *Le Zani*, while the arcaded building next to it comes from Serlio's Comic Scene, a little regularized. The third house with its balcony is transposed from the right side of *Le Pantalon*, and the fourth comes directly from the deepest part of *Le Capitan*. From *Le Capitan* also come the three secular buildings to the right, though in a different order from their source; the temple is borrowed from Jones's setting for *Artenice* (plate 12).

On the backshutters of the Comic Scene appears a view of a town, much like that seen beyond the arcade which closes the scene derived from *Albion's Triumph*. It seems possible, therefore, that Webb chose the great columns of Parigi's *cortile*, interpreted by Jones as a Roman atrium, as a suitable background for tragedy, and that the whole set of drawings represents a coherent (and, in tune with the annotations on the plan and section, all-purpose) group of Tragic, Comic and Satyric Scenes together with their common frontispiece. The stage plan makes provision for sets of sliding changeable wings housed in clusters, and it may be that Webb intended the three generic sets to be permanent installations, ready to be changed between productions but not as part of a single performance. None possesses the architectural vigour of Jones's Tragic Scene, nor is their open, wide-spreading formation arresting as scenic display. The Satyric Scene, derived perhaps from Parigi's Mount Ida for *Il Giudizio di Paride*, is more energetic than the architectural settings, but overall there is something touchingly lofty about these designs, a little vapid perhaps, and aloof from the theatrical fray that was to spill across the Hall Theatre's stage.

11 Conclusion

As EARLY AS 1615, on his return from Italy, Inigo Jones set down a memorandum describing his attitude to the mannerist design of Michelangelo and his followers. He found their ornaments unsuitable for what he called 'sollid Architecture and ye fasciati of houses', consigning them instead to gardens and 'the inner parts of houses' such as chimney-pieces. He likened architecture to the behaviour of a wise man, who maintains a grave public presence even while his imagination burns within with extravagant, delightful and moving fancies. The outward ornaments ought to be 'sollid' like the body of the building itself. But he was far from denying the power of the imagination, and it is typical of the man that as he noted down its workings his language took on the spirited vigour of its subject:

For as outwarly every wyse man carrieth a graviti in Publicke Places, whear ther is nothing els looked for, yet inwardly hath his immaginacy set on fire, and sumtimes licenciously flying out, as nature hir sealf doeth often tymes stravagantly, to dellight, amase us sumtimes moufe us to laughter, sumtimes to contemplation and horror, so in architecture ye outward ornaments oft [ought] to be sollid, proporsionable according to the rulles, masculine and unaffected.[1]

It would be an error to suppose that Jones, the maker of masques, was always devoted as an architect to work that was 'proporsionable according to the rulles'. The fire within him was a liberating one.

Nevertheless the humanist principles of the 'masculine and unaffected' architecture of the Renaissance, so well described by Rudolf Wittkower,[2] connect the work of Jones and Webb to the example of Palladio and to his antecedents, men like Alberti and Serlio. Together with his imaginative vision Jones brought to the design of the theatres the rational habits of proportion and construction which he found in the evidence of antiquity, in the ruins of Rome as much as in Vitruvius, and he had in Webb a follower who was prepared to extend this side of his work with zeal. Palladio's illustrations of the ancient theatre for Daniele Barbaro's commentary on Vitruvius[3] were too antiquarian to be of much use to the theatre designer of the seventeenth century, though his own Teatro Olimpico – seen and admired by Jones in 1613 – stood as an example of what might be done to revive the ancient forms in the modern world. The theatrical demands of the English Court were better met by the example of Serlio's theatre scheme, with its large unified perspective scene and its capacious auditorium designed to accommodate an ancient *cavea* within the narrow limits of a modern structure. The essence of theatre design is to bring the players and the audience together in a fruitful collaboration,

186

never allowing the two elements to become remote from each other, nor yet so mingling them together that the audience loses its capacity for wonder. The houses constructed by Jones and Webb from 1632 onwards show a good deal of tact in the pursuit of this elusive ideal. The actors were seldom forced to remain in the raked area between the wings and behind the frontispiece; in most of the theatres the main acting area was either a level forestage or else the orchestra, reached by steps whose various types of disposition had been taught by Serlio. From Serlio also were derived the often meticulous systems of modular proportioning which served to unite the stage and auditorium as parts of a single organism. Of course it is true that, apart from the Cockpit in Drury Lane, no theatre by Jones is known to us directly from drawings in his own hand, and we therefore often have no certain way of discovering how careful he was to construct stages and auditoria according to the architectural principles he espoused in his more permanent buildings. The drawings for the Drury Lane theatre are instructive in this respect, because they give evidence of a thorough and probably routine modularity of design, in which the depth of a seating degree coincides with a unit which is repeated, in various multiples, throughout the house. Such commensurate orderliness of planning is little more than we should expect to find in an architect devoted to the rational reinterpretation of ancient practices. The modular unit itself, however, is of a specialized kind and originates probably in the theatre scheme published by Serlio, where the depth of a seating degree equals the size of the square units into which the forestage is divided and which form the scale by which the whole is measured. In Jones the modular regime is flexibly administered, and departures from its organizing scheme are frequent. Webb followed similar principles, but his drawings are often sufficiently detailed to show him developing complete and independent modular systems of some complexity. The design of the Paved Court Theatre follows Serlio's *ad quadratum* scheme but is also informed by a strictly maintained modular standard of planning. Much the same is true of the working plan for the staging of *Florimène* at Whitehall and of the unidentified project which derives directly from the Teatro Olimpico. In all Webb's plans, with their frequent dimensional notations, one finds a certain humanistic pedantry at work, reducing the posts, brackets and boards to a neatly mathematical harmony. No auditoria drawings survive from his later projects at Rutland House and the Hall Theatre, but there it seems likely that lower budgets and the need to reuse old materials may have forced more flexible practices on him, willy nilly. It cannot however be said that either of these auditoria was more successful as a result, Davenant finding reason to cavil at the one and Pepys at the other.

Sometimes indeed the most revealing architectural drawings are those that represent ideal or theoretical schemes rather than ones that stand a chance of being built. Webb's 'Palladian' project makes few concessions to the mundane business of audience circulation or accommodation for the actors, and appears to be just such a theoretical study. The emphasis is on the *frons* as a piece of architecture, as an exercise in superimposed orders and in the play of solid and void. The great stage wall is penetrated by a single but huge recessed arch, filled with Serlian scenery whose airy perspective foreshortening contrasts with the stable weight of the architectural forms in a *tour de force* that has more to do with the values of pure design than the practical demands of a playhouse. The same modular rigidity that informs Webb's realized theatre designs is also evident here, associated with the modularity of the Palladian model by a series of marked dimensions and a common scale.

It is not surprising that Webb should yield to the architectural glamour of the Teatro Olimpico. Jones himself had made his pilgrimage to the Palladian shrine, and at the Cockpit-in-Court paid his tribute handsomely in a theatre whose every part signals the one-sided compromise between a dominant archaeological spirit and the concrete but often unaccommodated requirements of the public players of Caroline London. On this occasion Jones weighted the balance firmly in favour of learning and antiquity, but his customary habit was less scholarly and more attentive to actual theatrical needs. Both he and Webb normally preferred the Serlian model to the Palladian, recognizing its ready adaptability to the appetite for the scenic drama that prevailed at Court. Webb's unidentified scheme, in attempting to wed a stage of Serlian angled wings to a *frons scenae* derived from the Olimpico, aims for an ambitious but inevitably sterile conjunction. The scenic architecture is dwarfed by that of the monumental *frons*, reduced almost to a part of the decoration, its scale even slightly absurd when pitched against the great architectural orders surrounding it.

Jones would not have made such a mistake. His theatres were usually fully scenic, and of course elaborately so in the case of the masques. Only at the non-scenic Cockpit-in-Court did he turn to the Palladian example; at the equally non-scenic (but adaptable) Cockpit in Drury Lane he seems to have been content to let the forms developed by the Elizabethan and Jacobean 'private' theatres speak in their own idiom, though dressing them, to be sure, in decent architectural clothing, and casting the auditorium in a Serlian mould. Webb was always a competent architect, but in his work for the theatre function was sometimes obscured by his preoccupation with technique, whether of planning, of articulation or merely of modular drafting. Jones was less enthralled by theory, and though by no means always attentive to the demands of the actors he was alert to the complex interplay of stage and auditorium, player and audience.

The natural inheritor of Jones's masque conventions was the spectacular drama and opera of the Restoration. Webb's particular achievement was to convey Jones's example to the public theatres, for in his work for Davenant he carried his art easily from the Court productions of *Salmacida Spolia* and *Cleodora* to the simpler stages at Rutland House and the Drury Lane Cockpit. When *Mustapha* was acted at the Hall Theatre in 1666 it had already been staged at the Duke's Theatre, with scenes presumably by Webb. In these and other similar productions to which his contributions have not been explicitly recorded[4] he passed freely from the Court to the commercial playhouses and back again, bearing gifts from one to the other that remain to be assessed. If it could be proved – as perhaps one day it will – that he was the designer of the Duke's Theatre as well as the provider of scenes for *The Siege of Rhodes* and *Mustapha* it would be necessary to revise our judgment of him; the work more certainly from his hand, at the Drury Lane Cockpit in 1658, the Cockpit-in-Court in 1660 and the Hall Theatre in 1665, gives evidence neither of a large original talent in matters of the theatre, nor of a flexibility sufficient to find much challenge in the commercial realities of a new sort of drama. For *The Siege of Rhodes* at Rutland House and the Cockpit he erected a scene modelled on that of the Paved Court Theatre at Somerset House, constructed more than a quarter of a century earlier, its frontispiece containing a shallow raked stage with flat wings leading to the backshutters and relieves, and with no upper stage for sky effects. Only in containing the players within the scene does the later theatre alter the characteristics of the earlier, and hardly to much advantage. In refitting the Cockpit-in-Court in 1660 Webb introduced only minor variations on Jones's original Palladian theatre; and at the Hall Theatre his new construction of a complete playhouse within the scope of the palace hall so far lacked innovation that his designs for it reverted to the *Florimène* scheme of 1635, not only in the general arrangements of the parts of the two-level stage, but even in the deliberate modular development of its design. The project for a theatre based on the Teatro Olimpico shows Webb at his most innovative, but the pressure of his imagination is sustained only within the architectural context provided by the Palladian model and its Serlian predecessor; the design has nothing to contribute to the practical realities of staging a drama with scenes in post-Restoration London, leaving the technical details of the stage unexplained and reverting to the old-fashioned Serlian type of angled wing. Even in the Hall Theatre, where Webb introduced 'belconies' for the players to either side of the stage, probably to acknowledge a similar development at the patent theatres, his treatment of them was inadequate and unconvincing, their purpose neutered by the failure to provide anything more than a token forestage or apron beneath. For this theatre he designed the set of Comic, Tragic and Satyric Scenes which show that he lived still within the imaginative realm of Serlio and the Renaissance architect/designers who based their work firmly on the authority of Vitruvius.

   Yet without Webb the Restoration theatre would have had little direct contact with the scenic traditions of the earlier part of the century. Though he did not innovate, he was faithful to Jones's achievements, and conveyed them to a new public. It was Jones, not Webb, who naturalized the system of sliding flat wings on the English stage, and brought to it also the changeable back and upper scenes, with their deeper scenes of relieve. At the Cockpit in Drury Lane Jones constructed a theatre whose rounded auditorium, possibly confirming a pattern already established at the Blackfriars, anticipated similar continental models and stood among the streets of Restoration London to influence the builders of the new generation of scenic houses.[5] Much of what the Restoration playgoer found on the stages of the Duke's and the King's Theatres had first been brought to London in the Court theatres of Whitehall and Somerset House. Webb systematized what

Jones invented or adopted, and in the course of his quite deliberate studies became technically more adept perhaps than even Jones had been, especially in the design of auditoria. Yet he never passed beyond the circumference of Jones's talented invention in matters relating to the stage. In architecture it was different: his independent achievement is assured in the completed King Charles block at Greenwich, part of a larger scheme which marks him as an accomplished Baroque architect in his own right and a significant precursor of Wren's confident adventures in London building. His theatre work is less original, and it is to Jones, therefore, that we must turn if we are to find the sources of the revolution in production technique which was fully effected only in the decade after his death.

Notes

1 Introduction

1. For a detailed description of the Hall Theatre, and of the documents on which it is based, see chapter 10.
2. The interpretation of Webb's drawings for *Mustapha* is based on the technical account of movable scenery given in Richard Southern, *Changeable Scenery* (London, 1952).
3. Public Record Office (PRO) E351/3237.
4. Betterton was probably in Paris in the spring of 1662. See Philip H. Highfill, jun., Kalman A. Burnim and Edward A. Langhans, *A Biographical Dictionary of Actors . . . in London, 1660–1800*, 8 vols. (Carbondale and Edwardsville, 1973), II, 76.
5. For the Comédiens de Mademoiselle d'Orléans see chapter 3, pp. 65–6.
6. John Freehafer, reviewing the evidence with great thoroughness, is able to list only a few scenic productions in the regular playhouses before 1642, and several of these have been disputed. See 'Perspective Scenery and the Caroline Playhouses', *Theatre Notebook*, 27 (1973), pp. 98–113.
7. *Inigo Jones: The Theatre of the Stuart Court*, 2 vols. (London and Berkeley, 1973).
8. Historical Manuscripts Commission, *Rutland*, iv, 446.
9. John Harris, pers. comm. See also Harris's *The Palladians*, RIBA Drawings Series (London, 1981), p. 12.
10. John Webb, *A Vindication of Stone-Heng Restored*, 2nd edn (London, 1725), p. 119.
11. For the account of Jones at Oxford, see chapter 2.
12. Orgel and Strong, *Inigo Jones*, no. 14 (O & S 14).
13. O & S 61–4.
14. Cited by J. Alfred Gotch, *Inigo Jones* (London, 1928), p. 44.
15. A warrant for payment to Jones 'for carreinge of *Letteres* for his ma*jesties* service into ffraunce' was issued on 16 June 1609. PRO E351/543, p. 214.
16. The visit to Provence is usually dated 1614, but evidence produced by Gordon Higgott supports the earlier date: 'Inigo Jones in Provence', *Architectural History* 26 (1983), pp. 24–34.
17. George Chapman, *The Memorable Maske of . . . The Middle Temple* (London, 1613), sig. A1ᵃ.
18. *Dudley Carleton to John Chamberlain 1603–1624: Jacobean Letters*, edited by Maurice Lee, jun. (New Brunswick, New Jersey, 1972), p. 145.
19. Andrea Palladio, *I Quattro Libri dell'Architettura* (Venice, 1601). Jones's copy is at Worcester College, Oxford.
20. H. M. Colvin, general editor, *The History of the King's Works: Volume III 1485–1660 (Part I)* (London, 1975), p. 127.
21. At this date he already possessed Palladio's drawing of the *frons scenae* of the Teatro Olimpico, for he refers to it in his dated note in his copy of Palladio as 'the designe I haue'.
22. After the death of Arundel's widow, Alethea, Countess of Arundel, in Amsterdam in 1654 an inventory was drawn up listing her effects. At the head of the part concerning works of art is an item referring to the Scamozzi drawings: 'Casse con disegne tra gli

quali sono 2 forcieri con disegni d'Architettura de Vincenzo Scamozzi.' In the margin is the note '12' (presumably the 'casse') and '2 forcieri' (the chests of Scamozzi drawings). PRO *Delegate's Processes*, vol. vii, transcribed by Mary L. Cox and cited by Lionel Cust, 'Notes on the Collections formed by Thomas Howard, Earl of Arundel and Surrey', *Burlington Magazine* 19 (1911), p. 282. While some Scamozzi drawings survive in the Burlington–Devonshire collection it appears that the Countess of Arundel's two chests were lost.

23. In *The King's Arcadia: Inigo Jones and the Stuart Court* (London, 1973); John Harris and A. A. Tait, *Catalogue of the Drawings by Inigo Jones, John Webb and Isaac de Caus at Worcester College, Oxford* (Oxford, 1979); see also John Peacock, 'Inigo Jones's Stage Architecture and its Sources', *Art Bulletin* 64 (1982), pp. 195–216.

24. PRO E403/2730, fol. 181^b: 'Players imployed in the Barriers . . . xv^{li}/ ffor their Spanishe lether boot*es* bought by themselves . . . xlviij^s.' These items are included among accounts covering both *Prince Henry's Barriers* and *Oberon*.

25. Cited by C. H. Herford and Percy and Evelyn Simpson, *Ben Jonson*, 11 vols. (Oxford, 1925–52), X, 520.

26. For an account of the relationship between Jones and Jonson see D. J. Gordon, 'Poet and Architect', *Journal of the Warburg and Courtauld Institutes*, 12 (1949), pp. 152–178.

27. PRO A03/908/13, cited by E. K. Chambers, *The Elizabethan Stage*, 4 vols. (Oxford, 1923), IV, 171–2.

28. PRO E351/3255.

29. PRO E351/544, fol. 145^a, printed in Malone Society *Collections*, VI, 120.

30. PRO E351/3255.

31. Thus the seated auditorium took up four-fifths of the length of the room (88 ft out of 110 ft) and was bounded by a rectangle 88 ft by 55 ft in the proportion 8:5, a common Renaissance approximation of the Golden Section.

32. Scott McMillin, 'Jonson's Early Entertainments: New Information from Hatfield House', *Renaissance Drama*, n.s. 1 (1968), p. 160.

33. Jones's name appears ninth in a list of fifteen signatories of the foundation document of Alleyn's College in 1619. W. Young, *The History of Dulwich College*, 2 vols. (London, 1889), I, 49. In June 1623 Jones and Alleyn travelled together to Southampton with the Duke of Richmond. Ibid., II, 34–5.

34. PRO E351/3389.

35. G. E. Bentley, *The Jacobean and Caroline Stage*, 7 vols. (Oxford, 1941–68), VI, 271 and 282.

36. Selections from the Works accounts, transcribed by F. P. Wilson and edited by R. F. Hill, are printed in 'Dramatic Records in the Declared Accounts of the Office of Works 1560–1640', Malone Society *Collections*, X; extracts from the Chamber accounts, edited by David Cook and F. P. Wilson, are given in 'Dramatic Records in the Declared Accounts of the Treasurer of the Chamber 1558–1642', Malone Society *Collections*, VI.

37. *Triumph of Peace: A Study of the Whitehall Banqueting House* (Stockholm, 1956), pp. 119–20.

38. PRO LC5/132, in Malone Society *Collections*, II (part 3), p. 351. For the tentative identification see Orgel and Strong, *Inigo Jones*, I, 397.

39. Orgel and Strong, *Inigo Jones*, II, 787–91.

40. BL Add. MS 12498, fol. 124^a: 'The Roome for ye pastorall at Somsetthowse Cxxvj^{li} xxiij^d.'

41. Archivio di Stato, Turin. Lettere ministri: Gran Bretagna, mazzo 1, dispatch of G. B. Gabaleone dated 16 February 1614 (6 February, old style).

42. De' Servi arrived in London in June 1611 and is last heard of as the designer of *The Somerset Masque* in December 1613. See Colvin, general editor, *History of the King's Works*, III, 125–6.

43.   PRO SP29/5, no. 74(1), cited by Howard Colvin, *A Biographical Dictionary of British Architects 1600–1840* (London, 1978), p. 870.

44.   Colvin, general editor, *History of the King's Works*, III, 137.

45.   The exact date of Webb's entry into the office is unknown, but a drawing, dated 1628, of a design for the river stairs at Somerset House is probably from his hand.

46.   'Inigo Jones and St Paul's Cathedral', London Topographical Society *Record*, 18 (1942), p. 42, cited by Colvin, general editor, *History of the King's Works*, III, 150.

47.   PRO 351/3241.

48.   PRO 351/3272 (1638–39).

49.   Webb drawings dated 1638 for a lodge at Hale in Hampshire and a stable for a Mr Fetherstone are extant. See Colvin, *Biographical Dictionary*, p. 870.

50.   Peacock, 'Inigo Jones's Stage Architecture', *passim*.

51.   BL Add. MS 27962 H, fol. 79ᵃ, dispatch dated 28 November 1637 (18 November, old style) and fol. 205ᵃ, dispatch dated 19 November 1638 (9 November, old style). The work Jones waited for was Giovanni Carlo Coppola, *Le nozze degli dei* (Florence, 1637).

52.   *The Moderate Intelligencer*, no. 33 (9–16 October 1645): BL Thomason Tracts E 305; and *Mercurius Britannicus*, no. 101 (13–20 October 1645): BL Thomason Tracts E 305; both cited in Colvin, general editor, *History of the King's Works*, III, 156.

53.   *Vertue Note Books, Volume 1*, Walpole Society 18 (1930), p. 91.

54.   PRO SP23/G177, p. 781.

55.   Aubrey's sketch of the monument is reproduced in Harris, Orgel and Strong, *The King's Arcadia*, no. 405. Vertue reports a tradition that the second building represented was St Paul's, Covent Garden: *Vertue Note Books, Volume 1*, p. 99.

56.   PRO SP23/G177, p. 781.

57.   BL Lansdowne MS 1171.

58.   A second group, neatly inscribed by Webb in ink, includes a more balanced selection of masque and play designs: O & S 386, *Luminalia* (1638), a relieve; O & S 405, *Salmacida Spolia* (1640), a full scene; O & S 413, *Salmacida Spolia*, upper cloud scene; O & S 445, *Cleodora* (1640), a relieve; O & S 446, *Cleodora*, a shutter. All of these drawings are by Webb.

59.   Of *The Somerset Masque* Campion wrote, 'The work-manship . . . was undertaken by M. *Constantine*, an Italian, Architect to our late Prince *Henry*; but he, being too much of him selfe, and no way to be drawne to impart his intentions, failed so farre in the assurance he gave, that the mayne invention, even at the last cast, was of force drawne into a farre narrower compasse then was from the beginning intended.' Thomas Campion, *Works*, edited by Walter R. Davis (New York, 1970), p. 268. De' Servi was so secretive that he had Italian source material sent to him through the city merchants, concealed in bales of cloth. See my article, 'The London Stage in the Florentine Correspondence, 1604–1618', *Theatre Research International*, n.s. 3 (1978), pp. 170–1.

60.   *The Most Notable Antiquity of Great Britain vulgarly called Stone-Heng.*

61.   'John Webb's Drawings for Whitehall Palace', in Walpole Society, 31 (1946), pp. 45–107. See also John Summerson, *Inigo Jones* (London, 1966), pp. 127–34.

62.   William Kent, *Designs of Inigo Jones* (1727), Isaac Ware, *Designs of Inigo Jones and Others* (n.d.), John Vardy, *Designs of Mr. Inigo Jones and Mr. William Kent* (1744).

2 The theatre at Christ Church, Oxford

1.   Herford and Simpson, *Ben Jonson*, VII, 171–2.

2.   Herford and Simpson, *Ben Jonson*, X, 448.

3.   The account was printed by John Nichols, *Progresses . . . of King James the First*, 4 vols. (London, 1828), I, 530–59, and there ascribed to Philip Stringer. Nichols's copy was a modernized transcript of the original document made by the Cambridge academic

Thomas Baker and now in the British Library, Harleian MS 7044. It was Baker who, judging the seventeenth-century original in his possession to be in the same hand as a similar narrative of 1592 which was signed by Philip Stringer, concluded that Stringer was the author of the 1605 report also. But the two originals are extant – in Cambridge University Library Add. MS 34 – and are not in the same hand; Stringer's authorship of the present account must therefore be doubted. My quotations are from the original.

4.   Cambridge University Library Add. MS 34, fol. 44ᵇ.
5.   For Basil, see Colvin, general editor, *History of the King's Works*, III, 106–12.
6.   BL Add. MS 15505, fol. 21, top.
7.   Historical Monuments Commission, *City of Oxford* (London, 1939), p. 34.
8.   Bodleian Twyne MS 17, p. 201. See chapter 8 above, p.157.
9.   Sebastiano Serlio, *Tutte l'opere dell'architettura* (Venice, 1566), fol 43ᵇ.
10. M. Girouard, 'Designs for a Lodge at Ampthill', in *The Country Seat: Studies in the History of the Country House*, edited by H. M. Colvin and John Harris (London, 1969), pp. 13–17.
11. *Architecture in Britain, 1530–1830*, 4th edn (Harmondsworth, 1969), p. 22.
12. *Vertumnus* is extant and in Latin. Anthony Nixon wrote that *Alba* was 'a Comedie . . . in Latine', *Oxfords Triumph* (London, 1605), sig. B3ᵃ. It is highly unlikely that *Ajax Flagellifer* was in English, since such a departure from usual practice would have been noted, just as Daniel's pastoral was recorded as 'an English playe' in the Cambridge report (fol. 39ᵇ).
13. See John Chamberlain to Ralph Winwood, letter dated 12 October 1605, in Norman Egbert McClure (ed.), *The Letters of John Chamberlain*, 2 vols. (Philadelphia, 1939), I, 208; a similar judgment is perhaps implied by Sir Thomas Bodley writing to Sir John Scudamore, 20 September 1605: 'Their tragedy and comedies were very clerkly penned, but not so well acted, and somewhat over tedious, one only excepted.' H. R. Trevor-Roper, 'Five Letters of Sir Thomas Bodley', *Bodleian Library Record*, 2 (1941–9), p. 135.
14. Serlio, *Architettura* (Venice, 1551), fol. 31.
15. William E. Miller, 'Periaktoi: Around Again', *Shakespeare Quarterly* 15 (1964), pp. 60–5.
16. *The Ten Books on Architecture*, trans. Morris Hicky Morgan (Cambridge, Mass., 1914), p. 150.
17. Barbaro, *M. Vitruvii Polionis de Architectura*, p. 256. Jones's annotated copy is at Chatsworth.
18. Cited by Herford and Simpson, *Ben Jonson*, X, 413.
19. For *Tethys' Festival* see Orgel and Strong, *Inigo Jones*, I, 193–6.
20. *Le due regole della prospettiva pratica*, p. 91.
21. The lists, taken from the Oxford University Archives, were published by F. S. Boas, 'James I at Oxford in 1605', Malone Society *Collections*, I (part 3), 247–59. They show that many costumes for *Alba*, some for *Arcadia Reformed* and possibly a few for *Ajax Flagellifer* were hired for the occasion from Edward Kirkham and Thomas Kendall at Blackfriars. The Revels Office was also involved, as an entry in its accounts for 1605 reveals: 'Tape threed and workmanshipp of the garments sente to Oxforde at the Kinges being there . . . xxˢ' (PRO AO1/2046/11). The college accounts, on the other hand, are scant and lack detail. See R. E. Alton, 'The Academic Drama in Oxford: Extracts from the Records of Four Colleges', Malone Society *Collections* V, 60 and 72.

3 The Cockpit in Drury Lane

1.   For a contemporary account of de' Servi's ill success see my note, 'The Agent of Savoy at *The Somerset Masque*', *Review of English Studies* n.s. 28 (1977), pp. 301–5.

2. The dates of these two masques, long disputed, are confirmed by the reports of the Savoy agent in London. See my article, 'The London Court Stage in the Savoy Correspondence, 1613–1675', *Theatre Research International* 4 (1979), pp. 83–4.

3. D. F. Rowan, 'A Neglected Jones/Webb Theatre Project: "Barber-Surgeons' Hall Writ Large"', *New Theatre Magazine* 9 (1969), pp. 6–15.

4. 'Inigo Jones – Theatre Architect', *TABS* 31 (1973), pp. 101–4.

5. See chapter 1, pp. 8–10.

6. G. L. Hosking, *The Life and Times of Edward Alleyn* (London, 1952), pp. 177 and 213; and see above, chapter 1, n. 33.

7. Harris, Orgel and Strong, *The King's Arcadia*, p. 109.

8. D. F. Rowan, 'A Neglected Jones/Webb Theatre Project: "Barber-Surgeons' Hall Writ Large"', *Shakespeare Survey* 23 (Cambridge, 1970), p. 127.

9. These drawings are reproduced in *The King's Arcadia*, pp. 105 and 107.

10. *Jacobean and Caroline Stage*, VI, 77–86.

11. Harris and Tait, *Catalogue of the Drawings by Inigo Jones . . . at Worcester College, Oxford*, pp. 14–15. Not everybody agrees with Harris's dates. In a detailed study of Jones's architectural drawings undertaken for a Ph.D. thesis, as yet unpublished, Gordon Higgott has surveyed the canon and extensively reordered it, guided by such carefully chosen touchstones as the type of implements employed in the drafting, the competence of outline technique, the handling of hatched lines and wash, etc. Higgott redates several drawings, long thought to be in Jones's earlier hand, to the late 1630s; the present 'Cockpit' set he assigns to 1638 or shortly thereafter. A proper analysis of the evidence must await the full publication of Mr Higgott's thesis, but he has generously shown me the part relating to the 'Cockpit' drawings. It will of course be judged by specialists, but if the date *c.* 1638 is correct it may indicate that the drawings were made in connection with the establishment of the new company of the King's and Queen's Boys at the Cockpit in 1638. The sheets are highly finished presentation pieces, containing none of the cancellations, second thoughts or carefully stated alternatives often found when original designs have been worked up to presentation standards. If late in date they are probably fair copies of earlier working designs.

12. Leslie Hotson, *The Commonwealth and Restoration Stage* (Cambridge, Mass., 1928), pp. 88–99.

13. Cited in *Jacobean and Caroline Stage*, VI, 55.

14. Ibid., VI, 50.

15. (London, 1935), pp. 80–100.

16. *Acts of the Privy Council, 1616–17*, p. 36, dated 7 October 1616.

17. Ibid., p. 334, dated 29 September 1617.

18. London County Council *Survey of London*, V, 36.

19. *Middlesex County Records*, II, 125–6.

20. Ibid., n.s. III, 310.

21. *Jacobean and Caroline Stage*, VI, 54.

22. For Derby and Leicester see John Speed, *The Theatre of the Empire of Great Britaine . . .* (1611). 'The Cock Pitt' is keyed no. 26 in the 'Darbye' map in error for 27. The Leicester pit, on the outskirts of the town, is drawn very large, but it clearly bears no relation to the scale of the rest of the map. The Oxford pit stood at the corner of Holywell and Church Streets, and appears in D. Loggan, *Oxonia Illustrata* (Oxford, 1675), plate II. On its orgins see H. E. Salter (ed.), *Surveys and Tokens* (Oxford, 1923), p. 101. For the Dartmouth Street pit see LCC *Survey of London*, X, part 1, p. 81. It may have been built when Sir Edward de Carteret leased the site from Christ's Hospital in 1671. It is illustrated in Kip's 'View of Westminster' (1710). The Gray's Inn Gardens pit was called 'new' in an advertisement of 1700 cited by J. P. Malcolm, *Anecdotes of the Manners and Customs of London during the Eighteenth Century*, 2nd edn (London, 1810), II, 115. It appears in the background of the 'Prospect of Gray's Inn' engraved by Sutton

Nicholls for John Stow, *A Survey of the Cities of London and Westminster*, edited by John Strype (London, 1720), book IV, plate facing p. 69. In 1731 Nicholls engraved another view which shows the cockpit in rather more detail. It is reproduced in Hugh Phillips, *Mid-Georgian London* (London, 1964), pp. 202 and 203. In an article in *Notes and Queries* 7th series 9 (1890), p. 258, S.A.T. claimed that the Gray's Inn pit was built well before 1660, but gave no source for his information.

23. Both the Hogarth and the Rowlandson prints are reproduced by Glynne Wickham, *Early English Stages 1300 to 1660*, 3 vols. (London, 1959–81) II (part 2), plates XVI and XVII.

24. Clare Williams, *Thomas Platter's Travels in England* (London, 1937), pp. 167–8.

25. *London in 1710*, translated by W. H. Quarrell and M. Mare (Oxford, 1928), p. 48.

26. Early cockpit tables seem to have been smaller than many of those set up in the nineteenth century, for which the records are less scanty. The circular pit at Tufton Street, Westminster, which flourished *c.* 1816–28, had a 'mound of earth about 20 ft across' at the centre, surrounded by boards and covered with matting (Sir Walter Gilbey, *Sport in the Olden Time* (London, 1912), p. 93). A New York rule of 1859–60 required that 'The pit shall be a circular pit, at least 18 feet in diameter, and not less than 16 inches high' (Herbert Atkinson, *Cock-Fighting and Game Fowl* (Bath, 1938), p. 120). These articles referred to permanent cockpits, whereas a set of rules drawn up in England in the nineteenth century to govern mains held in taverns called for something smaller, and perhaps more old-fashioned: 'Rule I.–The pit shall be circular, twelve feet in diameter, and eighteen inches high . . .' (Frederick W. Hackwood, *Old English Sports* (London, 1907), pp. 262–3). Earlier accounts of cockfighting, such as that in the *Sportsman's Dictionary or, the Country Gentleman's Companion* (London, 1735), COCK-PIT, s.v., are not specific as to the size of the pit, though a large structure is hardly intended: 'COCK-PIT, a place made for cocks to fight in, being usually a house or hovel covered over . . .'

27. PRO E351/3216 and 3238.

28. PRO E351/3244.

29. PRO E317/Cambs. 4.

30. *Victoria County History: Cumberland*, II, 479.

31. BL Harleian MS 642, fol. 241.

32. Bentley, *Jacobean and Caroline Stage*, VI, 50. The Benchers' complaint to Queen's Council is recorded in *Records of the Honorable Society of Lincoln's Inn*, 5 vols. (London, 1897–1968), II, 186, dated 15 October 1616; their Black Book also contains a copy of a letter sent by the Lords of the Privy Council to the J.P.s of Middlesex, dated 4 September 1613, recording the Benchers' complaint about new building (ibid., pp. 158–9); their resolution to press the magistrates directly is minuted on 26 November 1613 (ibid., p. 160). The society was itself engaged in extensive building throughout this period, but if it suffered any qualms of conscience they are not minuted in the Black Book. In 1618 the Benchers asked Inigo Jones to design their new chapel, but in the event the plans were drawn by the Oxford mason, John Clarke.

33. PRO E351/3389, 'Chardges of a Maske at Denmarke house in the yeare 1616'. The text of the entry is given in chapter 4, p. 81.

34. For an analysis of the plan see Tomaso Buzzi, 'Il "Teatro all' Antica" di Vincenzo Scamozzi in Sabbioneta', *Dedalo* 8 (1927–8), pp. 488–524; Franco Barbieri, *Vincenzo Scamozzi* (Verona and Vicenza, 1952), p. 104; and G. Ricci, *Teatri d'Italia* (Milan, 1971), pp. 98–104.

35. For Arundel's '2 forcieri con disegni d'Architettura de Vincenzo Scamozzi' see above, chapter 1 n. 22.

36. Buzzi, 'Il "Teatro all' Antica" . . .', p. 504.

37. Campion's *Somerset Masque*, staged at Whitehall on 26 December 1613, was equipped by its Italian designer, Constantino de' Servi, with a regular proscenium arch: 'At the

lower end of the Hall [the Banqueting House], before the Sceane, was made an Arch Tyumphall, passing beautifull, which enclosed the whole Workes . . .' *Campion's Works*, edited by Percival Vivian (Oxford, 1909), p. 149. John de Critz, the Sergeant Painter, was paid 'for payntinge of a great arche with two spandrell*es*, two figures and two pillasters on eyther syde for the maske in the Banquettinge house . . .' (PRO E351/3248).

38. *Elements of Architecture* (London, 1624), p. 17.
39. For the *ad quadratum* method see Paul Frankl, 'The Secret of the Mediaeval Masons', *Art Bulletin* 27 (1945), pp. 46–60; James S. Ackerman, '"Ars sine scientia nihil est": Gothic Theory of Architecture at the Cathedral of Milan', *Art Bulletin* 31 (1949), pp. 84–111; and Howard Saalman, 'Early Renaissance Architectural Theory and Practice in Antonio Filarete's *Trattato di Architettura*', *Art Bulletin* 41 (1959), pp. 89–106.
40. The method included in the d'Honnecourt MS is described in detail by Paul Frankl, *The Gothic: Literary Sources and Interpretations during Eight Centuries* (Princeton, 1960), p. 50.
41. Matthias Roritzer, *Von der Fialen Gerechtigkeit* (Regensburg, 1486).
42. 'Premieramente la parte C. e quel' suolo piano et ponian caso che vno quadro sia dua piedi . . .' (Paris, 1545), fol. 65ᵇ.
43. *L'idea dell'architettura universale* (Venice, 1615), p. 40. Compare Cesare Cesariano, *Di Lucio Vitruvio Pollione de Architectura* (Como, 1521), III, fol. 1.
44. 'Staging of Plays at the Phoenix in Drury Lane, 1617–42', *Theatre Notebook* 19 (1964–5), pp. 146–66.
45. *Inigo Jones*, II, 786–8.
46. 'Inigo Jones – Theatre Architect', p. 104.
47. (London, 1658), sig. A2ᵃ.
48. (London, 1659), sig. A2ᵃ.
49. Malone Society *Collections*, II (part 3), 382.
50. *Jacobean and Caroline Stage*, VI, 68.
51. Malone Society *Collections*, II (part 3), 389.
52. (London, 1659), sig. A1ᵃ.
53. (London, 1658), p. 6.
54. Bodleian Library Malone 220 (5), pp. 4 and 6.
55. H. Liebrecht, *Histoire du Théâtre Français à Bruxelles au XVIIᵉ et au XVIIIᵉ Siècles* (Paris, 1923), p. 59.
56. Frederic Faber, *Histoire du Théâtre Français en Belgique*, 5 vols. (Paris, 1878–80), IV, 225–6.
57. *The Diary of Samuel Pepys: Volume II, 1661*, edited by Robert Latham and William Matthews (London, 1970), p. 165.
58. BL Add. MS 27962 Q, fol. 102ᵇ and Q, fol. 104ᵇ, dispatches dated 23 and 30 September 1616 (13 and 20 September old style).
59. Bodleian Library, Malone 161.8.
60. Faber, *Histoire du Théâtre Français en Belgique*, IV, 227.
61. See the account in Liebrecht, *Histoire du Théâtre Français à Bruxelles*, pp. 38–41, and J. Fransen, *Les Comédiens Français en Hollande au XVIIᵉ et au XVIIIᵉ Siècles* (Paris, 1925), pp. 101–3.
62. *Jacobean and Caroline Stage*, VI, 74–5.
63. *Commonwealth and Restoration Stage*, pp. 133–66.
64. Ibid., pp. 43 and 96.
65. BL Lansdowne MS 1171, fols. 11ᵇ and 12ᵃ.
66. (London, 1656), sig. A2ᵃ.
67. Webb had inherited Jones's drawings in 1652. See Harris and Tait, *Catalogue of the Drawings by Inigo Jones . . . at Worcester College, Oxford*, pp. 1–3.
68. The title page of the second edition (London, 1659) reports that the work was

performed 'At the Cock-Pit in DRURY Lane', where the first edition of 1656 had named Rutland House. A variant of the 1656 edition, noted by Wing (D340) as among the Dyce collection at the Victoria and Albert Museum, is reported to have been sold from the Cockpit, but it seems that this is a ghost: no such volume exists in the Dyce collection.

69.   (London, 1659), p. 2.

70.   A drawing at Chatsworth in Webb's hand showing one set of these rock wings is published by Orgel and Strong (O & S 464) as an unidentified design of mountains, possibly for a scene of relieve. It clearly belongs to *The Siege of Rhodes*.

71.   *Changeable Scenery*, p. 109–16.

72.   'John Jolifus "English and Roman Imperial Comedian" sent an application from Strasburg to the Council of Basle in the beginning of 1654, with the tempting assurance that with his well-practised company, not only by means of good instructive stories, but also with repeated changes of expensive costumes, and a theatre decorated in the Italian manner, with beautiful English music and skilful ("rechten") women he would give universal satisfaction to the lovers of plays. In spite of all these fine promises, the request was refused.' Albert Cohn, *Shakespeare in Germany in the Sixteenth and Seventeenth Centuries* (London, 1865), pp. cii–ciii.

73.   Webb's petition of 1668, abstracted in *C.S.P. Domestic 1668–69*, p. 132, is printed in full in *The Wren MS 'Court Orders'*, Wren Society 18 (London, 1941), Appendix part II, p. 156.

4 Perspective scenes at Somerset House

1.   Herford and Simpson, *Ben Jonson*, VII, 463. In its stylistic treatment of the architecture Jones's design is influenced also by a woodcut (1589) of Bartolomeo Neroni's scene, itself developed from Serlio, for Piccolomini's comedy *L'Ortensio*, performed in Siena in 1560. See John Peacock, 'New Sources for the Masque Designs of Inigo Jones', *Apollo* 107, no. 192 (February 1978), pp. 98–111. In the disposition of the scene, however, Jones adopts Serlio's conventions rather than Neroni's.

2.   Wake, *Rex Platonicus*, p. 46.

3.   Herford and Simpson, *Ben Jonson*, VII, 351.

4.   Dispatch dated 22 February 1619 (12 February 1618/19 old style). See my article, 'The London Court Stage in the Savoy Correspondence, 1613–1675', pp. 84–6.

5.   Summerson, *Architecture in Britain 1530–1830*, pp. 16–17.

6.   RIBA Drawings Collection. See Colvin, general editor, *History of the King's Works*, IV, 255 and plate 20. The plan is probably based on a survey made *c.* 1609 by Edward Basil, the brother of the Surveyor. Compare the eighteenth-century plan printed by John Charlton, 'Royal Palaces in England from Norman to Victorian Times', *RIBA Journal*, 3rd series 67 (1960), p. 84.

7.   PRO E351/3246: 'Paule Warde Carpenter for frameinge sawinge raylinge and planckinge the hall floore at Somersetthouse conteyninge in length lx.ᶠᵒᵒ & in breadth xxxj.ᶠᵒᵒ . . .'

8.   Malone Society *Collections*, VI, 110.

9.   BL Harleian MS 1653.

10.   A transcript of the entries relating to Somerset House is given in John Orrell, 'Court Entertainment in the Summer of 1614: the Detailed Works Accounts', *Records of Early English Drama Newsletter* (1979: 1), pp. 6–7.

11.   Chambers, *Elizabethan Stage*, IV, 183, and J. D. Alsop, 'A Sunday Play Performance at the Jacobean Court', *Notes and Queries* 224 (1979), p. 427.

12.   PRO E351/3389, 'Chardges of a Maske at Denmarke house in the yeare 1616'.

13.   Colvin, general editor, *History of the King's Works*, IV, 260.

14.   PRO E351/3253.

15.   PRO E351/3259.
16.   Orgel and Strong, *Inigo Jones*, I, 385.
17.   The year is given in the Annunciation style, referring to February 1625/6.
18.   The ratio is 1:1.632; the Golden Section is 1:1.618.
19.   PRO E351/3259.
20.   The design of the border is based on Andrea Andreani's woodcut of Bartolomeo Neroni's standing scene for *L'Ortensio*, a comedy attributed to Piccolomini and staged at Siena on 26 January 1560. In the woodcut, however, the border is an entablature supported by decorated pilasters to either side.
21.   Nicola Sabbatini, *Practica di Fabricar Scene e Machine* (Ravenna, 1638), pp. 73–5, describes an ungainly way of changing angled wings by means of cloths fitted over them, but there is no evidence that Jones ever used such a device.
22.   PRO E351/3259. In the same account Hooke was also paid for 'turning three greate Collombes of ffir Tymber at iijˢ iiijᵈ the peece', and 'for turning of xviijᵉⁿ ballasters at iiijᵈ the peece . . .' 4d was the usual price for a baluster, far less than the cost of turning the substantial columns of fir, 3s 4d each. The 'pillers for the Tabernackle' cost 4d apiece and must have scaled more like balusters than real columns.
23.   This item appears among the Lord Chamberlain's Wardrobe warrants for the year ending Michaelmas 1627, in a list of costumes for 'the Queenes Masque performed at Xpmas 1626', Malone Society *Collections*, II (part 3), 332–4. Bentley, *Jacobean and Caroline Stage*, VII, 63, takes the list to refer to the queen's masque staged in the Banqueting House at Whitehall on 14 January 1627, but the present item indicates that it alludes rather to the unknown masque presented by the queen at Somerset (i.e. Denmark) House to mark her birthday, 16 November 1626, and loosely presented in the warrants years later as belonging to 'Xpmas'. The Chamber accounts mention making ready 'of Denmarke house for her Majesty with the presence, and other Roomes for a Maske on her Majesties Birth Day . . . mense November *1626*' (PRO E351/544, fol. 221ᵃ). Salvetti dates the performance one day after the actual birthday, on Friday 17 November, BL Add. MS 27962 D, fol. 298ᵇ, dispatch dated 4 December 1626 (24 November old style).
24.   Colvin, general editor, *History of the King's Works*, IV, 261–6.
25.   PRO LC5/132, p. 154, cited in Malone Society *Collections*, II (part 3), 351.
26.   PRO E351/3263.
27.   Orgel and Strong, *Inigo Jones*, I, 401, corrected against the drawing.
28.   Peacock, 'New Sources of the Masque Designs of Inigo Jones', pp. 100–1.
29.   Peacock, 'Inigo Jones's Stage Architecture', p. 209.
30.   Warrant to Jones, dated 28 December 1638, 'to cause a scene to bee made at Sommerset houe [*sic*] in yᵉ Chamber of Presence there for A Pastorall to bee acted before the Queene & degrees to be made in such manner as it hath formerly beene done'. PRO LC5/132, p. 348, printed in Malone Society *Collections*, II (part 3), 361.
31.   '. . . fframing and making all the Carpentry woorke of a Sceane with diverse motions in the presence Chamber for a Pastorall to be presented there before the kinge and Queene fitting and putting vpp Degrees round aboute the same roome . . .' PRO E351/3267 (1633–4).
32.   For the productions of this play at the Cockpit in Drury Lane and Somerset House, see Bentley, *Jacobean and Caroline Stage*, I, 232–3. Raymond C. Shady, 'Stage History of Heywood's *Love's Mistress*', *Theatre Survey* 18 (1977), pp. 88–91, proposes that three Jones drawings (O & S 113, 473 and 452), being more or less suitable to the locations and characters of the play, are in fact designs for it, and concludes that 'we should consider these drawings "identified"' (p. 91). O & S 113, an architectural scene labelled 'Cupids Pallas', seems to be earlier in style and is a problematical composite drawing. The grotesque man and fat woman in O & S 473 might belong in any one of a number of masques. The proposal that the 'Temple of Apollo' (O & S 452) is a relieve design

for *Love's Mistress* is attractive, but not capable of proof on the present evidence.

33. 'The comedy that was presented yesterday before the Queen by the ladies was very lovely.' Dispatch of the Savoy agent, Benedetto di Cize, dated 22 August 1635 (12 August old style): Turin, Archivio di Stato, Lettere ministri: Gran Bretagna, mazzo 5.

34. Jones was paid £150 'for makeing of severall Sceanes for a Play to be Acted in the hall at Somersett house the xxvjth day of July 1638. hee findeing all Cloth Coloures Gould and Workemanshipp excepting the Carpenters worke Smythes worke and such thinges as have byn usually provided by his Majestie in former Masques and playes . . .' Orgel and Strong, *Inigo Jones*, II, 725, citing accounts of Sir Richard Wynn, Master of the Household, National Library of Wales, Aberystwyth.

35. PRO E351/3272.

5 The Cockpit-in-Court

1. PRO E351/3264.
2. At Berkeley Castle; the painting is reproduced in London County Council, *Survey of London*, XIV, plate 2.
3. LCC *Survey of London*, XIII, plate 1. For a summary of the complicated evidence relating to this print see ibid., pp. 41–4; and Colvin, general editor, *History of the King's Works*, V, 264–5.
4. Worcester College, Oxford, Jones/Webb 1/27.
5. Some indication of the uses to which the cockpit was put between 1603 and 1622 is given in the Chamber Accounts, published in the Malone Society *Collections*, VI. In all the room was made ready 74 times, 39 of which are specified as for plays and only one for a cocking. The remaining 34 are unspecified, but because most entries in the Chamber Accounts for buildings other than the cockpit and tiltyard are careful to specify the nature of the occasion for which preparations were to be made, it seems likely that these two specialized locations were thought to be self-explanatory. If so, the majority of the unspecified occasions at the cockpit will presumably have been cockfights. No records survive of preparations at the cockpit between 1622 and 1629.
6. Wyngaerde's drawing is at the Ashmolean and is reproduced in LCC *Survey of London*, XIV, plate 9; for John Thorpe's see John Summerson (ed.), *The Book of Architecture of John Thorpe in Sir John Soane's Museum*, Walpole Society 40 (1966), T 147 (i), p. 84 and plate 66. The drawing has been covered by another pasted over it, but is revealed by infra-red photography.
7. PRO Works 5/15, cited by LCC *Survey of London*, XIV, 27–8.
8. PRO E351/3216: 'one Bulrushe matt for the Cockpitt being iij yeardes everie way – x^s', and E351/3239: 'for enlardging the round oulde Matt upon the Cockpitt being broken and torne withe Cockeffighting there'.
9. Reproduced in Wickham, *Early English Stages*, II, part 2, plates XVI and XVII.
10. See chapter 3, pp. 46–8 above.
11. PRO E351/3216. There seems to be no good reason for believing that 'settelles' were necessarily movable benches, as John Astington does in 'The Whitehall Cockpit: The Building and the Theater', *English Literary Renaissance* 12 (1982), p. 311.
12. PRO E351/3224.
13. Accounts of James Nedam, March–May 1533, Bodleian Library Western MSS Rawl. D775, cited by J. W. Kirby, 'Building Work at Placentia 1532–1533', Greenwich and Lewisham Antiquarian Society *Transactions* 5 (1954–6), pp. 44–5.
14. At the beginning there was also a cockpen on the roof, presumably constructed on the leads of the outer part of the building. BL Add. MS 20030, cited in LCC *Survey of London*, XIV, 24.
15. Réné Graziani, 'Sir Thomas Wyatt at a Cockfight', *Review of English Studies* n.s. 27 (1976), pp. 299–303.

16. BL Add. MS 20030, fol. 150.
17. Cited by W. H. Hart, 'The Parliamentary Surveys of Richmond, Wimbledon and Nonsuch, in the County of Surrey', *Surrey Archaeological Collections* (1871), p. 80.
18. See the plan of Nonsuch in Summerson, *Architecture in Britain 1530–1830*, p. 9.
19. BL Royal MS 14B.IVB and Add. MS 20030, fol. 150.
20. In 1584 Lupold Von Wedel visited the 'great garden' at Whitehall: 'in it there are thirty-four high, painted various animals of wood with gilt horns placed upon columns. On these columns are, further, banners with the Queen's coat-of-arms.' Victor von Klarwill (ed.), *Queen Elizabeth and Some Foreigners* (London, 1928), p. 319.
21. 'Fittinge and settinge a newe Lyon on the toppe of the Cockpitt', PRO E351/3238 (1602–3).
22. PRO E351/3216. For an alternative interpretation of this document see Astington, 'The Whitehall Cockpit: The Building and the Theater', pp. 302–4.
23. PRO E351/3263.
24. Ibid.
25. PRO Works 5/17, cited in LCC *Survey of London*, XIV, 27–8.
26. PRO Works 5/1, cited by Eleanore Boswell, *The Restoration Court Stage (1660–1702)* (Cambridge, Mass., 1932), p. 239.
27. PRO E351/3255.
28. BL Harleian MS 1656, fol. 153[b].
29. PRO E351/3263. Compare E351/3255: 'two boordes nayled upon every brackett'.
30. PRO Works 5/4, cited by Boswell, *Restoration Court Stage*, p. 241.
31. PRO E351/3265.
32. Ibid. The frames for the Titians were especially ornate: the account was for painting 'in a sadd [= dense] wallnuttree cullor & guilding ouer those frames in diuers places with fine gould in oyle and one broad carued edge next all aboue the picture togeather with the Maskeheades ffestons Draperies the greater fflowers & the lesser flowers the greater & lesser Scrowles & the edges betwixt the flutes all guilt with fine gould varnished with the best varnish'.
33. Bentley, *Jacobean and Caroline Stage*, VI, 278; compare Wickham, *Early English Stages*, II (part 2), 120.
34. See Mary Edmund, *Limners and Picture Makers: New Light on the Lives of Miniaturists and Large-scale Portrait Painters Working in London in the Sixteenth and Seventeenth Centuries*, Walpole Society 47 (1980), p. 211, n. 500.
35. Victoria and Albert Museum Library MS 86. J. 13, fols. 103–11; in Oliver Millar (ed.), *Abraham Van Der Doort's Catalogue of the Collections of Charles I*, Walpole Society 37 (1960), pp. 226–8. The inventory of St James's was probably made by Sir James Palmer. Ibid., p. xxiv.
36. Titian's Emperors were half-figures, and survive in many copies and a set of engravings by Egidio Sadeler. In all the greater dimension is the vertical one. See Corrado Cagli, *L'Opera Complete di Tiziano* (Milan, 1969), p. 109. The Palmas are now in the Prado.
37. The drawings were first published, in the form of a small diagram based on them, by J. R. Lethaby, 'Inigo Jones and the Theatre', *Architectural Review* 31 (1912), p. 190. In 1931 the Works accounts connected with the conversion were published (LCC *Survey of London* XIV, 24–5) and associated with the Webb drawings; but the importance of the accounts went unnoticed by theatre historians until 1968, when G. E. Bentley's description of the Cockpit-in-Court appeared in *Jacobean and Caroline Stage*, VI, 268–81.
38. Hamilton Bell, in 'Contributions to the History of the English Playhouse', *The Architectural Record* 33 (1913), pp. 262–7, took the scale of the overall plan to be half that of the stage drawings and published the dimensions thus arrived at. He missed the pricked-out scale below the overall plan. The faulty dimensions were reported by Bentley, *Jacobean and Caroline Stage*, VI, 277. An undated plan of the Cockpit

accompanying a grant to the Earl of Danby in March 1676 shows new buildings abutting a square-planned structure, presumably the old cockpit itself. The scale appears to confirm the accuracy of Webb's drawing. See LCC *Survey of London*, XIV, 28 and plate 37.

39.   PRO E351/3263.

40.   Colvin, general editor, *History of the King's Works*, IV, 335.

41.   *Ars Poetica*, 333–4.

42.   The inscriptions are not easy to read. Hamilton Bell, spotting '—phocles' on one of the niches assumed that the series would be Aeschylus, Euripides, Sophocles and Aristophanes. Bentley, *Jacobean and Caroline Stage*, VI, 276, found Agath—, –ectan–, Sophocles and Antiph—. On the brackets beneath the busts he read 'Thespis' and 'Epicar—'. But the right hand niche is certainly labelled 'Aristo–', and the second from the left, being much cross-hatched, is almost impossible to make out. If the inscriptions record the state of the *frons* in 1660 they must orginally have been rather different, for in 1633–4 de Critz and Gooryicke were paid 'for mending the Statues in the Cockpitt altering the inscriptions and clenzing other woorke there'. PRO E351/3267.

43.   PRO E351/3264.

44.   Cited in Colvin, general editor, *History of the King's Works*, IV, 336n.

45.   On the fifth flyleaf, verso, transcribed by Bruce Allsopp, *Inigo Jones on Palladio* (London, 1968), I, 1.

46.   Vitruvius, *Ten Books of Architecture*, trans. Morgan, p. 146, and Ottavio Bertotti Scamozzi, *Le Fabbriche e i Disegni di Andrea Palladio* (London, 1968 [Vicenza, 1796]), I, 34–8.

47.   Andrea Palladio, *Quattro Libri dell'Architettura* (Venice, 1601), I, 37 and 44.

48.   Sebastiano Serlio, *The Five Books of Architecture* (New York, 1982 [London, 1611]), Book III, fol. 25^b.

49.   Biblioteca Communale, S. IV, 17, carta 33 [40]^b.

50.   Webb's petition is printed in full from the State Papers in *The Wren MS 'Court Orders'*, Wren Society 18, Appendix part II, p. 156. The claim in a petition of June 1660 to have 'prepared Whitehall in a fortnight for His Majesty on his own account' (*C.S.P. Domestic 1660–61*, p. 76) antedates the work on the Cockpit. The Cockpit drawings are dated at the Restoration by Harris and Tait, *Catalogue of the Drawings by Inigo Jones . . . at Worcester College, Oxford*, pp. 11–12.

51.   See, for example, Wickham, *Early English Stages*, II (part 2), 121, fig. 14; and Richard Leacroft, *The Development of the English Playhouse* (London, 1973), p. 77, figs. 52–4.

52.   PRO Works 5/1, cited by Boswell, *Restoration Court Stage*, p. 239.

53.   *OED Pendent s.v.* (3).

54.   'putting up a boarded partition . . . in a lower roome next vnto the pitt'. Works 5/17, cited by LCC *Survey of London*, XIV, 28.

55.   PRO E351/3263.

56.   The posts served to brace the rear access gangway and the joists supporting the degrees. See plate 7, chapter 3 above.

57.   PRO E351/3263.

58.   Ibid.

59.   Ibid.

60.   PRO LC5/60, p. 390, cited by Boswell, *Restoration Court Stage*, p. 18.

61.   The screen resembles some designs by Jean Barbet and includes a decorated frieze in its lower order closely like that in the *frons* at the Cockpit. See Summerson, *Architecture in Britain 1530–1830*, p. 73 and plate 44. The treatment of the upper level opening in the *frons* is similar to that of several overmantle designs in Barbet's *Livre d'Architecture*, especially that in his plate 13. Barbet's book was not published until 1633, in Paris, but it is possible that French designers in the queen's service were doing similar work at Somerset House before 1629.

62.   PRO E351/3265.

63.   Ibid. The emptions include 'Copper Rings – xv:ᵉⁿ dozen at viij.ᵈ the doz*en* – xˢ One
        Lardge Hamper – ij.ˢ Counters one Sett – v.ˢ wier greate and small – xv.ˢ x.ᵈ . . .
        whalebone for the Sceane in the Cockpitt – iijˢ Assidue ijˡᵇ di*midium* at iiij.ˢ the pound –
        xˢ . . .'

64.   Among the emptions in the Cockpit Works account for 1631–2 are 'Canvas and Callicut
        viz: lxx:ᵉⁿ yardes Callicutt at xvj.ᵈ the yarde – iiij.ˡⁱ xiij.ˢ iiijᵈ and viij ells of broad Canvas
        at xxᵈ thell – xiij.ˢ iiij.ᵈ' PRO E351/3265.

65.   Allsopp, *Inigo Jones on Palladio*, I, I.

66.   PRO E351/3265.

67.   Ibid.

68.   PRO E351/3266 (Whitehall emptions).

69.   Leonie Star has made the tentative but unacceptable suggestion that the 1639 sketch
        was intended as a scene to be erected at the back of the stage in the Cockpit-in-Court,
        immediately in front of the central section of the *frons*. This arrangement would bring
        the sky borders, cloudrows and backcloth hard up against the entablature and pediment
        of the lower storey; the proscenium arch would reach unhappily to the sill of the
        'window'; the wings would be compressed tightly one against another; and the 'citti of
        rileve' would have no space at all if it were to be set up in front of the backcloth. See
        'Inigo Jones and the Use of Scenery at the Cockpit-in-Court', *Theatre Survey* 19 (1978),
        pp. 42–4.

70.   Orgel and Strong, *Inigo Jones*, II, 726–7 and O & S 397, inscribed by Webb as 'The
        wood 6 sceane / the wood a shutter in yᵉ 2ᵈ part of Mr Lodowicks play'.

71.   John Orrell, 'Amerigo Salvetti and the London Court Theatre, 1616–1640', *Theatre
        Survey* 20 (1979), pp. 24–5.

72.   O & S 450; the unruled drawings, of 'A Palace' and 'An Army', are O & S 448 and 449.

73.   PRO LC5/60, p. 63, cited by Boswell, *Restoration Court Stage*, p. 15.

74.   Ibid., pp. 16–20.

6 The Paved Court Theatre at Somerset House

1.   *Albions Trivmph* (London, 1631), p. 3.

2.   John Newman, 'The Inigo Jones Centenary', *Burlington Magazine* 115 (1973), p. 561.

3.   PRO LC5/132, p. 309, printed in Malone Society *Collections*, II (part 3), 359.

4.   BL Add. MS 27962, F fol. 368ᵇ, dispatch dated 19 November 1632 new style
        (9 November old style) and fol. 370ᵇ, dated a week later.

5.   PRO E351/3266.

6.   Printed by Charlton, 'Royal Palaces in England from Norman to Victorian Times',
        p. 84.

7.   Similar errors were made by Webb at the left end of his Hall plan for *Florimène* (plate
        20), but were in that case corrected by pasted cancellations.

8.   See my note, 'Productions at the Paved Court Theatre, Somerset House, 1632/3' *Notes
        and Queries* n.s. 23 (1976), pp. 223–5.

9.   PRO E351/3404. Compare the plan of the chapel in the Chambers survey cited in note 6
        above and that reconstructed by John Summerson, *Inigo Jones* (Harmondsworth,
        1966), p. 76.

10.   See the plan of Somerset House in Samuel Pegge, *Curialia* (London, 1806), part 5, plate
        facing p. 93. Pegge – or his engraver, Longmate – includes the note: 'Lower Court two
        Stories lower than yᵉ upper Court.'

11.   Yale Center for British Art, Rare Books Collection: 'Inigo Jones and John Webb.
        Manuscript account book for work in the 1630s. A building compendium with
        measurements for quantities, the earliest extant' (typed transcript).

12.   Colvin, general editor, *History of the King's Works*, IV, 270. The entry refers to 'worke

done' and the amount of lumber 'spentt' on it; clearly it is a draft bill, not an estimate as Colvin and Summerson supposed.

13.   BL Add. MS 27962 F, fol. 384ᵃ⁻ᵇ, dispatch dated 21 January 1632/3 (11 January old style).

14.   BL Stowe MS 976, Sloane MS 3649 and Add. MS 41617.

15.   Orgel and Strong, *Inigo Jones*, II, 506.

16.   The drawing is reproduced full size by Orgel and Strong, *Inigo Jones*, II, 510.

17.   PRO A03/908/18.

18.   Upholsterers were paid for sewing, straining and setting up 'the Canvas for the Ceeling for the great Banquetting house', and Leonard Frier, the Sergeant Painter, 'for laying upon Canvas in the Ceiling of the great Banquetting house vᶜxxxij yardes square of worke called the Cloudes in distemper': PRO E351/3239.

19.   A pastoral scene of trees with a temple thrust out between the wings is tentatively assigned by Orgel and Strong to *Artenice* in 1626 (O & S 136). As we saw in chapter 4, the size of this drawing is 119 mm by 169 mm, precisely the same as the scenic opening in the proscenium design for *The Shepherd's Paradise*. Its trees spring from banks like those of the latter design, and unlike the few trees whose trunks are visible in the standing scene for *Artenice* (plate 12). The drawing should be reassigned to the Paved Court Theatre, and represents what Stowe MS 976 calls 'the sheapherds paradise', the standing scene of tree wings with rural cottages on the backshutters.

20.   See n. 19 for the assignment of this drawing.

21.   The three shutter drawings tentatively associated with *The Shepherd's Paradise* by Orgel and Strong include depictions of the rear wings to either side, and the shutter grooves appear to be located above the ruled base lines, one square high in O & S 251 and 252, one and a half squares high in O & S 253.

22.   On the plan the proportions are as follows, measured directly in millimetres: the orchestra, 76.0 mm wide; the distance of the 'piazza' from the centre, 54.0 mm; the width of the auditorium between centres, 151.0 mm (interior 147.5 mm, exterior 154.5 mm); the width of the stage end between centres, 214.75 mm (interior 211.5 mm, exterior 218 mm). An *ad quadratum* sequence beginning with three inches (the width of the orchestra) would produce the series 76.2/152.4/215.53 mm, and would give the distance between the centre and the 'piazza' as 53.88 mm. Allowing for the fact that the sheet has been silked and folded, with some distorting effect on the measures taken from it, the correspondence between the plan's actual proportions and those theoretically yielded by the *ad quadratum* construction is remarkably close (within one per cent at the furthest) and shows with what precision Webb might produce such a working drawing as this.

23.   The relevant measures taken directly from the drawing are: width of house at the base, between centres, 151.0 mm; distance of centre from the interior of the base wall, 131.0 mm. The corresponding altitude of an equilateral triangle of sides of 151.0 mm is 151.0 $\times \frac{\sqrt{3}}{2} = 130.77$ mm.

7 The 'Florimène' Theatre at Whitehall

1.   *The Argvment of the Pastorall of 'Florimene' with the Discription of the Scoenes and Intermedij* (London, 1635). The play was possibly one in which the queen had acted when she was a girl at the Louvre: see my note in 'The London Court Stage in the Savoy Correspondence', p. 91.

2.   British Library Lansdowne MS 9, fols. 198ᵇ–199ᵇ.

3.   PRO E351/3243 (1607–9).

4.   PRO E351/544, p. 14ᵇ, printed in Malone Society *Collections*, VI, 57.

5.   PRO E351/3206 (1571–2).

6. British Library Lansdowne MS 9, fol. 198[b].
7. PRO E351/3204 (1567–70).
8. PRO E351/3229.
9. PRO E351/3247.
10. PRO E351/3271.
11. PRO E407/59, fol. 8[b] (February and March, 1602).
12. PRO E351/3242 (1606–7).
13. PRO E351/3239 (1603–4).
14. Ibid.
15. PRO E351/3259 (1625–6).
16. PRO E407/59, fol. 8[a] (February and March, 1602).
17. For a contemporary description of the 1619 masque, the last to be staged in the old Banqueting House before it was destroyed by fire, see above, chapter 4, p. 79. The description was unknown to Orgel and Strong when they associated O & S 100 with this lost masque on stylistic grounds alone, but it precisely confirms the attribution. It seems likely that O & S 101 is connected with the restaging of the masque at Shrovetide in the hall after the fire. O & S 101 is squared up with incised lines, 30 units wide and 30 high. O & S 110, attributed to the lost masque of 1621, shows a proscenium frontispiece similarly squared up, its opening again 30 units by 30. If each unit expresses one foot the frontispiece would be some 38 ft wide overall, the same width as a frontispiece designed by Webb for the hall in 1665 (plate 29).
18. British Library Lansdowne MS 1171, fols. 5[b]–6[a].
19. British Library Lansdowne MS 1171, fols. 7[b]–8[a] (310 mm by 395 mm).
20. Orgel and Strong, *Inigo Jones*, II, 642–3. The section was used by Richard Leacroft in his reconstruction of the *Florimène* theatre in *The Development of the English Playhouse*, p. 60.
21. The warrant is printed in Malone Society *Collections* II (part 3), 376.
22. *The Ten Books on Architecture*, trans. Morgan, pp. 103–4 (Book IV, Chapter I).
23. The measures have been taken where possible from Webb's annotations; otherwise they have been scaled from the original drawings and are cited here in millimetres. Photographs are treacherous for this kind of work, and in an attempt to minimize the distortions which occur in printing I publish the two halves of the plan in two separate plates. That Webb intended it to be used in this way is evident from his heavy inking of the pricked-out scale bar so that it appears on both sides of the paper. When the left side of the sheet is folded over the scale on its verso is brought close to the stage and the scene.
24. The section gives no indication of the gallery heights, but in the plan the two indications of stairs by which the upper level was reached show twenty-three risers. This figure is clearly deliberate, because although both lead and ink schemes include the same number of risers, they dispose them differently about a quarter-landing, so that while their plans differ their total rise remains the same. If the risers were the customary 8 in each, the total ascent – the height of the gallery floor above that of the hall – would have been 15 ft 4 in, the same dimension as the width of the orchestra and half the height of the frontispiece.
25. The annotation '3 f 4' in one of the half-bays designates the interval between the surfaces of the posts, as may be confirmed by means of the scale.
26. The scenic openings in two Jones designs associated with the hall (O & S 101 and 110) are each squared 30 units wide. See above, n. 17. An opening 30 ft wide seems to have been almost *de rigueur* in the 1620s and 30s: it was provided by the Tragic Scene, probably at Somerset House in 1629–30, and there achieved by the omission of support pilasters at the sides. The 30 ft opening for *The Shepherd's Paradise* in the Paved Court was flanked by unusually slender supports.
27. One curious feature of these steps, which Jones copied directly from Neroni, is that the bottom one is hollowed out, apparently making progress down them difficult. Perhaps

Neroni intended the bottom tread to be recessed below the projecting sides of the lowest visible flier. That Jones did mean to include the steps in the stage as built is possibly confirmed by the fact that he drew them also in the half-scene sketch for *Florimène*, O & S 325. For Neroni's design see above, chapter 4, n. 20. It is reproduced by John Peacock, 'New Sources for the Masque Designs of Inigo Jones', p. 99.

28.   *On Painting and On Sculpture*, translated by Cecil Grayson (London, 1972), p. 55.

8 The Masquing House at Whitehall

1.   Malone Society *Collections*, II (part 3), 385.
2.   *A Brief Discourse Concerning the Three Chief Principles of Magnificent Building* (London, 1662), p. 40.
3.   A drawing by Webb for a hunting lodge is at the RIBA; it is endorsed in his hand: 'ffor Mr Penruddock . 1638 for a Lodge in a Parke in Hampshire'. The house was at Hale Park, Hampshire. Jones had built the church at Hale in 1631. Webb's drawing is reproduced in Harris, *The Palladians*, p. 50.
4.   If Gordon Higgott is correct in dating what I have called the Cockpit drawings at 1638 or shortly after they will have been drawings of record made for presentation, probably at Court. No specific provisions are made in them for scenery, and the audience surrounds the stage on all sides. For that reason they are most unlikely to represent an original design made in the late 1630s. See above, chapter 3, note 11.
5.   Davenant, *Luminalia* (London, 1637), p. 21.
6.   Davenant, *Britannia Trivmphans* (London, 1637), pp. 3–4.
7.   PRO C115/N8/8810, cited by Bentley, *Jacobean and Caroline Stage*, VI, 285–6.
8.   PRO E351/3271, first printed by Wickham, *Early English Stages*, II (part 2), 225.
9.   Arthur M. Hind, *Wenceslaus Hollar and his Views of London and Windsor in the Seventeenth Century* (London, 1922), plate L, no. 85.
10.   In the Van der Hem Atlas at the National Library, Vienna, and at the Albertina. See P. H. Hutton (ed.), *Drawings of England in the Seventeenth Century by Willem Schellinks, Jacob Esselens & Lambert Doormer*, Walpole Society, 35 (1959), plates 27 and 28.
11.   Sir John Summerson prints a scaled section of the Banqueting House in *Inigo Jones*, p. 50, fig. 14.
12.   Letter of 1 November 1637, cited by Bentley, *Jacobean and Caroline Stage*, VI, 285.
13.   PRO E351/3271.
14.   The document is reproduced and transcribed by Orgel and Strong, *Inigo Jones*, II, 694–5.
15.   The scale bar represents 30 ft in 302.5 mm, or very nearly 1 ft.
16.   *Love's Mistress* (London, 1640), sig. A3ª.
17.   Oxford University Archives, Register R, fol. 133ᵇ.
18.   Bodleian Twyne MS 17, p. 201, cited by John R. Elliott jun., 'Plays at Christ Church in 1636: a New Document', *Theatre Research International* (forthcoming).
19.   Twyne's original manuscript makes no mention of the scene designer, but Peter Heylyn, who as Charles's chaplain was probably present at the performances, attributed the scenes for *The Royal Slave* to Jones: '. . . they were feasted after Supper with another Comedy, called, *The Royal Slave*; the Enterludes represented with as much variety of Scenes and motions as the great wit of *Inigo Jones* (Surveyor General of his Majesties Works, and excellently well skilled in setting out a Court-*Masque* to the best advantage) could extend unto . . .' (*Cyprianus Anglicus* (London, 1668), p. 319). Anthony Wood copied both Twyne's and Heylyn's accounts into his *History and Antiquities of the University of Oxford*, edited by John Gutch (Oxford, 1792), II, 411, and also included – perhaps very late, since it does not appear in the Latin translation of the first version of the *History* which was published in 1674 – the claim that the designs for

The Floating Island were 'originally due to the invention of Oxford scholars' (II, 408). This attribution is found in neither Twyne nor Heylyn, and is probably unreliable. Professor John Elliott, who kindly drew my attention to the Heylyn passage, has recently discovered an itemized account relating to the plays among the Christ Church archives (D.P. xi. a. 15, fol. 23ᵇ). The document names many of the performers, musicians and tirewomen, but fails to identify 'the Designers for the Sceenes, with all things thereunto belonging', who were paid £260 for their work. But a contemporary set of Latin verses issued in connection with the royal visit names Inigo Jones as the designer of the scenery used in the plays: see *Coronae Carolinae Quadratura* (Oxford, 1636), sig. D2ᵃ.

20. The stage in Serlio's theatre plan is 34 units wide (see plate 3) and, because there is no frontispiece, it represents the overall width of the scene. Jones may have taken his inspiration directly from this source. The stage at the Cockpit-in-Court was also 34 ft wide.

21. The frontispiece designs for *Coelum Britannicum* (O & S 277 and 278) are difficult to measure precisely because of the freedom of their handling, but the design of ruins for the first scene is carefully squared up and numbered, 34 squares wide by 30 tall (O & S 279).

22. *Salmacida Spolia* (London, 1639), sig. D4ᵃ.

9 An unidentified theatre project

1. 'A Theatre Project by Inigo Jones', *Burlington Magazine* 31 (1917), pp. 61–70 and 105–11.

2. RIBA Drawings Collection, B.D. XIII/5.

3. D. F. Rowan, 'Inigo Jones and the Teatro Olimpico', *The Elizabethan Theatre VII*, edited by George Hibbard (Port Credit, 1980), p. 72.

4. Simpson and Bell, *Designs of Inigo Jones*, Walpole Society 12 (1924), p. 27; Colvin's conclusions are cited in Harris and Tait, *Catalogue of Drawings by Inigo Jones . . . at Worcester College, Oxford*, p. 18.

5. Harris and Tait, *Catalogue of Drawings by Inigo Jones . . . at Worcester College, Oxford*, pp. 17–18 and 92–3.

6. Keith, 'A Theatre Project by Inigo Jones', plates I and IV; Lily B. Campbell, *Scenes and Machines on the English Stage during the Renaissance* (Cambridge, Mass., 1923), plate V and pp. 204–5; and Leacroft, *The Development of the English Playhouse*, p. 69.

7. As built, the Teatro Olimpico followed neither alternative completely, though closely reproducing the right side of the design. Webb's studies derive from Palladio's drawing and not from the actual building in Vicenza. Perhaps for this reason no distinction is made on the sheet between Vicenzan and English feet.

8. Jones already possessed a 'designe' of the Olimpico when he visited it in 1613, for he alludes to it in his notes on the theatre, transcribed by Allsopp, *Inigo Jones on Palladio*, I, I.

9. Doors in this position are found also in Serlio's theatre scheme (plate 3); with so much precedent in the obvious Italian sources of Webb's project there seems little reason to connect his flanking doors with the 'doors of entrance' found in London theatres of the Restoration, unless these also originated in the Italian designs. Webb's drawings do not indicate whether he intended to provide balconies over the side doors, as at the Olimpico. His door openings are 5 ft wide, like those in Palladio's drawing and Webb's copies of it.

10. '. . . poniamo caso che vn quadro sia due piedi', *Architettura* (Venice, 1619), fol. 44ᵃ. This was the edition owned by Webb.

11. In fact the inscribed '24½' in the arch on Palladio's drawing appears to extend to an

arrowhead at the foot of the stage, thus including the 3 ft 6 in height of the stage in the dimension. Comparison with other marked dimensions shows that this is an error, as Webb saw. In his copy of the left elevation he marks the arch as 24 ft 6 in high above the stage. The matter is complicated somewhat by a scale bar on Palladio's sheet which does not accurately correspond to the inscribed dimensions. Webb appears to have ignored this scale, following instead the written annotations.

12.   Dimensions scaled from the drawings use measurements taken directly from Webb's sheet to the nearest 0.5 mm and are kindly supplied by Professor Richard C. Kohler in an unpublished paper, 'Vitruvianism in Shakespeare's England'. The chief measures are: the scale bar of 40 ft, 79 mm; width of orchestra in the project plan, 97 mm; height of arch in the project *frons*, clear space, 55 mm; width of the project *frons* in elevation, 110.5 mm. The present chapter is much indebted to Professor Kohler's paper which, however, it does not follow in all particulars.

13.   Aldrich misses the curved plan of the splay, drawing straight angled walls instead.

14.   Webb's early design, of 1638, for a lodge for a Mr Penruddock contains many inscribed dimensions together with a scale bar and the note: 'The measures are writt down iustly though they agree not with this scale.' See the reproduction in Summerson, *Inigo Jones*, p. 123.

10 The Hall Theatre at Whitehall

1.   See chapter 3 for the French players' season at the Cockpit in Drury Lane.

2.   See Highfill, Burnim and Langhans, *A Biographical Dictionary of Actors*, II, 76.

3.   BL Add. MS 27962 Q, fol. 33ª. Dispatch of Giovanni Salvetti dated 27 January 1661 (17 January, old style).

4.   This description by Lorenzo Magalotti is ostensibly of the King's Theatre, but Magalotti, travelling in the train of Cosimo de' Medici, confused the names of the two patent houses. See my article, 'Filippo Corsini and the Restoration Theatre', *Theatre Notebook* 34 (1980), pp. 4–9.

5.   Balthazar de Monconys, *Journal des Voyages de Monsieur de Monconys* (Lyons, 1666), part 2, pp. 25–6. However Monconys also used the phrase 'en Amphitheatre' to describe the 'rangs de degrez . . . disposez en Amphitheatre' in the Parliament chamber at Westminster, where they were ranged straight along the walls. Ibid., p. 35.

6.   Samuel Chappuzeau, *L'Europe vivante* (Geneva, 1667), p. 214. Chappuzeau's description of the London theatres deliberately parallels them with those of Paris, and his assessment of them is of some value: 'Il y a donc à Londres trois Troupes d'excellens Comediens; la Troupe Royale qui jouë tous les iours pour le public, & ordinaire tous les Ieudys apres soupé à Vvitthal: la Troupe de Monsieur Frere vnique du Roy dans la place de Lincolne, qui reüssit admirablement dans la machine, & qui va maintenant du pair auec les Italiens: & vne troisième en Drury-lane, qui a grand abord . . . . Il faut ájoûter, Que ces trois Maisons de Londres sont pouruûes de gens bien faits, & surtout de belles femmes; Que leurs Theatres sont superbes en decorations & en changemens; Que la Musique y est excellente & les Ballets magnifiques; Qu'elles n'ont pas moins de douze violons chacune pour les Preludes & pour les Entr-actes; Que ce seroit vn crime d'employer autre chose que de la cire pour éclairer le Theatre, & de charger les Lustres d'vne matiere qui peut blesser l'odorat; & enfin, quoy qu'on iouë tous les iours, que ces Maisons ne desemplissent iamais & que cent carrosses en barricadent les auenues' (pp. 214–15). Chappuzeau returned to London shortly after the Fire, and then found only two playhouses active: '. . . la comedie se jouoit en deux maisons, & l'amphiteatre ne desemplissoit iamais' (*L'Evrope vivante*, 2nd edn (Geneva, 1669), p. 7).

7.   *The Restoration Court Stage*, pp. 37–40.

8.   Ibid., pp. 22–55.

9.   Ibid., pp. 243–71.

10.   Ibid., pp. 31–2.

11.   Ibid., p. 256.

12.   Ibid., p. 31.

13.   In November 1677 the Works account records 'takeing the bourds and joysts from under the stage and laying it [sic] even with the stage for the Danceing for the Queenes birth day at night' (ibid., p. 260).

14.   See chapter 6 above. When its brief life as a theatre was over Richard Ryder was paid for 'inlarding the roome with ioisting and bourding it for a Maske . . .' (PRO E351/3266).

15.   In November 1697.

16.   Pepys, *Diary*, 29 October 1666.

17.   *The Restoration Court Stage*, p. 46.

18.   In 1584–5 the Elizabethan Banqueting House was cleared of the ivy and other evergreens installed in the roof and a canvas ceiling was stretched there, painted 'with Diamondes frutages and other kinde of woorke' (PRO E351/3219). For the Cockpit-in-Court see PRO E351/3265; here the ceiling was of calico as well as canvas. At the Paved Court there was a 'Cloth in the Ceeling' (PRO E351/3266).

19.   *A Description of the Painting of the Theater in Oxford* (Oxford, 1673), p. 1.

20.   *The Restoration Court Stage*, p. 249.

21.   David V. Illingworth, 'L'Hotel de Bourgogne: une salle de théâtre "à l'italiene" à Paris en 1647?' *Revue de l'Histoire du Théâtre* 23 (1971), pp. 40–9, largely confirmed by the discovery by Graham Barlow of a plan of the theatre, 'The Hotel de Bourgogne according to Sir James Thornhill', *Theatre Research International* 1 (1976), pp. 86–98.

22.   *The Restoration Court Stage*, p. 39n.

23.   It is reproduced by Orgel and Strong, *Inigo Jones*, II, 585.

24.   Curiously enough the identification is neither acknowledged nor even mentioned by Orgel and Strong, *Inigo Jones*, II, 830.

25.   *The Restoration Court Stage*, p. 243.

26.   The total elevation is 4 ft for the stage + 23 ft for the opening + 3 ft 9 in for the frieze; the height is diminished a little by the forward tilt of the frieze.

27.   *Inigo Jones*, II, 554–9 and 830.

28.   Parigi had shown a Doric frieze with a Composite order in the great bays of architecture; Jones corrected the solecism by substituting a frieze of masques and consoles in imitation, and by the authority, of a marble in the Arundel collection. See John Peacock, 'Inigo Jones's Stage Architecture', p. 207, and John Harris, 'The Link between a Roman Second-Century Sculptor, Van Dyck, Inigo Jones and Queen Henrietta Maria', *Burlington Magazine* 115 (1973), pp. 526–30. Jones, in a note in his copy of Vitruvius, recorded that the marble came from Smyrna, and it may be that Webb in the present design sought to register a further decorum. He knew the marble well, having drawn it in 1639 (Ashmolean Museum, Larger Talman Album, 69), and in the scene he retains its pattern on the frieze but transposes the order into the Roman Ionic, perhaps to acknowledge its provenance from a city that had belonged to the Ionian League and been a part of the Roman Province of Asia. Webb had also used the frieze, probably for strong emblematic purposes, in his design for the title page of Bishop Brian Walton's *Biblia Sacra Polyglotta* (London, 1657). See Harris and Tait, *Catalogue of Drawings by Inigo Jones . . . at Worcester College, Oxford*, plate 87.

29.   Percy Simpson and C. F. Bell, *Designs by Inigo Jones for Masques & Plays at Court*, Walpole Society 12 (1924), p. 80.

30.   *The Trivmph of Peace* (London, 1633), pp. 6–7.

31.   Webb's shutter and relieve designs for *Mustapha* are at Chatsworth, and are reproduced in *The Dramatic Works of Roger Boyle, Earl of Orrery*, edited by William Smith Clark, 2 vols. (Cambridge, Mass., 1937), I, frontispiece, 244, 268 and 280. A further relieve scene, ruled up like the *Mustapha* designs 15 by 11½, but not endorsed by Webb, was

assigned to the production by Allardyce Nicoll, *British Drama* (London, 1925), p. 222. It is not easily identifiable with any scene in *Mustapha* and probably belongs to some other play at the Hall Theatre. Eleanore Boswell printed a reconstruction by E. C. Northover which treats this relieve design as if it were for a full scene, with misleading results: *Restoration Court Stage*, p. 110.

32.   'Inigo Jones's Stage Architecture', p. 209.

11 Conclusion

1.   Cited from Jones's Roman notebook by John Summerson, *Architecture in Britain, 1530–1830*, p. 67. Like many of Jones's designs the passage derives from a specific source. His lightly annotated copy of Vasari's *Vite* (1568) is now at Worcester College, and in vol. III (part 1), p. 282 contains a marginal note, in Jones's early hand, of a translation of part of the life of Giuliano d'Agnolo: 'Architecture must be masculine fear*me* Simpell And Inriched with ye grace of desine and of a varried suiecte in the Compossit*ion* that wh*ich* nether too littell nor to much alterithe ye order of architecture not ye sight of ye Iuditious.' Between the words 'fear*me*' and 'Simpell' he inserted, possibly later on, the word 'Sollid', reinforcing the idea already conveyed by 'fear*me*', and planting the idea that was to be expressed in the Roman notebook. The significance of this marginal note was first pointed out by Palme, *Triumph of Peace*, p. 93.

2.   *Architectural Principles in the Age of Humanism*, 3rd edn (London, 1962).

3.   *M. Vitruvii Polionis de Architectura Libri Decem* (Venice, 1567), p. 188.

4.   Several shutter designs by Webb at Chatsworth remain unassigned. Some are the same size as those for *Mustapha*, and may have been intended for other plays at the Hall Theatre; others, including a 'Shutter for the village', may have been meant for the Duke's Theatre.

5.   Evidence relating to the rounded shape of the auditoria at Blackfriars and Salisbury Court is given in my article, 'The Private Theatre Auditorium', *Theatre Research International* 9 (1984), pp. 79–92.

Index